THE FINANCIAL TIMES
GUIDE TO

USING AND
INTERPRETING

COMPANY
ACCOUNTS

THE FINANCIAL TIMES
GUIDE TO
USING AND INTERPRETING COMPANY ACCOUNTS

WENDY McKENZIE

PITMAN PUBLISHING
128 Long Acre, London WC2E 9AN

A Division of Pearson Professional Limited

First published in Great Britain 1994

British Library Cataloguing in Publication Data
A CIP catalogue record for this book can be obtained from the British Library.

ISBN 0 273 60728 6 Cased
1 3 5 7 9 10 8 6 4 2
ISBN 0 273 60727 8 Paperback
7 9 10 8 6

Typeset by Northern Phototypesetting Co Ltd, Bolton
Printed and bound in Great Britain by
Bell & Bain Ltd, Glasgow

*The Publishers' policy is to use paper manufactured
from sustainable forests.*

CONTENTS

Part I

WHAT INFORMATION WILL I FIND IN THE ACCOUNTS?

1

INTRODUCTION

PREFACE TO THIS BOOK

If you have ever asked yourself these questions:

'Is my income large enough to cover my costs?'
'Can I afford to buy a better car?'
'How much am I worth?'

then you have prepared accounts. Probably only mentally, and certainly not in any formal way. We all prepare accounts in one form or another. In essence company accounts are no different to the ones that we prepare for ourselves, even though the format is more complicated and formalised. Yet most people believe that company accounts are hard, if not impossible, to understand.

All senior managers should be able to understand and analyse company accounts. This book shows you how. It shows you what you will find in a set of accounts and how to analyse the data so that you understand how the company is performing. Although it is primarily concerned with UK accounts it also discusses the major differences you would find in looking at accounts prepared in other countries.

The book is organised into three sections.

- The first section answers the question 'What information will I find in the accounts?'. This shows you:
    - what documents you will find,
    - what these documents are trying to show you,
    - the way these documents are prepared,
    - the judgements involved in preparing these documents,
    - the main differences between UK accounts and those prepared in other countries.
- The second section answers the question 'How do I analyse the accounts?' and works through a set of published accounts, from the engineering company IMI plc, to show you:
    - the way to approach and structure the analysis,
    - the ratios to use,
    - what the ratios do and do not tell you.
- The third section answers the question 'How can I use my analysis?' by

looking at four different applications:
- – analysing suppliers' accounts,
- – analysing customers' accounts,
- – analysing competitors' accounts,
- – identifying the acquisition potential of a company.

INTRODUCTION TO THE ACCOUNTS

All accounts contain broadly the same information, small private companies show less detail and public companies that are listed on a Stock Exchange will give additional information.

The amount of detail disclosed in the accounts is influenced by four factors:

- the Companies Act,
- the accounting rules,
- a Stock Exchange listing,
- the company's size and ownership.

These four factors combine to determine the amount of detail required in the accounts. If we consider each in turn:

The Companies Act

All companies have a legal requirement to prepare accounts that are 'true and fair' and, with the exception of very small companies, have been audited by an independent accountant. Until the implementation of the Fourth and Seventh EC Directives (in 1981 and 1989) there were no detailed rules on accounting layout or measurement in British law. The Companies Act 1985 now identifies the minimum information that must be disclosed in the accounts and filed at Companies House. It also requires that the accounts should include a directors' report, a profit and loss account, a balance sheet, an auditor's report and notes to the accounts.

The accounting rules

These are called Accounting Standards and are set, in the UK, by the Accounting Standards Board. Accounting rules issued before August 1990 are called Statements of Standard Accounting Practice (SSAPs), subsequently they have been called Financial Reporting Standards (FRSs). These rules cover things that would be set in law in other countries. (There are also some International Accounting Standards, most UK standards are broadly in line with the international view.)

They clarify the way that profit should be measured, assets and liabilities should be valued, and require that more information should be disclosed in the notes to the accounts. In addition to those documents required by the Companies Act, Accounting Standards require the publication of a number of other documents – a cash flow statement, a note of historical cost profits and losses, and a statement of total recognised gains and losses.

A Stock Exchange listing

Companies listed on a Stock Exchange must disclose additional information concerned with the company's status, affairs and activities, directors, shares and shareholders, and loans and interest.

Company size and ownership

Until recently the accounts prepared by small and large companies were broadly similar, although smaller private companies were exempt from some accounting standards. (For example they do not have to prepare a cash flow statement.)

In 1992 an amendment to the Companies Act introduced substantial disclosure exemptions for small companies. We are currently seeing the evolution of two different sets of generally accepted accounting practices. Larger companies being required to comply with all statutory provisions and accounting standard requirements, whereas smaller private companies comply with a shorter, restricted set of rules that reduce the amount of disclosure in the accounts. The size of the company is determined by its turnover, total assets and average number of employees. (A small company is currently one where two out of the three following conditions are met. The turnover must be less than £2.8 million, the total assets less than £1.4 million and the average number of employees must be below 50. If these conditions are satisfied the company will qualify for the small company disclosure exemptions under the Companies Act.)

> The November 1993 budget continued the divergence between small and larger companies' accounting practices by modifying the audit requirement for smaller companies. Companies with a turnover below £90,000 do not need to have their accounts audited. Those with a turnover between £90,000 and £350,000 only require an independent accountant to verify that the accounts accurately reflect the books.

Consequently the amount of detail that you will find in the accounts varies from one type of company to another; dependent on size, ownership and whether the company is listed on a Stock Exchange.

THE BASES USED IN PREPARING ACCOUNTS

There are two fundamentally different ways in which accounts can be compiled in the UK.

- **Historical cost**: based on the costs the company has incurred during the year.
- **Current cost**: based on year end costs.

Historical cost is the most commonly used basis for preparing accounts. Utilities are the only large group of companies to use current cost accounting, and then usually only in their regulatory accounts. Current cost accounting is an attempt to cope with inflation, using the rate of inflation that is specific to the business. Current cost accounts adjust the historical cost accounts to show the real profit, assets and liabilities for the year. We do exactly the same when we consider our salary increase. If inflation is running at 3 per cent, and we are offered a 4 per cent pay rise, we would consider that we are only 1 per cent better off.

Current cost accounting looks at the areas that are affected by inflation in the business.

- **Fixed Assets**: these are bound to increase in cost because of inflation.
- **Stocks**: if we are paying more for our materials, labour and overheads it will be reflected in higher stock values when based on a current cost.
- **Trade Credit**: if the difference between our debtors and our creditors was £100, and inflation was running at 3 per cent, we wouldn't be surprised to see the difference increase to £103.

Profit is reduced by these additional costs and balance sheet values are increased to reflect the assets and liabilities at year end values.

THE ACCOUNTING PRINCIPLES

There are six accounting principles or concepts that determine the way that the accounts are prepared. The first four are incorporated into SSAP 2 (which looks at accounting policies) and the last two are reflected in many other accounting standards:

- matching/accruals,
- prudence,
- consistency,
- going concern,
- substance over form,
- materiality.

It is important to understand these principles if you want to understand accounts.

The matching/accruals principle

This matches costs to revenues and brings them into the profit and loss account in the period to which they relate. This means that the profit and loss account does not necessarily reflect the cash that has come in and gone out of the business. The sales are the sales that have been legally made in the period and the costs are those that relate to these sales.

The fact that we have to consider the costs that relate to the sales in the period means that we make judgements about what those costs are. We shall consider these judgements later in Chapter 2; they are important as they give companies the opportunity to engage in creative accounting.

The prudence principle

This is the most important principle. All others are subordinate to it. Prudence means you must take into the profit and loss account potential losses, but you can't take potential gains. Consequently companies must make provisions for items such as possible bad debts, but can't include increases in asset values in the profit and loss account.

The consistency principle

Items should be accounted for in a consistent manner within a period and from one period to the next.

The going concern principle

This assumes that the business will continue in existence for the foreseeable future.

Substance over form

This tries to ensure that accounts reflect the commercial reality rather than the strict letter of the law. If a company has all the risks and rewards associated with owning something it should be included in the accounts, regardless of the legal position. The way that long-term leases (finance leases) are treated in the accounts is a good example of this. Finance leasing is just another form of borrowing, which can be particularly attractive to companies with tax losses. The company leasing the assets has all the benefits and risks that are associated with owning the assets. So although the leasing company legally owns the assets, they are shown in the company's accounts as fixed assets and depreciated in the usual way. The amount owed to the leasing company, over the life of the lease, is included in creditors.

Materiality

Accounts do not include items that are considered to be immaterial, but it is not possible to give a precise definition of what is and is not material. In some situations an error of less than 5 per cent would be considered satisfactory, but in another situation any error would be unacceptable. For example in a business with a multi-million pound turnover a £10,000 error in the materials cost is unlikely to be material. But a £10,000 error in the chairman's salary, which is subject to specific disclosure requirements, would be classed as material.

Accountants regard an item as material if there is a statutory requirement to disclose it accurately, or knowing about that item would influence your view about the company.

In conclusion these six accounting principles ensure that the accounts reflect an accountant's view of reality:

- Profitable businesses can go into liquidation – cash transactions are not necessarily reflected in this period's profit and loss account.
- Companies are required to make judgements in arriving at the costs that relate to the sales.
- The book value of a company is unlikely to be realised if there is a liquidation.
- The accounts are not totally accurate, they are subject to approximations and may not reflect the legal position.

THE ACCOUNTS

Most larger companies follow the same format and their accounts will contain:

- a chairman's statement,
- a directors' report,
- a profit and loss account,
- a statement of total recognised gains and losses,
- a balance sheet,
- a cash flow statement,
- an auditor's report,
- notes to the accounts.

Some of these will be discussed in detail in later chapters, but a summary of the things that you can expect to find is given here.

The chairman's statement

The chairman's statement is a marketing document that larger companies use to satisfy the statutory requirement for a business review. It tries to present the company's performance in the best light and usually contains information on:

- the company's strategy and business plans,

- the general trading performance of the company in the context of the economic and competitive climate,
- the prospects for the next year,
- the performance of specific businesses within the company,
- any items of special interest during the year (for example acquisitions).

The directors' report

This contains statutory information that may be found elsewhere in the accounts. In the directors' report you should find information on the following subjects:

- Principal activities of the company and the business review, if not disclosed elsewhere in the accounts.
- Proposed dividend and the amount of profit that will be transferred to reserves if the proposed dividend is paid.
- Major changes in fixed assets and any significant difference between the market value and the book value of the assets.
- Directors, directors' interests and shareholdings, and any changes in directors.
- Employees, employee involvement in the running of the company, policies relating to equal opportunities and the employment of disabled persons.
- Any political or charitable donations made during the year, over £200.
- Insurance taken out for directors or auditors against liabilities in relation to the company.
- Company status. Companies are required to disclose whether they are 'close company'. An unquoted company would be classed as a close company if it is in the control of five, or fewer, persons or it is under the control of the directors. A listed company is not classed as a close company if more than 35 per cent of the voting power is held by the public.
- The appointment of the auditors.

The profit and loss account

The profit and loss account shows whether the company has been selling its goods and services for more, or less, than it costs it to make and deliver them to the customer. It takes the income from sales made in the period and then deducts the costs that relate to those sales.

When looking at a profit and loss account it is important to remember three things:

(a) **It is historical**. All profit and loss accounts will tell you what has happened, not what is happening now. It usually takes a UK company three months, after the year end, to publish their profit and loss account. To reinforce the fact that they are historical, profit and loss accounts always say something like 'for the year ending . . ., for the six months ending . . ., for the period ending'.

(b) **It does not include capital expenditure**. The only impact that capital expenditure has on the profit and loss account is the depreciation charge. Consequently a business can be profitable but run out of cash because of a capital expenditure programme.

(c) **It is not concerned about whether the cash has been received from customers or paid to suppliers, just that the sale has been made**. If I buy an apple for 5p and sell it for 8p, the profit and loss account records a profit of 3p. But I may have paid cash to buy the apple, and sold it on credit. The profit remains the same even though my cash is now at −5p. Consequently a business can be profitable but run out of cash if the customers haven't paid for the sales in the period.

Therefore a 'profitable' business in the accounts may be loss-making today and can easily go into liquidation, because it's skint!

The way a profit and loss account is laid out varies from one company to another. There are a number of different formats, and costs can be looked at in different ways. The costs of materials, labour and overheads used in sales (the operating costs) can be calculated in two ways.

- We can look at what we have spent the money on:
  - materials,
  - wages,
  - overheads.

or

- We can look at why we have spent it:
  - cost of sales,
  - administration expenses,
  - selling and distribution expenses.

If the company has sold assets that have previously been revalued, the profit and loss account will be followed by a note of historical cost profits and losses. This shows what the profit would have been had there been no revaluations of assets and is discussed in Chapter 6.

The profit and loss account is discussed in detail in Chapter 2.

The statement of total recognised gains and losses

This is a new document, much burdened by its title. It forms a bridge between the profit and loss account and the balance sheet bringing together profit, asset valuations and currency adjustments. The information found in the statement of total recognised gains and losses is not new. It has always been in the accounts, buried in the notes.

It is concerned with movements on reserves and recognises that a non-professional reader of the accounts may not read all the notes. It ignores any transactions with the shareholders and any premiums that have been paid for acquisitions (what accountants call goodwill). By looking at this statement the reader can see instantly:

- whether the company has made a profit, before paying dividends,
- whether the fixed assets have been revalued during the year,
- the impact of any currency movements on the overall worth of the company.

The statement of total recognised gains and losses is discussed in more detail in Chapter 5.

The balance sheet

This shows what the business is worth at the end of the year, given a set of assumptions detailed in the notes. The balance sheet represents a picture of the business on a certain day, identifying the assets and the liabilities. Like any picture, there are a number of different views you can have. A UK balance sheet identifies how much the business is worth to the shareholders; we shall see that other countries look at the business from a different perspective.

The directors of the company know how important the balance sheet is. It will be used to determine things like:

- how much credit the company will get,
- how much money can be lent to the company,
- the rate of interest that will be charged on borrowings,
- whether someone is going to invest their life's savings in this company.

An important document indeed!

As a snapshot on a certain day, it can be 'managed'. Companies will pick the best day in their year to take the snapshot, and always remember they have 364 days notice of that day arriving! It may well be as like the business for the rest of the year as our passport photographs represent true and fair views of us! Balance sheets should be read very carefully, and we should always remember to look for trends. Every year the company tries to show the best picture. Is the best picture getting better or worse?

The balance sheet is discussed in detail in Chapter 3.

The cash flow statement

The cash flow statement shows the movement of cash in the business in the past year. It identifies where the money has come from and where the business has spent the money. Looking at the cash flow statement helps us see if the company is living within its means.

It is probably the most important document of all; profit can be created, but you either have cash or you don't. You can always spot a business engaging in creative accounting – the cash runs out!

The cash flow statement is discussed in detail in Chapter 4.

The auditor's report

With the exception of very small companies, the accounts will include a report from the auditors. Auditors are required to state if the financial statements give a true and fair view of the company's financial position and profit or loss. If the auditor is unable to state that the accounts represent a true and fair view, he will qualify the accounts by referring to all material matters that he has reservations about. He should tell us why he is qualifying the accounts and, if it is relevant and practicable, quantify the effect of the qualification on the accounts.

There are two types of qualified audit report; the auditors may feel uncertain about whether the accounts are a true and fair view or they could disagree with the view given by the company's accounts.

The auditors could be uncertain for a number of reasons. Qualifications resulting from uncertainties could have arisen from:

- inherent uncertainties, for example concern about the continued support of the company's bankers or the outcome of a major litigation,
- a lack of information to support some of the items in the accounts.

The auditors could disagree with the view portrayed in the accounts for a number of reasons, including:

- the company has not complied with legislation, or accounting standards,
- the company has inappropriate accounting policies,
- the auditors disagree with the amounts, or the facts, disclosed in the accounts,
- the auditors disagree with the way things have, or haven't, been disclosed in the accounts.

The qualification could be at two degrees of severity. It could be fundamental (it is so important that it undermines the view given in the accounts) or material.

There is a recommended wording for the qualification of accounts:

- Fundamental disagreement *'do not give a true and fair view'*
- Material disagreement   *'except for'*
- Fundamental uncertainty   *'unable to form an opinion as to . . .'*
- Material uncertainty   *'subject to'*

The notes to the accounts

These should probably be read first of all. They tell you the accounting policies used in the preparation of the accounts and how all the numbers in the accounts have been calculated. Careful reading of the notes is essential if you want to spot creative accounting.

Thank you to IMI plc for their kind permission both to use and to analyse their accounts, which appear throughout this book.

2

THE PROFIT AND LOSS ACCOUNT

INTRODUCTION

The profit and loss account identifies whether the company is managing to sell its products/services for more or less than it costs to deliver them to the customer.

To do this it takes the sales in the period and deducts the costs that are associated with these sales to arrive at the profit, or the loss.

In this chapter we will be looking at the profit and loss account in detail. We will cover:

- The difference between capital and revenue costs,
- The things you can expect to find in a profit and loss account,
- The way a profit and loss account is laid out in the accounts,
- The judgements that accountants make when preparing the profit and loss account.

CAPITAL COSTS v. REVENUE COSTS

It is important to understand the way a company classifies its costs. Costs can be either:

- **capital costs**: relating to buying or improving assets,
- **revenue costs**: relating to the sales in the period.

We all understand the difference between capital costs and revenue costs. Decorating your home is a revenue cost, you don't get any more money for a well-decorated house! Putting in an extra bathroom is a capital cost, you can expect to recover the money when you sell the house. Even DIY dodgers can usually be talked into working on capital projects!

The distinction is important in accounting, as only revenue costs are included in the profit and loss account. Any capital costs are charged to the balance sheet. Consequently it is possible for companies to improve profitability (and apparent net worth) by capitalising costs. The opportunity for creative accounting arises because it is not always easy to work out what costs should be capitalised, even though the Companies Act defines what should comprise the cost of an asset:

(a) **Company purchases the asset**. If the company buys the asset it is relatively straightforward, it is the purchase cost plus 'any expenses incidental to its acquisition'.

(b) **Company builds the asset**. This is where the problems start as the company has to calculate the cost of production. The Companies Act defines the production cost as the price of raw materials and consumables used, plus additional costs that are 'directly attributable to the production of the asset'. During the period of production companies may also include 'a reasonable proportion of the costs' . . . 'which are only indirectly attributable to the production of the asset'. This includes 'interest on capital borrowed to finance the production of the asset'. The problem lies in the interpretation – what is reasonable? How do you calculate capitalised interest costs when the borrowings aren't necessarily specific to the construction of the asset?

UK accounting standards currently give little guidance on interpreting the Act, auditors rely on common sense and some limited guidance given by the International Accounting Standards.

THE ITEMS FOUND IN THE PROFIT AND LOSS ACCOUNT

We shall now consider the items that you could expect to find in the profit and loss account:

- turnover,
- operating costs,
- exceptional items,
- profit on sale of assets/subsidiaries,
- interest,
- income from interests in associated undertakings,
- extraordinary items,
- taxation,
- minority interests,
- dividends.

Turnover

Turnover is the total sales in the period, excluding any VAT or similar taxes. Group accounts show the sales to outsiders; inter-company sales do not show on the face of the profit and loss account, but may be disclosed in the notes.

Operating costs

These are the costs of materials, labour and overheads used in sales, excluding any VAT or similar taxes. We have discussed the two different ways that these can be calculated. Following the introduction of FRS 3 in 1993 the operating costs will include most exceptional items. Companies will include other operating income in their calculation of operating profit. Other operating income is income that doesn't fit into any other heading, for example royalty income.

Exceptional items

Exceptional items are things that you would expect to occur in the normal course of events, like bad debts, but because they are so large or unusual, they should be disclosed if the accounts are to give a true and fair view. Exceptional items used to be disclosed on the face of the profit and loss account, after operating profit, but this has changed following the implementation of FRS 3.

FRS 3 requires most exceptional items to be included in the relevant operating cost heading, and the details of the exceptional items disclosed in the notes to the accounts. The only exceptional items disclosed separately on the profit and loss account itself are profits and losses on sale of fixed assets and subsidiaries, together with provisions for losses on businesses to be discontinued. This means that reading of the notes is essential if you want to understand the underlying trends in the profitability of the company.

Profit on sale of fixed assets/subsidiaries

(a) **Profit on sale of fixed assets**. Fixed assets are by definition things the business means to keep. But all businesses sell assets when they reach the end of their useful life. The sale of assets will affect profitability if the company receives more or less than the asset value.

If the company bought a machine for £15,000 and has depreciated it by £10,000, it will be worth £5,000 on its books. If the asset is sold for £6,000, the company will have made £1,000 profit on sale of assets. If it was only sold for £3,000 a loss of £2,000 will be shown.

When assets are sold they have a value in the books. If the company receives more than the book value it shows as a profit, any less would show as a loss.

Therefore profits or losses on sale of assets are determined by the value of these assets in the accounts in the books.

(b) **Profit on sale of subsidiaries**. Following a ruling from part of the Accounting Standards Board that looks at the way the rules are interpreted it is more complicated to calculate the profit, or loss, on sale of subsidiaries. It all stems from the way that companies currently account for goodwill (the premium paid to acquire a company and access its future profits).

To illustrate the problem:

A predator wants to buy a company. This company is only worth £50,000 on paper (assets less liabilities) but last year made £20,000 profit. When the predator buys this company he will have to pay more than £50,000; as he will not just be buying the assets, but also buying the future profits. If the predator pays £90,000 for the company, he will have bought £40,000 'goodwill'. This is the premium paid on acquisition. (Goodwill will be discussed in more detail in Chapter 3.)

We will assume that the acquisition is consolidated into the predator's accounts at £50,000. (This may not be strictly true as asset values will probably be restated to reflect 'fair values' (replacement cost) when the acquisition is consolidated. This is determined by the method used to account for the acquisition.)

The predator has paid £90,000 to buy this company, which has a value on his accounts of £50,000. If he sells it for £70,000 next year has he made a profit or a loss? Common sense says that it is a loss of £20,000 and this is how he must account for it. (Before this ruling, some companies were saying they had made a profit . . . they had sold assets and liabilities worth £50,000 for £70,000, therefore there was a profit of £20,000!)

Profits or losses on sale of subsidiaries must consider goodwill, as well as the current value of the business.

Interest

The interest figure on the profit and loss account is the net interest figure, the notes will disclose how much interest has been paid, received, and capitalised. For example the note relating to £50,000 net interest payable might read:

	£
Interest paid	(80,000)
Interest received	20,000
Interest capitalised	10,000
Net interest paid	(50,000)

Of the £80,000 interest paid only £70,000 is charged to the profit and loss account, £10,000 is charged to the balance sheet.

The logic for charging the interest to the balance sheet goes like this. The business could buy a ready-built store from a construction company. This company would look at all the costs involved in constructing the store (land, materials, labour, etc.) in determining the price that they would charge. These costs would include interest on borrowings. If interest can be included if a store is purchased from a third party, surely the business should be able to capitalise interest if it builds the store? Well there isn't a rule that says you can't, and the Companies Act says you can!

The problem with capitalising interest is twofold:

- The cost of construction plus the capitalised interest could well exceed the market value of the property (we shall see in the next chapter that the book value of assets rarely coincides with the market value).
- The cash cost of interest is £60,000 (the £80,000 paid less the £20,000 received) and is totally unaffected by where the interest is charged. A company could be experiencing difficulties with its bankers even though when you look at the profit and loss account the interest is only a small proportion of the profit.

Income from interests in associated undertakings

Before we consider what an associate is, it is probably as well to reflect on the meaning of an undertaking. It is a term straight from the Companies Act. It is an all-embracing term covering companies, partnerships and associations carrying on a trade or a business. An undertaking does not have to be a company or have a profit motive.

An associated undertaking is one where the company has participating interest in a long-term investment. A participating interest is where the company can influence the operational and financial decisions of its investment. A 20 per cent, or more, shareholding in a company is assumed to represent a participating interest.

If an investment is classed as an associate, the company will bring its share of the pre-tax profit into its profit and loss account. (If the investment is not classed as an associate, or a subsidiary, only the income received from the investment will be shown in the profit and loss account.)

For example Company A buys a 30 per cent stake in company B. Before including Company B's results their summarised profit and loss accounts were as follows:

	Company A	Company B
	£000	£000
Turnover	1,000	700
Profit before tax	200	150
Tax	(60)	(30)
	———	———
Profit after tax	140	120
Dividend	(20)	–
	———	———
Retained profit	120	120

Company A will take its share of the pre-tax profits (£45,000) and tax charge (£9,000) into its profit and loss account:

	Company A
	£000
Turnover	1,000
Share of profits of associated undertakings	45
Profit before tax	245
Tax	(69)
	———
Profit after tax	176
Dividend	(20)
	———
Retained profit	156

Profit has been increased, but there will be no cash benefits to Company A as Company B is not paying dividends to its shareholders!

Extraordinary items

Following the implementation of FRS 3 in 1993, these have largely disappeared. FRS 3 defines extraordinary items as 'extremely rare' items that relate to 'highly abnormal events or transactions that fall outside the ordinary activities . . . and are not expected to recur'. The accounting standard thinks that they are so rare it doesn't even give an example of them!

Taxation

With the exception of small companies, the notes will detail the calculation of the charge for taxation. Small companies will only show the total tax charge. Tax on profit or loss from ordinary activities will be shown separately from tax on extraordinary profits or losses (these should be very rare now with the virtual disappearance of extraordinary items).

The notes will also disclose:

- UK corporation tax,
- double taxation relief,
- UK income tax,
- overseas tax,
- tax charge relating to associated undertakings,
- deferred tax,
- advance corporation tax (the tax on dividends).

Most of the tax note is self-explanatory, but three will be discussed in more detail:

- double taxation relief,
- deferred tax,
- advance corporation tax.

(a) **Double taxation relief**. Agreements have been made with most countries to ensure that overseas profits are usually subject to UK tax only to the extent that UK tax is higher than the overseas tax paid. This ensures that any dividends paid to the parent company will not be taxed again, unless the tax paid overseas is lower than UK tax. Then the company will be liable to pay the difference.

(b) **Deferred taxation**. In the UK, unlike other European countries (for example Germany), taxable profits are not the same as published profit before tax. Consequently it is not possible to take the pre-tax profits, multiply them by the tax rate and arrive at the tax charge. Therefore in the UK companies prepare two sets of accounts: the published accounts that we see and the accounts prepared for the Inland Revenue. Some things are required to be charged to the published profit and loss account (e.g. entertainment costs) that are not allowed for tax purposes. Other things have different values in the tax accounts and the published accounts.

These differences between the two sets of accounts are called timing differences. They can be either permanent, where they appear in one set of accounts, but not the other, or alternatively, they could be charged to the published accounts in a different year than to the tax accounts. Accountants talk about differences being either 'permanent' or 'timing'. A good example of a timing difference is the different fixed asset values found in the two sets of accounts. Companies are free to choose the rate of depreciation used in the published accounts. The Inland Revenue ignores the depreciation that the company has chosen, which can vary from one company to another, and gives all companies a standard tax allowance. This is called a 'capital allowance'. (Company tax allowances work essentially the same way as personal tax allowances, reducing the taxable profit.)

For example a company buys a machine for £5,000 and plans to keep it for 5 years. At the end of the 5 years they believe that the machine will be worth nothing. To the company, depreciation is a matter of simple arithmetic – they have £5,000 to write off over 5 years. They choose to depreciate the value of the machine £1,000 a year. This depreciation charge will be charged to the profit and loss account as an operating cost.

The machine qualifies for a 25 per cent capital allowance. Capital allowances are calculated in a different way to the way that most companies calculate depreciation. Most companies make an equal charge over the life of the asset, using a method of depreciation called the straight line method. Capital allowances work on a 'reducing balance'. In the first year the allowance would be 25 per cent of £5,000 = £1,250, giving a residual value of the asset of £3,750. In the second it would be 25 per cent of £3,750 = £938. Consequently the depreciation charge would differ from the capital allowance. In the early years depreciation would be lower than the tax allowance, in the later years it would be higher.

Deferred tax brings the tax accounts and the published accounts into line. It adjusts the tax charge to reflect the tax that would have been payable if the tax allowances had been the same as the depreciation charge. This has the effect of equalising the tax charged to the profit and loss account over the life of the asset.

(c) **Advance corporation tax**. Dividends are taxed at source. Therefore the company pays tax on behalf of its shareholders. If a company pays dividends to its shareholders it will need to pay advance corporation tax (ACT) to the Inland Revenue. ACT is currently charged at 20 per cent of gross dividend. So the ACT on a £40,000 net dividend would be:

$$(\text{£40,000/80 per cent}) \times 20 \text{ per cent} = \text{£10,000}$$

This £10,000 is paid on behalf of the shareholders, and is not a tax liability of the company. It represents an advance payment of corporation tax, and can be used to offset the corporation tax handed over to the Inland Revenue. However there are restrictions on the amount of ACT that can be recovered and a company may be unable to offset all the ACT if:

- dividends are very high,
- a lot of their profit is generated outside the UK and is taxed overseas.

It would pay ACT, but be unable to use it to reduce its corporation tax bill. The company would then have 'irrecoverable ACT'. This does not mean that the tax can never be recovered, only that it can not be recovered this year. Any that can not be used this year can be carried back for six years and carried forward indefinitely. It can also be handed over to other members of the group, subject to certain restrictions.

Consequently irrecoverable ACT can be an important factor when a company with an ACT problem is considering an acquisition. The GKN bid for Westland in 1994 arose primarily because of GKN's problem with irrecoverable ACT. Another example is Tomkins's acquisition of Rank Hovis McDougall. Tomkins used to make most of their profits overseas, and had built up a lot of irrecoverable ACT. When they decided to make a bid for Rank Hovis McDougall they were able to offer more than their bid rivals Hanson. Rank Hovis McDougall made most of its profit in the UK, and a UK acquisition would allow Tomkins to recover their erstwhile irrecoverable ACT, thus reducing the cash cost of the acquisition.

Minority interests

These occur because companies consolidate subsidiaries that are not wholly owned, consequently some of the profits shown in the profit and loss account do not belong to its shareholders. Where one company controls another it must prepare consolidated accounts to show the results and financial position of both companies.

If a company's results are consolidated, all its sales and costs will be taken into the profit and loss accounts and all its assets and liabilities will be taken into the balance sheet. Any of the profits, or net assets, that do not belong to the 'parent' company's shareholders will be shown as minority interests.

To illustrate this we will consider our previous example, and now assume that Company A owns 60 per cent of Company B:

	Company A	Company B
	£000	£000
Turnover	1,000	700
Profit before tax	200	150
Tax	(60)	(30)
Profit after tax	140	120
Dividend	(20)	–
Retained profit	120	120

The consolidated profit and loss account would be:

	£000
Turnover	1,700
Profit before tax	350
Tax	(90)
Profit after tax	260
Minority interests	(48)
Profit attributable to shareholders	212
Dividend	(20)
Retained profit	192

[handwritten annotations: "profit/net assets not belonging to Co. 'parent'", "120 × 40%", "(48) →", "(260-48)", "< (20)", "∧ 192"]

The rules on consolidation used to be linked to the size of the stake in the company; if you had more than 50 per cent shareholding the company would be consolidated. This meant that companies could be excluded from consolidation if the shareholding was 50 per cent or less, even though they were effectively part of the group. Since the Companies Act 1989 and the implementation of FRS 2 in 1992, the rules on consolidation also include effective control of the company. Usually control and ownership go together, but the change in the rules was necessary as some companies were using the fact that control was not part of the rules to get 'off-balance sheet funding'. They were excluding companies they controlled from the group accounts by keeping the size of the ownership at 50 per cent, or below. Consequently both the law and the accounting standard now talk about 'dominant influence'.

Company A must consolidate the results of Company B if:

- it has the majority of the votes in Company B,
- it is a shareholder of Company B and has the right to appoint, or remove, the majority of the directors,
- it has the right to exercise dominant influence over Company B. (Dominant influence is defined as influence that can be used to achieve the operational and financial objectives of Company A, regardless of whether it is in the best interests of Company B.) Dominant influence does not have to be interventionist, it may be simply the setting of targets, with direct intervention occurring rarely. It could arise from:
  - provisions laid down in the companies Memorandum or Articles of Association,
  - the two companies are being managed as a single unit ('on a unified basis'),
  - a contract. this is probably illegal in the UK, because of the rules on directors' obligations. (This provision comes from European Community law. Control contracts are common in Germany.)

This means that effectively there can be large minority interests showing on accounts where the company has been forced to consolidate because of its dominant influence over the subsidiary, rather than its ownership of the company and its profits.

Dividends

There are legal restrictions on the amount of dividend that can be paid by the company. It is possible to pay dividends out of losses, but only if there are enough accumulated profits from previous years to cover the dividend.

For example, consider the following:

	Retained profits
	£
Year 1	10,000
Year 2	5,000
Year 3	7,000
Year 4	2,000
Total	24,000

In the fifth year the company makes a loss before dividend of £8,000, but still wishes to pay a dividend of £10,000. This would take the retained loss for the year to £18,000, which can be absorbed by the accumulated profits. These accumulated profits are known in law as 'distributable reserves'; dividends can be paid until these reach zero. Therefore the company could pay up to £16,000 in dividends.

The payment of dividends does not necessarily require shareholder approval. As long as it does not contravene the law, interim dividends can be paid by the directors without the approval of the shareholders. The final dividend does require shareholder approval at the Annual General Meeting, and the directors will devote a lot of time in determining how much should be paid. Only private companies like paying dividends, although they are likely to have taken money out of the business well before we reach dividends! Private companies are generally paying dividends out to themselves. Public companies are different – dividends are paid out to strangers. The more the company pays, the less it can keep in the business for the next year's development and growth. Public companies use the same underlying principle to determine the size of the dividend that they use to decide the level of salary increase for employees – the least they can get away with! In fact the same things influence dividend decisions as influence salary decisions. It is a balance. They can't afford to disappoint the shareholders (they will vote with their feet and sell their shares). But neither can they afford to create unsustainable expectations (shareholders look for dividend growth, the dividend paid this year creates expectations about the dividend that will be paid next year). To try to reduce the cash impact of paying dividends, a number of companies now offer a 'scrip dividend'. A scrip dividend is where the shareholder receives extra shares instead of cash. This is often an attractive option for smaller shareholders as it enables them to build up their stake in the company without paying dealing fees. The company also benefits from the payment of a scrip dividend as ACT is not payable on scrip dividends and no cash leaves the business. So everyone wins! To encourage shareholders to take the scrip dividend alternative it is often 'enhanced'. The shareholder receives more if he takes the shares, rather than the cash.

Most companies follow the Articles (the rules that govern the operation of the company) laid out in the Companies Act. If these Articles are followed, the only way the shareholders can change the dividend is to reduce it (probably as likely as us asking for a reduction in the size of our next salary increase)!

The dividends that appear on the profit and loss account are the net dividends that are proposed to be paid, the tax liability having been included in the tax charge.

THE FORMAT OF THE PROFIT AND LOSS ACCOUNT

Having seen what we might find in the profit and loss account, we will now look at how it is laid out. The layout of the profit and loss account varies slightly from one company to another. But one thing will be common to all companies reporting in the UK, the costs will be considered in a standard order and then deducted from turnover to arrive at different levels of profit.

	Turnover
−	Operating costs
+	Other operating income
=	OPERATING PROFIT (a profit figure shown by companies, but not required by the Companies Act)
+/−	Profits and losses on sale of fixed assets or subsidiaries
+/−	Interest
=	PROFIT BEFORE TAX
+/−	Tax
=	PROFIT AFTER TAX
−	Dividends
=	RETAINED PROFIT

Within the EEC there are four different ways of presenting the profit and loss account, and these are reflected in the Companies Act. Only two formats are used in the UK, the others being more popular in continental Europe. The formats used in the UK present the profit and loss account vertically and differ only in their approach to calculating the operating costs:

● **Format 1**: this is a functional presentation answering the question 'Why have we spent the money?'
● **Format 2**: this is a factual presentation answering the question 'What have we spent the money on?'

Formats 3 and 4 are essentially horizontal presentations of Formats 1 and 2, with costs and income grouped separately.

A 'Format 1' profit and loss account

This is the most commonly used format in the UK and classifies costs into:

- cost of sales,
- administrative expenses,
- distribution costs.

Unfortunately these terms are not defined in the Companies Act. Some companies include their sales and marketing costs in distribution costs, others in administrative expenses. Some retailers define cost of sales as the cost of merchandise, others add distribution costs and store operating costs to the cost of merchandise.

Consequently it is not possible to compare costs between companies; only within a company over time.

An example of a Format 1 profit and loss account is given below:

PROFIT AND LOSS ACCOUNT – FORMAT 1

	£000
Turnover	1,000
Cost of sales	(600)
Gross profit	400
Distribution costs	(140)
Administrative expenses	(70)
Other operating income	10
Operating profit	200
Profit on sale of fixed assets	10
Net interest payable	(50)
Share of profits of associated undertakings	20
Profit on ordinary activities before taxation	180
Taxation	(40)
Profit on ordinary activities after taxation	140
Minority interests	(10)
Dividend	(40)
Retained profit for the financial year	90

A 'Format 2' profit and loss account

This classifies costs as materials, staff costs (which include social security and pension costs), other external costs, and depreciation. As these costs are often the costs of purchases in the period, two adjustments will probably be made:

- to exclude costs relating to stock – 'changes in stock and work in progress',
- to exclude staff costs spent on installing or improving capital items – 'own work capitalised'.

If we look at the same profit and loss account in a format 2 presentation:

PROFIT AND LOSS ACCOUNT – FORMAT 2

	£000
Turnover	1,000
Raw materials and consumables	(470)
Staff costs	(195)
Other external charges	(100)
Depreciation	(90)
Changes in stock and work in progress	20
Own work capitalised	25
Other operating income	10
Operating profit	200
Profit on sale of fixed assets	10
Net interest payable	(50)
Share of profits of associated undertakings	20
Profit on ordinary activities before taxation	180
Taxation	(40)
Profit on ordinary activities after taxation	140
Minority interests	(10)
Dividend	(40)
Retained profit for the financial year	90

Historically companies only disclosed total revenues and costs on the face of the profit and loss account. (The notes would usually detail a divisional and geographical analysis.) There was no requirement to identify how much of the profit came from recent acquisitions or from businesses closed down, or sold, during the period. This meant that it was often impossible to identify how much of the profit had been generated by acquisitions and disposals, and how much from 'normal activities'.

Since 1993 (following the implementation of FRS 3) acquisitive companies have been required to show a more detailed profit and loss account, as illustrated in the following example:

	Continuing operations	Discontinued operations	Total
		Acquisitions		
	£000	£000	£000	£000
Turnover	500	300	200	1,000
Cost of sales	(280)	(160)	(160)	(600)
Gross profit	220	140	40	400
Distribution costs	(70)	(40)	(30)	(140)
Administrative expenses	(35)	(15)	(20)	(70)
Other operating income	10	~	~	10
Operating profit	125	85	(10)	200
Profit on sale of fixed assets	5	2	3	10
Profit before interest	130	87	(7)	210
Net interest payable				(50)
Share of profits of associated undertakings				20
Profit on ordinary activities before taxation				180
Taxation				(40)
Profit on ordinary activities after taxation				140
Minority interests				(10)
Dividend				(40)
Retained profit for the financial year				90

You can see how this gives us a much clearer idea of where the profits have been made this year and what the profits might be next year. Following the acquisitions and the businesses discontinued (whether from closure or sale) during the year we could expect turnover to fall next year and profits to rise.

THE ACCOUNTING JUDGEMENTS – DEFINING THE COSTS THAT RELATE TO THE SALES

All companies make five major accounting adjustments to ensure that the costs charged to the profit and loss account are those that relate to the sales made in the period:

Charges are made to the profit and loss account to include:

- provisions for likely costs,
- accrued expenses,
- depreciation,

and the following are not included in the profit and loss account:

- stock,
- prepayments.

In addition companies involved in trading overseas must find a way to deal with exchange rates. All of these adjustments impact on both the profit and loss account and the balance sheet, but will be dealt with in detail in this chapter.

Provisions

All companies must make provisions to cover likely future costs that relate to the sales made in the period. Typical provisions would cover:

- bad and doubtful debts,
- obsolete stock (this may not be obsolete in the literal sense, stock must be shown on the accounts at the lower of cost or net realisable value),
- warranty claims,
- litigation,
- rationalisation.

To illustrate the way provisions impact on the accounts we will look at a doubtful debt provision. Provisions can be either:

- specific, where each debtor is considered individually,
- general, where the same level of provision is applied to all debtors,

or

- a combination of the two, where perhaps large customers would be considered on an individual basis and smaller customers on a general basis.

Let us consider a company that has decided to make a provision of 4 per cent to cover doubtful debts, and look at the impact on the accounts over a period of two years.

	Year 1 £	Year 2 £	Profit Growth
Outstanding invoices	100,000	110,000	
Less 4 per cent provision	(4,000)	(4,400)	
Debtors on balance sheet	96,000	105,600	
Profit before provisions	110,000	115,500	5%

If we consider two different scenarios.

(a) The company collects £98,000 from the first year's debtors.
(b) They only collect £94,000.

The profit after provisions would be:

	Year 1	Year 2	Profit Growth
(a)	£106,000	£113,100	6.7%
(b)	£106,000	£109,100	2.9%

In the first option they overprovided £2,000 in the first year and so only needed to charge £2,400 into the second year's profit and loss account to bring the provision to £4,400 (4 per cent of £110,000). In the second option they had underprovided and had to increase the charge to the profit and loss account, to bring the provision to the 4 per cent required.

Provisions are only the managers' best guesses and are unlikely to be a totally accurate reflection of what will happen. As provisions can only reflect approximations they are often used by companies to move profit from one year to the next. An overprovision in one year can be written back in the next.

The writeback of provisions, and its impact on reported profits, can be illustrated by London International Group. In their 1993 interim results on their health and personal products business they reported that

> Operating results for the half year, compared with the corresponding half year have been depressed by two additional factors. Firstly, operating results last year were helped by the release of surplus provisions and the benefit of favourable exchange variances, following the UK's exit from ERM. In total these benefits amounted to £5 million compared to this year. Secondly, the adoption of more conservative accounting policies have adversely affected results by circa £2 million.

Operating profits for the half year in this division had fallen from £16.1 million to £3.5 million.

Accrued expenses

These are outstanding invoices that relate to costs for items used in the period. We all know about accruals, even if we have never used the term. A lot of our personal costs are accrued . . . gas, electricity, telephone, we pay them quarterly in arrears. If, as individuals, we were trying to prepare a profit and loss account for the year ending 31st December we would find it difficult to estimate our costs accurately. We would have to try to work out what proportion of our next gas bill etc. related to this period's sales. Companies have to make similar provisions to reflect their accrued expenses – the costs of items used, but not invoiced in the period.

For example:
A company has used and paid for electricity as follows:

	Year 1 £	Year 2 £
Electricity used	80,000	84,000
Electricity invoiced and paid for	65,000	83,000
Charge to the profit and loss account	80,000	84,000
Accrued expenses (included in creditors on the balance sheet)	15,000	16,000

(handwritten annotation: 68,000 of this year paid)

The charge to the profit and loss account will always be the costs *used*, not the costs paid for. It will include any outstanding invoices.

On the balance sheet creditors are divided into those where we have received the invoice and those where we haven't (the accrued expenses). The accrued expenses in the second year are £16,000. £15,000 of the £83,000 paid during the second year related to the first year, so only £68,000 of this year's electricity has been paid for. Consequently the outstanding invoices, which relate to costs charged to the profit and loss account, were £84,000 − £68,000 = £16,000.

Depreciation

Depreciation is something we all know about. We buy something today, and it's not worth the same tomorrow. Some things depreciate more than others. Cars and computers generally depreciate faster than our other assets. The Companies Act requires companies to make a charge for depreciation in their accounts to reflect the shrinking in value of their assets. This is not a cash cost to the business. (We don't pay depreciation in the same way that we pay rent, we physically pay depreciation when we trade our car in. That's when we find that it isn't worth what we paid for it.)

The charge to the profit and loss account should take account of:

- cost,
- asset life,
- net residual value (scrap value, at the end of the asset life).

For example: a company buys a machine for £10,490, believes it will last for 5 years and will have a scrap value of £490 in 5 years time. It has £10,000 to depreciate over 5 years, and would probably make an annual charge to the profit and loss account of £2,000. This is called the straight line method of depreciation and is the most popular method of depreciating in the UK. The depreciation charge is constant at £2,000 per year and the value of the asset is reducing in a straight line:

$$(10490 - 490)/5 = 2,000 \text{ p.a}$$

	Depreciation	Asset value
Year 1	£2,000	£8,490
Year 2	£2,000	£6,490
Year 3	£2,000	£4,490
Year 4	£2,000	£2,490
Year 5	£2,000	£490

This is not the only method of depreciating, there are many others:

- **Reducing balance**. This is sometimes called the double declining balance method. We looked at this method in our discussions on taxation on page 11. This uses a fixed percentage each year and applies this to the reducing value of the asset. The percentage is calculated using the following formula, which will give the chosen residual value at the end of the life.

$$1 - n\sqrt{\dfrac{\text{residual value}}{\text{cost}}}$$

where n is the anticipated life. Using the example above, the percentage that would be used is 45.8 per cent. Don't let the formula fool you, although it has a root sign in it, it is no more accurate. All it does is calculate the percentage that would allow us to arrive at what, for the UK, is a purely arbitrary residual value.

This would give the following depreciation charges and asset value:

		Depreciation	Asset values
Year 1	£10,490 × 45.8%	£4,805	£5,685
Year 2	£5,685 × 45.8%	£2,604	£3,081
Year 3	£3,081 × 45.8%	£1,411	£1,670
Year 4	£1,670 × 45.8%	£765	£905
Year 5	£905 × 45.8%	£414	£491

(rounding error of 1)

Some companies prefer the reducing balance method, as they believe it gives a closer approximation to 'real' depreciation.

- **Sum of the digits**. In the UK this method is largely used only by leasing companies, but it is widely used overseas, particularly in the US. It gives a depreciation charge between the straight line method and the reducing balance method. The sum of the digits is simply the total of the number of years the asset is expected to last ($1 + 2 + 3 + 4 + 5 = 15$) and can be found quickly by using the formula:

$$\dfrac{n(n + 1)}{2}$$

where n is the anticipated life.

Having found the sum of the digits, the next step would be to find the depreciation factor for each year. In the first year depreciation is calculated at 5/15 × £10,000, in the second 4/15 × £10,000 and so on:

		Depreciation	Asset values
Year 1	5/15 × £10,000	£3,333	£7,157
Year 2	4/15 × £10,000	£2,667	£4,490
Year 3	3/15 × £10,000	£2,000	£2,490
Year 4	2/15 × £10,000	£1,333	£1,157
Year 5	1/15 × £10,000	£667	£490

Some companies prefer this method as it reflects the reducing balance method, but is less extreme.

- **Usage-based methods**. This method of depreciation is based on the usage of the asset, expressing the life in production units, or hours, rather than years. This method of depreciation is often used for machinery and planes. Continuing our example, if the company believed that the machine would last for 20,000 hours, the annual depreciation charge would be based on the usage, at 50 pence an hour.

	Usage (hours)	Depreciation charge £
Year 1	3,600	1,800
Year 2	4,400	2,200
Year 3	3,800	1,900
Year 4	4,200	2,100
Year 5	4,000	2,000
	20,000	10,000

In calculating the charge for depreciation companies have four variables to consider:

- cost,
- asset life,
- net residual value,
- depreciation method.

Any change in these will affect both profitability and asset values. For example we could use the straight line method, instead of the reducing balance method, depreciate over 10 years instead of 5 and have a net residual value of £2,490. This would improve profitability and asset values:

	Depreciation		Asset values	
	Reducing balance over 5 years residual value: £490	Straight line over 10 years residual value: £2,490	Reducing balance over 5 years residual value: £490	Straight line over 10 years residual value: £2,490
Year 1	£4,805	£800	£5,685	£9,690
Year 2	£2,604	£800	£3,081	£8,890
Year 3	£1,411	£800	£1,670	£8,090
Year 4	£765	£800	£905	£7,290
Year 5	£414	£800	£491	£6,490
Year 6	–	£800	£491	£5,690
Year 7	–	£800	£491	£4,890
Year 8	–	£800	£491	£4,090
Year 9	–	£800	£491	£3,290
Year 10	–	£800	£491	£2,490

Companies can change the way they depreciate assets if they believe it gives a truer and fairer view.

Stock

By definition stock has yet to be used and therefore must be excluded from the costs in the profit and loss account. Therefore any costs charged to stock will not be included in the profit and loss account. Consequently the valuation of stock is an important determinant of the costs of sales.

Stock can be analysed into its component parts, starting with raw materials and adding labour and overhead costs as the materials move through the production process.

Stock should be shown on the balance sheet at the lower of cost and net realisable value. (Net realisable value is defined as the selling price less any further costs to completion, and sales, marketing and distribution costs.) This limits the costs that can be charged to stock.

To calculate the value of goods used in sales companies have to:

● measure the volume of units used in sales,
● calculate their value.

Measuring the volume of goods used in sales is theoretically very simple, all companies use some form of stocktaking:

	Opening stock
Plus	Purchases
Equals	Goods available
Less	Closing stock
Equals	Goods used in sales

However anyone who has been involved in stocktaking knows just how imprecise it can be!

Once the company has measured how many units it has in stock it then has to value them. Valuing stock accurately is important, small changes in stock values can have a disproportionate impact on reported profits in businesses where the materials cost is a large proportion of the total costs.

In practice valuing stock can be difficult. Some guidance is given in the accounting standard (SSAP 9). Companies have to cope with changing prices, and manufacturing businesses have to find a basis to value work in progress and finished goods.

To illustrate the difficulties we will consider three different types of company:

- **a retailer**: holding goods for resale,
- **a manufacturer**: with materials stock, work in progress and finished goods stock,
- **a construction company**: with long-term contracts.

(a) **The retailer**. The retailer has fewer problems as there is only one type of stock, the goods for resale. A number of retailers (for example Marks and Spencer) find it useful to show stock at resale value in their internal accounts. When they publish their accounts they adjust this figure to arrive at 'cost'. They deduct the gross margin they would expect to make on the product. For example if they had a dress that would retail at £70.00 and the estimated gross margin was 50 per cent, the stock value would be £35.00. The accounting standard requires companies using the estimated margin method of valuing stock to test that this is a 'reasonable approximation of the actual cost'.

(b) **The manufacturer**. Manufacturing businesses experience a number of problems when trying to determine the cost of goods sold and the value of stock.

- Most manufacturers carry stock for longer than retailers, and so are more likely to have goods in stock at different prices.
- They have different types of stock, at the year end they are likely to have materials stock, work in progress, and finished goods stock. Labour and overhead costs need to be added to the value of the materials as they move through the production process.

To cope with these difficulties accountants have developed a number of different approaches to valuing stock. The most common methods are:

- first in first out (FIFO),
- average cost,
- last in first out (LIFO).

We will use the following example to illustrate the impact of using the different methods:

		Units	Unit cost £	Total £
1st January	Opening stock	1,500	1.00	1,500
28th February	Purchases	2,000	1.05	2,100
1st April	Purchases	1,500	1.06	1,590
30th June	Purchases	2,000	1.08	2,160
31st August	Purchases	2,200	1.10	2,420
30th November	Purchases	1,500	1.13	1,695
		10,700		11,465
31st December	Closing stock	1,000		

To determine the cost of sales we must ascertain the value of the closing stock.

(i) *First in first out*. This applies the principle of stock rotation to stock valuation. The first goods into the warehouse are assumed to be the first despatched to the customer, therefore it will be the latest deliveries that will be in stock.

The value of stock shown on the balance sheet will be £1,130 and the cost of sales charged to the profit and loss account will be £10,335.

(ii) *Average cost*. A weighted average is used, as a simple average will not give the degree of accuracy required.

A simple average cost per unit would be:

$$\frac{£1.00 + £1.05 + £1.06 + £1.08 + £1.10 + £1.13}{6} = £1.07 \text{ per unit}$$

This would mean that £10,379 would be charged to the profit and loss account and stocks would be £1,070. You may notice that using a simple average doesn't cover the total cost of purchases, £11,465. The stock and the cost of sales total £11,449. To be exactly right a weighted average must be used.

A weighted cost per unit would be:

$$\frac{(1,500 \times £1.00) + (2,000 \times £1.05) + (1,500 \times £1.06) + (2,000 \times £1.08) + (2,200 \times £1.10) + (1,500 \times £1.13)}{10,700}$$

$$= £1.0714953$$

The extra decimal places ensure the accuracy!
Cost of sales will be £10,393.504 and stock £1,071.4953

(iii) *Last in first out*. Last in first out charges the most recent deliveries into the profit and loss account. In our example the closing stock on the balance sheet will be shown at £1,000 and the cost of sales in the profit and loss account will be £10,465. As this doesn't reflect the commercial reality, where the oldest will be used first, the accounting standards only allow this if it is necessary to ensure the accounts show a true and fair view. Last in first out is, however, widely used in the United States.

Using our example, the cost of sales would be £10,465 and the stock £1,000. However our example is too simple, to operate LIFO properly companies would have to calculate the last in at the time of making the sale. This means that they would have to have a complicated accounting system to cope with the demands of operating LIFO.

The three methods of valuing stock will give different profits and different stock values on the balance sheet:

	Cost of sales £	Stock values £
First in first out	10,335.00	1,130.00
Weighted average	10,393.50	1,071.50
Last in first out	10,465.00	1,000.00

These methods give us the basis for calculating the costs of goods used in sales, but do not cope with the problem of including labour and production overhead costs into the value of work in progress and finished goods stock. Most companies' accounting procedures allow them to build in the cost of labour and production overheads as the materials move through the production process. But problems can occur when production falls or rises dramatically, as the procedures assume 'normal' production levels.

(c) **The construction company**. Construction companies experience slightly different problems, as large construction contracts often span a number of years. If the company waited until the completion of the project before including the contract in the profit and loss account, the accounts would not reflect a true and fair view of their financial performance. They could complete no contracts in one year and three in the following year. Treating companies who are involved in long-term contracts in the same way as other companies would render their accounts meaningless. Consequently construction companies include uncompleted long-term contracts in their profit and loss account. Therefore we need to consider how they incorporate turnover and profit into the profit and loss account.

Turnover is recorded as the contract progresses and profit is recorded as it arises.

However identifying the turnover is only simple if the contract is 'cost plus' one or where the contract is divided into easily identifiable parts. A number of methods have evolved to cope with this situation, but all have problems associated with them:

- **Valuation by an independent surveyor**: the surveyor certifies the percentage of the contract that has been completed. However this certificate may pre-date the end of the financial year.
- **Valuation by the management**: the management estimate the percentage of contract completion. This would allow all turnover to be included in the profit and loss account, but it is not an independent valuation.
- **Cost basis**: there are a number of different formulas that can be used including:

$$\frac{\text{Costs to date}}{\text{Anticipated total costs}} \times \text{Anticipated total contract value}$$

This method would only be appropriate if the costs were incurred evenly over the period of the contract and there is a direct relationship between the degree of completion and the level of costs.

$$\frac{\text{Labour costs to date}}{\text{Anticipated total labour costs}} \times \text{Anticipated total contract value}$$

This would only be appropriate where the labour costs were a fair reflection of the completion of the project.

The contract turnover is allocated to the profit and loss account independently of the calculation of any attributable profit. On long-term contracts profit is calculated before the cost of sales, the reverse of the normal procedure. SSAP 9 provides no guidelines for the calculation of cost of sales, only of profit (and these are somewhat imprecise). Profit is usually calculated on the percentage of completion basis, unless there are any uncertainties about the apportionment of the profit. Profit should only be recorded when the profitable outcome of the contract is reasonably certain. A lot of companies believe that profitability can be assessed with some certainty when more than 30 per cent of the contract has been completed. When a contract is believed to be profitable the profit should be allocated fairly over the different time periods. It is not the same for losses. Any losses should be taken to the profit and loss account as soon as they are foreseen.

Once the company has decided that the contract is reasonably certain to be profitable it must decide how much profit to attribute to this period's profit and loss account. There are many different ways to calculate this, auditors encourage companies to use methods similar to those used to calculate turnover.

Prepayments

Prepayments is one of the few accounting terms that means what it says. Prepayments are payments made for goods that the business hasn't used during the year. Again, these are something we are all familiar with. Insurance and road tax are both prepayments, we pay before we get the benefit.

As prepayments are payments in advance, they are not charged to the profit and loss account because they do not relate to the sales made in the period.

For example. A company with a 31st March year end pays insurance premiums on the 1st January.

On 1st January 1993 the insurance premium cost £2,000. On 1st January 1994 it had risen to £2,800. The charge for insurance in the accounts for the year ending 31st March 1994 would be £2,200 (threequarters of the payment made in 1993 – £1,500, and a quarter of the payment made in 1994 – £700). The balance of the 1994 payment (£2,100) would be charged to the 1995 profit and loss account. It would show on the 1994 balance sheet as a prepayment and is included with debtors, although some countries show prepayments separately on the balance sheet.

Currency adjustments

Any company that exports or imports goods or has foreign operations in a subsidiary or associate has to find a way of incorporating different currencies into the accounts. With the increasing globalisation of capital markets companies have had to deal with the erratic behaviour of exchange rates.

We need to consider the exchange rate accounting problems that face companies and how these are accounted for in individual companies and in groups.

(a) **Exchange rate accounting problems**. There are two problems with dealing with exchange rates:

- which rate do you use?
- how do you account for any exchange differences?

We have the same problem on a foreign holiday when we buy our souvenirs. In calculating the cost, should we use the rate that we can get at the hotel or the rate we are likely to get on our credit card? We've all experienced exchange differences when we find that the rate that we thought we would get is different from the rate that appears on the credit card bill. Like companies, sometimes we win and sometimes we lose!

There are four possible exchange rates that can be used:

- **the closing rate**: the rate ruling at the end of the financial year,
- **the average rate**: the weighted average exchange rate during the year,

- **the historical rate**: the rate ruling at the date of the transaction,
- **the forward/contracted rate**: the rate that the company actually gets.

The accounting standards (SSAP 20) give some guidelines about accounting for foreign currencies, both the rates that should be used and the treatment of exchange differences. The rules are slightly different for individual companies and groups.

(b) **Individual companies**. For profit and loss account items individual companies should use either the rate of exchange at the date of the transaction or, if there are no significant fluctuations, average exchange rates. SSAP 20 allows, but does not require, forward rates to be used in trading transactions. Exchange differences can arise from the movement in exchange rates between the date of invoicing and the date when the invoice is paid. Exchange differences that derive from trading transactions are charged to the profit and loss account. The way that exchange differences deriving from balance sheet transactions are accounted for is determined by the nature of the asset/liability.

Assets and liabilities are classified by the accounting standard as either monetary (e.g. deposits and loans), non-monetary (e.g. plant and machinery) or shares in foreign companies.

(i) *Monetary assets and liabilities*. These are translated at the closing rate and any exchange differences are reported in the profit and loss account.

(ii) *Non-monetary assets and liabilities*. Once these are recorded their value is set, the value of the assets and liabilities don't change to reflect any differences in exchange rates.

(iii) *Foreign equity investments*. Foreign equity investments are usually shown at the rate of exchange when the investment was made. The only exception to this is if the investment is financed by foreign borrowings, in which case they may be translated at the closing (year end) rate. Any exchange differences are taken to reserves on the balance sheet, where any differences arising from the borrowings may be offset against them. The borrowings used to finance the investment don't have to be in the same currency as the investment.

(c) **Groups**. Groups must use the net investment method, also known as the closing rate method. This uses closing or average rates for the translation of profit and loss account items for most subsidiaries. Most companies use average rates, believing that this is more representative of the actual rates during the year. Any difference between the average rate and the closing rate is taken to reserves.

Balance sheet items are translated using closing rates. Any differences in the net investment (the parent's share of the capital and reserves) is taken to reserves. The only exception to this is where the subsidiary/associate is not independent and its activities are interlinked with those of the parent. In this case the trade of the subsidiary is a direct extension of the trade of the parent company. They are treated as though they were part of the parent, with historical or average rates being used. This is called the temporal method.

IMI's PROFIT AND LOSS ACCOUNT

A copy of IMI's profit and loss account is shown below. The profit and loss account follows format 1, with the cost of sales, administration expenses and distribution costs being disclosed in the notes to the accounts.

There are three things to note on the profit and loss account.

- They have two exceptional items, and any analysis of profit trends would have to take account of this.
- The loss on disposal relates to the sale of Brook Street Computers. This was sold in February 1994. Companies may make provisions for businesses that they have decided to discontinue, either by closing them down or selling them. These provisions can comprise both the anticipated losses until the disposal or termination and anticipated losses on disposal. These provisions are shown after operating profit, and are disclosed on the face of the profit and loss account. As the business was sold in February this represents the actual losses rather than the provision.

    The loss 'comprises losses arising and goodwill of £2.5 million previously deducted from reserves.' This means that they paid £2.5 million more for the company than they received when they sold it!
- They have now decided to account for their investment in International Radiator Services Ltd as an associated undertaking. International Radiator Services Ltd is a subsidiary of BTR, and is involved in the manufacture and sale of parts for motor vehicles. P. Fisken, who runs IMI's Special Engineering division, was appointed to their board on 6th February 1992. IMI has 30 per cent of the shares in International Radiator Services Ltd and a director on the board, therefore it has a participating interest. The £2.1 million represents IMI's share of their profits. The £4.4 million, shown as an exceptional item, is their share of International Radiator Services Ltd's retained profits that were not previously consolidated.

IMI plc
Group profit and loss account
FOR THE YEAR ENDED 31 DECEMBER 1993

		Continuing operations			
	Notes	Before exceptional items 1993 £m	Exceptional items 1993 £m	Total 1993 £m	Total 1992 £m
Turnover	2	1,064.6		1,064.6	1,005.6
Net operating costs	3	(984.9)		(984.9)	(930.0)
Operating profit	2	79.7		79.7	75.6
Loss on disposal	4	–	(5.9)	(5.9)	–
Share of profits of associated undertakings	5	2.1	4.4	6.5	–
Income from current asset investments		0.1		0.1	0.8
Profit before interest		81.9	(1.5)	80.4	76.4
Net interest payable	8	(10.2)	–	(10.2)	(8.4)
Profit before taxation	6	71.7	(1.5)	70.2	68.0
Tax on profit	9	(24.6)	(0.6)	(25.2)	(23.8)
Profit after taxation		47.1	(2.1)	45.0	44.2
Minority interests		(0.1)	–	(0.1)	(0.1)
Profit for the financial year	10	47.0	(2.1)	44.9	44.1
Dividends	11	(32.5)	–	(32.5)	(32.4)
Retained profit for the financial year	23	14.5	(2.1)	12.4	11.7
Earnings per share	12	14.5p	–	13.8p	13.6p

The results of acquisitions are not material to the results of the Group and no significant operations have been discontinued during the year.

The movements in reserves are set out in notes 23 and 24.

3

THE BALANCE SHEET

INTRODUCTION

The balance sheet is probably the only document that everyone has regularly prepared, and yet it is the one that most managers find the hardest to understand! Everyone has prepared a balance sheet in the last month, if not the last week.

Have you ever compared your lifestyle to someone else's? Have you ever looked at a friend and wondered how they can afford the flash car and the fabulous holiday? Have they come into some money, or is it all on credit cards? If you have, then you have prepared a balance sheet, in fact a balance sheet prepared in exactly the same way as a UK company. You look at what your friends have got, knock off what you reckon they might owe, to find out what they are worth. That's a balance sheet!

All of us are pretty much the same. We have a group of friends who we believe are intellectually similar, and willing to work about as hard. If they seem to be doing better than us we become dissatisfied and look for another job!

We all prepare our own balance sheets and compare our balance sheets with those of our friends. Our parents can tell us how well off we are, but we don't believe them if all our friends have better standards of living and aren't up to their ears in debt. Some of our friends can have better houses and cars, but they probably have bigger mortgages and credit card bills. We all have different levels of debt that we feel comfortable with (that's why you end up having rows with your partner about money – their debt comfort level is different to yours). Companies are exactly the same.

Balance sheets tell us what the company has (the assets) and what it owes (the liabilities) on a certain day. It is a snapshot of the business and is the best measure that we have for looking at the financial health of the company. By looking at what the company has got and what it owes we can see whether the company can pay its debts when they fall due. Company balance sheets do appear more complicated than the ones we prepare for ourselves, and sometimes these detailed differences can obscure the more obvious similarities. The company does exactly the same as we do, it looks at what it has got, knocks off what it owes, to find out what it is worth.

There are three main differences between our personal balance sheets and the ones prepared by companies.

- The format is more complicated, with sub-totals that are only useful when you understand what the balance sheet tells you.
- The jargon is unfamiliar, even though what it describes isn't.
- Companies can get different types of loans and company treasurers are becoming increasingly innovative, often constructing debt to appeal to a specific type of lender or investor.

It is further complicated by the fact that you often see two balance sheets. Most public companies are not individual companies, but a group of companies. Group accounts will have two balance sheets in accounts; one for the parent company (or holding company), and the other the consolidated balance sheet for the group. In financial analysis it is the consolidated balance sheet for the group that is important, as this will relate to the consolidated profit and loss account. (Only a group profit and loss account is prepared, the Companies Act does not require the parent company to disclose its profit and loss account.)

In this chapter we will look at the balance sheet in detail. We will cover:

- the things you can expect to find in the balance sheet. These will be discussed in detail, to enable you to understand both the balance sheet and the wealth of information to be found in the balance sheet notes,
- the way the balance sheet is laid out in the accounts.

THE ITEMS FOUND IN THE BALANCE SHEET

The balance sheet identifies the company's assets, and liabilities. The assets are sorted into long-term assets (fixed assets) and short-term assets (current assets). Within the European Community the liabilities are sorted in a similar way, into long-term liabilities (creditors: amounts falling due in more than a year) and short-term liabilities (creditors: amounts falling due within a year). Outside the Community these short-term liabilities are called current liabilities.

In the UK, the balance sheet deducts the assets from the liabilities in order to show what the company is worth to the owners – adopting a 'net worth' format.

Fixed assets are defined by the Companies Act as assets that the company intends to use on an ongoing basis. All other assets are current assets. The fixed assets are sorted into three categories on the face of the balance sheet:

- **Tangible assets**: this is the term used within the EC to describe land and buildings, plant and machinery, and vehicles etc.
- **Intangible assets**: this term covers items like brand-names or patents which have a value to the company, but that value is more difficult to determine objectively.
- **Investments**: these are the long-term investments that the company intends to keep for more than a year.

Current assets comprise cash and assets held for resale. They would normally include:

- **stock,**
- **debtors,**
- **investments,**
- **cash at bank and in hand.**

The creditors falling due within a year are often shown as a total on the face of the balance sheet, with details in the notes to the accounts. It would include anything that might represent cash, or services, expected to go out of the business in the next twelve months.

The creditors falling due in more than a year are largely debt, but we will see that this could cover other cash, or services, that are not due to leave the business within a year.

The capital and reserves represent the owner's stake in the business. We will see that it includes the cash received from the shareholders, the profits ploughed back into the business and any revaluations of assets.

Each item you would find on the balance sheet is discussed in detail in this chapter, including the more recent innovations. Once you have read this chapter you will have a thorough understanding of balance sheets and should be able to look at any company's accounts without trepidation.

Fixed assets

There are three types of fixed assets shown on UK accounts:

- tangible assets,
- intangible assets,
- investments.

(a) **Tangible fixed assets**. This is the EEC term for things that outside of the Community are called fixed assets. These assets are held by the business to use in generating sales, and are not held for resale. When the company intends to sell them they will be included within the current assets.

When we are doing our personal balance sheets and look at our friends' fixed assets, we have a fair idea of what they are worth. Unfortunately the book value of a company's assets rarely reflects the market value.

When looking at the tangible assets on a company's balance sheet you need to remember two things:

- these assets may not be owned by the company,
- their values are affected by the company's depreciation and revaluation policies.

(i) *Ownership of assets*. In the introductory chapter we discussed the accounting principle of substance over form. This says that if the company has the benefits, and risks, associated with owning an asset, the asset should be incorporated into the accounts, regardless of the legal position. This means that assets purchased under hire purchase agreements where the company doesn't own the asset until it has met certain conditions (normally when it has paid an agreed number of instalments) will be shown as part of the tangible assets. Assets leased on long-term leases (finance leases) will also appear as part of the tangible assets. Those leased on a short-term basis (operating leases) will not.

The accounting standard (SSAP 21) defines these two types of leases and the appropriate accounting treatment for them.

- **Finance leases**: the basic principle is that both the asset and the underlying liability should be shown on the balance sheet. Therefore assets leased under finance leases are capitalised and depreciated (the life must be the shorter of the lease term and the anticipated useful life). The capital amount owed to the leasing company is included in creditors, split between creditors due within a year and more than a year. The lease rental should be analysed into the capital element and the interest element. The capital repayment will reduce the amount owed to the leasing company, included in creditors, and the interest element of the lease rental is charged to the profit and loss account in the normal way.

  The allocation between capital and interest payments is not straightforward, as the standard requires companies to use net present value techniques to determine the split.

- **Operating leases**: these are treated in the same way as any other short-term hire agreement. The lease rental is charged to the profit and loss account as an operating cost. The notes to the profit and loss account will disclose the amount charged during the period, split between the hire of plant and machinery and other assets. Neither the asset, nor the commitment to the leasing company are shown on the balance sheet. As the leasing agreement represents a contractual liability, the notes will disclose the annual commitment for operating leases, analysed between:
  - leases expiring in one year,
  - leases expiring between two and five years,
  - leases expiring in more than five years.

Whether a lease is a finance lease or an operating lease is obviously important. The accounting standard tries to define the differences between the two, but stresses that it can only be a matter of degree, not a fundamental difference. The standard recognises that it is often difficult to decide whether the lease is a finance or an operating lease. This grey area has allowed finance companies to try and develop finance leases that can be classified as operating leases under the standard. This gives companies a source of 'off balance sheet funding'. However under FRS 5, this is unlikely to continue. If the company has the risks and rewards associated with ownership, it will be required to show the asset and associated liability on the balance sheet.

Whilst it is impossible to give a definitive definition of the difference between the two leases (the accounting standard defines an operating lease as 'a lease other than a finance lease'!) a summary of the major differences that you are likely to find is given below:

	Finance leases	Operating leases
Risks and rewards associated with ownership	Yes	No
Lease term	similar to asset life	shorter than asset life
Lease rental equivalent to	interest and repayment of at least 90% of cost	interest and repayment of depreciation of asset

(ii) *Depreciation of assets*. Most fixed assets must be shown at cost less depreciation. The only exception to this are investment properties, which are stated at market value, in the UK. The argument being that depreciating an asset being used directly to generate income would be illogical!

All other assets must be depreciated. The company's definition of costs (how much should be capitalised) and their depreciation policy affects not only the profitability of the company but also the valuation of the assets. We have already seen, in Chapter 2, how capitalising costs and extending asset lives can flatter both profits and net worth!

(iii) *Revaluation of assets*. If we think about our own assets, not all of them depreciate. Some, for example property assets, may increase in value. We have already seen that UK companies must show investment properties at market value. This means that they must conduct an annual valuation of these properties.

Most companies' properties are not held for investment purposes and whilst they must disclose any significant differences between book values and market values, they currently have the option on whether to incorporate this surplus in the accounts. (The Companies Act requires most companies to disclose in the directors' report any material difference between the book value and the market value of properties.)

If the company revalues its assets it must disclose in the notes to the balance sheet:

- the basis of the valuation,
- the name and qualifications of the valuer.

To illustrate how a company would account for the revaluation of assets we will consider the following example:

A company has tangible fixed assets of £100,000 and share capital of £100,000. The share capital has been used to buy the tangible assets, which include property costing £60,000. Property prices have been rising steeply and the company has had the property valued at £80,000 and decides to incorporate this into the balance sheet. The new balance sheet will be:

Tangible fixed assets £120,000

Share capital	£100,000
Revaluation reserve	£20,000
	£120,000

Three things should be noted:

- The revaluation does not affect the profit and loss account directly as it is not a realised gain (the principle of prudence means that only realised gains are shown in the profit and loss account). It may affect the profit and loss account indirectly, as the depreciation charge will be based on £80,000, not the original cost of £60,000.
- The revaluation reserve is not a distributable reserve, and therefore cannot be used for the payment of dividends.
- The net worth of the company has increased by £20,000. This will probably improve the company's borrowing powers and will affect the ratios calculated on the company's accounts (the impact of this will be discussed in detail in Chapter 11).

If the property subsequently falls in value (as commercial property did in the late 1980s, early 1990s), it should be recognised in the accounts if the fall is believed to be permanent. In our example above, the company could absorb a fall of £20,000 on the balance sheet. For example if the value of the property fell to £65,000, the revaluation reserve would fall by £15,000 to £5,000. But if the value of the property fell to £50,000 a charge of £10,000 would have to be made to the profit and loss account.

Revaluation deficits, which are believed to be permanent, can only be charged to the revaluation reserve to the extent of any revaluation surpluses that relate to those assets. This became a major problem for UK companies in the 1990s.

Trafalgar House is a good example of a company whose profits were hit by asset writedowns. Their hotels were revalued at open market value at 30th September 1993. This resulted in a 'writedown of their carrying values of £51.5 million of which £11.7 million has been charged to the profit and loss account and £39.8 million to the revaluation reserve.' Only part of the writedown could be absorbed by the reserves, the balance had to be charged to the profit and loss account.

A number of retailers had a similar problem in 1994. For example Sainsbury's charged their profit and loss account with £341.5 million (nearly 43 per cent of their operating profit before exceptional items) to cover property writedowns.

When we mentally revalue our own property we use an approximate market value for the valuation; for companies it is more difficult to calculate that value. The problems that Queens Moat Houses experienced in the valuation of their hotels illustrates the difficulties. Two firms of surveyors had put widely different values on the assets. Weatherall Green & Smith valued the hotels at £1.35 billion, following a draft valuation of £1.86 billion. Jones Lang Wootton valued the same assets at £861 million. Both of these companies had used the same basis for the valuations.

But different bases do exist. Should the company use an open market value based on existing use, or alternate use? Should it, as Trafalgar House did before 1993, underpin the valuations by indicative offers from potential purchasers?

Under current revaluation rules there is no requirement for the valuation to be either professionally conducted or independent. Revaluations by directors should be treated with suspicion.

(b) **Intangible assets**. Although most companies do not show any intangible assets on the balance sheet, there are a large number of items that could be included. For example:

- capitalised research and development costs,
- concessions,
- patents and trade marks,
- brand names,
- goodwill.

The Companies Act does give some limited guidance about the accounting treatment of intangible assets. It identifies the following categories of intangible fixed assets:

- development costs,
- concessions, patents, licences, trade marks and similar rights and assets,
- goodwill,
- payments on account.

Where an intangible asset has a finite life it must be written down in the same manner as tangible assets. (Companies talk about amortising, rather that depreciating, intangible assets.)

There is currently no accounting standard dealing with intangible assets as a whole. There is a draft rule (called an exposure draft or ED) covering the accounting treatment of intangible assets and research and development and goodwill are covered by separate accounting standards.

(i) *ED 52*. The exposure draft (ED 52) states that an intangible asset can only be recognised if:

- it can be clearly distinguished from other assets,

- it has a cost, or valuation, that can be measured,
- it is probable that the company will derive future benefits from the asset.

The exposure draft suggests that all intangible assets should be amortised, as they all have a finite life, and suggests that a twenty-year maximum asset life would be appropriate.

(ii) *Research and development.* Companies must disclose their accounting policy for research and development in the notes to the accounts. The fixed assets used for research and development are always included within the fixed assets and the other costs are normally charged to the profit and loss account in the year in which they are incurred. Both pure and applied research should always be charged to the profit and loss account. However the accounting standard (SSAP 13) does identify some specific criteria which, if met, would allow the company to show development expenditure as an intangible fixed asset. These criteria are if:

- there is a clearly defined project,
- the related expenditure is separately identifiable,
- it is reasonably certain that the project is both technically feasible and commercially viable,
- it is expected to be profitable, having considered all current and future costs,
- the company has the resources to complete the project.

If the company capitalises development costs, they should be amortised over the periods expected to benefit from their use.

(iii) *Goodwill.* Goodwill is simply the difference between the purchase price of a company and the value of the net assets on the balance sheet.

If we consider the following example:

A predator buys a company, with net assets of £50,000, for £90,000 cash. The goodwill is therefore £40,000. If we look at the two balance sheets before the acquisition:

	Predator £000	Victim £000
Tangible fixed assets	100	40
Current assets:		
Stock	30	20
Debtors	70	45
Cash	100	5
	200	70
Creditors: amounts falling due within a year:		
Creditors	(110)	(30)
Net current assets	90	40
Total assets less current liabilities	190	80
Creditors: amounts falling due in more than a year:		
Loans	(30)	(30)
	160	50
Capital and reserves:		
Share capital	50	10
Profit and loss account	110	40
	160	50

On acquisition the predator has spent £90,000 and gained net assets of £50,000. When the victim is consolidated into the predator's accounts the balance sheet won't balance because of the premium he has paid on acquisition – goodwill. This can be seen in the following balance sheet:

Consolidated balance sheet

	£000
Tangible fixed assets	140
Current assets:	
Stock	50
Debtors	115
Cash (100 + 5 − 90)	15
	180
Creditors: amounts falling due within a year:	
Creditors	(140)
Net current assets	40
Total assets less current liabilities	180
Creditors: amounts falling due in more than a year:	
Loans	(60)
	120
Predator's capital and reserves:	
Share capital	50
Profit and loss account	110
	160

The business has net assets of £120,000 and capital and reserves of £160,000. The balance sheet doesn't balance because the predator has paid £40,000 premium to acquire the victim.

There are two different ways to resolve the problem; either goodwill can be written off against reserves, or an intangible asset can be created to reflect the goodwill.

These are illustrated below as Option 1 and Option 2 respectively:

	Option 1	Option 2
	£000	£000
Tangible fixed assets	140	140
Intangible fixed asset – goodwill	–	40
		180
Current assets:		
Stock	50	50
Debtors	115	115
Cash	15	15
	180	180
Creditors: amounts falling due within a year:		
Creditors	(140)	(140)
Net current assets	40	40
Total assets less current liabilities	180	220
Creditors: amounts falling due in more than a year:		
Loans	(60)	(60)
	120	160
Capital and reserves:		
Share capital	50	50
Profit and loss account	(110−40) 70	110
	120	160

The first option writes goodwill off against *past* profits, the second option increases the assets and opens the debate about whether the goodwill should be amortised. Both the international accounting standards and the draft rule, published in 1989, suggest that goodwill should be amortised. This has the effect of charging goodwill against *future* profits. Most companies in the UK follow the preferred treatment in the current accounting standard, the immediate write-off of goodwill to reserves (the first option). Most companies overseas use the second option. This gives UK companies an acquisitive advantage, they can afford to pay more for a company than companies incorporated in other countries. Any goodwill arising on acquisitions will not subsequently be charged to their profits.

The accounting treatment of goodwill is one of the most controversial topics in accounting. It has been a major topic of debate since the Accounting Standards Board started in 1990 and the resolution of the debate still seems as far away as ever. UK companies will accept the capitalisation of goodwill (particularly when their distributable reserves are low) but are reluctant to accept the amortisation of goodwill. The impact on profits could be disastrous and it would highlight those acquisitions where the predator has overpaid, and the profits do not cover the amortisation of goodwill.

(iv) *Brand names.* The inclusion of brand names on company balance sheets is a recent phenomenon, and common practice in the food and drinks industry where brand names are a large hidden asset. At 30th September 1993 Grand Metropolitan had brands on their balance sheet of £2,924 million compared to net assets of £3,754 million. These brands obviously do have a value (we are talking about names such as Smirnoff, Pilsbury, Green Giant), the problem is – what value?

The accounting profession has yet to resolve the problem of brand accounting, although brand names, as an intangible asset, fall within the scope of ED 52. It states that an intangible asset can only be recognised if it can be clearly distinguished from any other asset, including goodwill. Whereas companies like Grand Metropolitan and Cadbury Schweppes turn all goodwill into an intangible asset, arguing that any payment above the net asset value is for the acquisitions' brands. By classifying the intangible asset as a brand they do not have to comply with the requirements for the amortisation of goodwill. They can revalue their brands on an annual basis, and argue that amortisation is irrelevant for brand accounting.

Most companies have their brands valued independently by companies like Interbrand Group. The valuation is derived from applying a multiple (based on the brand's strength in certain areas) to the brand's earnings. Both components of the formula (the multiple and the future earnings) are subjective.

Brands are undoubtedly important in some industries, and this is reflected in the amount of goodwill paid for the acquisition. But the valuation of brands is very subjective and the inclusion of brands in the balance sheet reduces the comparability of accounts and affects the ratio calculations.

(c) **Investments**. Investments can be found in two places on the balance sheet – fixed assets or current assets. Where they show on the accounts is determined by why the company is holding the investment, not what the investment is. An investment should be classed as a fixed asset when the company has an intention to keep it on a long-term basis, or where the company is forced to keep it on a long-term basis. (For example the company may be unable to sell it.)

Therefore an investment will be classed as a fixed asset if the company does not intend to, is not able to, or will not be required to, sell it in the next year. Otherwise it will be classed as a current asset investment.

Like any other fixed asset, investments must be shown at costs less any necessary provisions. Therefore if the net realisable value falls below the cost/valuation a provision will have to be made to cover the 'diminution in value'.

Companies may have three different types of fixed asset investments:

- investments in subsidiaries,
- investment in associated undertakings and other participating interests,
- other investments.

(i) *Subsidiaries*. Only the last two may be included in the investments of the group, subsidiaries will only show as a fixed asset investment in the parent company's balance sheet (usually published alongside the group balance sheet). They will not show as investments in the group's accounts as their assets and liabilities will have been consolidated.

(ii) *Associated undertakings*. The investment in associated undertakings must be accounted for using some version of the 'equity method'. It is shown at cost, plus the group's share of retained profits since acquisition.

To illustrate this our predator buys 30 per cent of the victim for £20,000. The total net assets of the victim were £50,000. Therefore the predator has paid £5,000 goodwill as its share of the net assets will be £15,000. (£20,000 − £50,000 × 30 per cent).

The balance sheets would show:

	Predator Pre-acquisition £000	Predator Post-acquisition £000
Fixed assets:		
Tangible fixed assets	100	100
Investments		20
		120
Current assets:		
Stock	30	30
Debtors	70	70
Cash	100	80
	200	180
Creditors: amounts falling due within a year:		
Creditors	(110)	(110)
Net current assets	90	70
Total assets less current liabilities	190	190
Creditors: amounts falling due in more than a year:		
Loans	(30)	(30)
	160	160
Capital and reserves:		
Share capital	50	50
Profit and loss account	110	110
	160	160

The predator and victim's profit and loss accounts for the year following the acquisition were:

	Predator	Victim
	£000	£000
Turnover	1,000	700
Profit before tax	200	50
Tax	(50)	(20)
Profit after tax	150	30
Dividends	(60)	–
Retained profit	90	30

We know that the predator will take its share of the victim's profits into the group profit and loss account:

	Predator (inc. victim)
	£000
Turnover	1,000
Share of profits of associated undertakings	15
Profit before tax	215
Tax	(56)
Profit after tax	159
Dividends	(60)
Retained profit	99

The value of the investment shown in the predators' balance sheet will rise to £29,000 – the £20,000 cost plus the £9,000 retained profit from the associate. The predator's proportion of the victim's profit, less any dividends paid from this profit, will be added to the value of the investment shown on the balance sheet. This ensures that the value of the investment increases to reflect both the cost and the predator's proportion of the victim's retained profit, or loss. If the victim had paid a dividend of £10,000, its retained profits would be £20,000 (£30,000 – £10,000 dividends paid). The predator would have received £3,000 cash from the dividend that wouldn't have shown on the profit and loss account, but will be reflected on the balance sheet in increased cash balances. Therefore he would increase the value of the investment on the balance sheet by £6,000 (£9,000 shown in the profit and loss account, less the £3,000 dividends received). This reflects his share in the victim's net worth. Therefore the value of the investment shown on the balance sheet would be £26,000 – the cost plus the predator's share of the retained profits.

(iii) *Other investments*. Usually these will be investments where the company owns less than 20 per cent. If the company has investments of 20 per cent or more and decides not to account for these as an associated company it must disclose the reason for its decision in the notes to the accounts. Investments in companies listed on a Stock Exchange will be shown at cost, and the aggregate market value will be disclosed if this differs from the cost. Unlisted investments should be shown at cost or valuation.

If an investment is deemed to be 'significant' under the Companies Act the company must disclose additional information about the investment. (A significant investment is where the company holds 10 per cent or more of the nominal value (this term is explained later in this chapter) of any class of shares, or where the investment represents more than 10 per cent of the company's assets.) In most situations companies will have to disclose:

- the name of the investment,
- the country of incorporation,
- the size and nature of the investment.

There is a possibility that the DTI will exempt companies from the disclosure requirements if the directors believe that it will be prejudicial and the company trades overseas.

Current assets

Current assets are the short-term assets and include:

- stock,
- debtors,
- investments,
- cash.

(a) **Stocks**. Companies will usually show the total stock on the balance sheet and will disclose the detail in the notes. The accounting standard (SSAP 9) requires the sub-classification of stocks to be 'in a manner which is appropriate to the business and so as to indicate the amounts held in each of the main categories'. The Companies Act is stricter than the standard, it requires stocks to be analysed under the following sub-headings:

- raw materials and consumables,
- work in progress,
- finished goods and goods for resale,
- payments on account.

Despite the lack of a clear definition of what constitutes stock, companies do not appear to experience any difficulty in determining which items should be classed as stock. In addition to the categories found in the Act it is not unusual to find assets previously classed as fixed assets included in stock if the company intends to sell them (for example properties and brands).

When looking at stock it should also be recognised that:

- not all items included as stock are intended for resale. Consumable stores would be included in stock, but will be used within the business.
- not all stock is tangible. For example work in progress will include work on long-term contracts.
- a company may hold stocks that are subject to reservation of title clauses. The accounting principle of substance over form means that it will still show on the company's accounts, unless they are part of consignment stock.
- consignment stock is treated slightly differently. Consignment stock is essentially the same as stock covered by a reservation of title clause. It is held by one party, but legally owned by another. Consignment stock is covered by one of the accounting rules (FRS 5). It says that consignment stock should show on the accounts of the party who has the risks and rewards of ownership. To help companies identify who has the risks and rewards four variables are identified:
  - the manufacturer's right of return,
  - the customer's right of return,
  - the stock transfer price and deposits,
  - the customer's right to use the stock.

FRS 5 becomes effective for accounting periods ending on, or after, 22nd September 1994. The accounting for consignment stock and sale and repurchase agreements (common in property companies and distilleries, where stock may be held for a number of years) will change significantly. The stock will have to appear on the accounts of the party who benefits from the stock and who has all the risks associated with ownership.

The valuation of stock has been discussed in Chapter 2.

(b) **Debtors**. Debtors represent amounts of money owed to the business. They will be shown as a total on the balance sheet itself, with a note to disclose how much falls due within a year and how much falls due in more than a year.

The notes to the accounts will subdivide debtors into:

- trade debtors,
- amounts owed by group undertakings (parent company balance sheet only),
- amounts owed by undertakings in which the company has a participating interest,
- other debtors,
- prepayments and accrued income.

Trade debtors relate to turnover, whereas other debtors relate to the sale of other items.

We saw in Chapter 2 how debtors are shown on the balance sheet net of any bad debt provisions. Therefore the size of the provision will affect the value of the asset shown on the balance sheet.

Factoring

The cash tied up in debtors can be a major problem for manufacturing companies and can lead to liquidation in times of expansion. We have seen the trend for large companies to delay paying smaller companies, recognising them as a source of interest-free borrowing (a practice not too dissimilar to our payments to the electricity companies – how many of us pay on the blue bill?!). This has led an increasing number of companies to turn to factoring as a way of releasing cash from the debtors.

In factoring the company sells the invoices to a factoring house (they are usually part of a bank or an international factoring organisation), who will give them up to 80 per cent of the invoice value as cash. The balance will be paid (less their fees) on payment of the invoice by the customer.

There are different types of factoring agreements.

- Disclosed (where the customer deals with the factor, who manages the sales ledger).
- Undisclosed (where the customer deals with the company, who still manage the sales ledger in the normal way). This is also called invoice discounting.
- With recourse (if the customer does not pay, either in full or by a certain date, the company will repay the advances from the factor).
- Non-recourse (the factor can not force the company to repay in the event of non-payment by the customer).
- With partial recourse (some non-refundable proceeds are received by the company).

FRS 5 discusses the accounting treatment of these different types of factoring agreements. When it becomes effective, all companies whose agreements have any recourse back to the company will have to disclose in the notes to the accounts:

- that they are factoring,
- the amount of factored debtors at the end of the year,
- the cost of factoring.

The specific accounting treatment will depend on the nature of the recourse involved in the agreement:

- **Non-recourse agreements**: neither the debtors nor the advance from the factor will show on the balance sheet. It will be 'derecognised'. The cost of factoring will be charged to the profit and loss account.
- **Limited recourse agreements**: the debtors will be reduced by the amount of non-recourse advances, to show a net debtor position. This is called a 'linked presentation'. This should only be used where the company selling

the invoices cannot be forced to re-acquire them in the future. The non-recourse advances could take several forms. For example, they could be in the form of credit insurance, or a credit protection policy.

The factoring cost will be split between any administration costs and interest charges, which should show on the appropriate lines of the profit and loss account.

- **Full recourse agreements**: the gross debtors will be shown on the balance sheet, less any provisions for bad debts, and the advances from factors will show as a separate line within the notes to the creditors. This is called 'separate presentation'. The factoring cost will be split between any administration costs and interest charges, which should show on the appropriate lines of the profit and loss account.

(c) **Investments**. Investments are shown at the lower of cost and net realisable value. The notes to the accounts will categorise the investments, with listed investments shown separately.

Creditors: amounts falling due within a year

These short-term creditors are required to be categorised as follows:

- bank loans and overdrafts,
- payments on account,
- trade creditors,
- bills of exchange payable,
- amounts owed to group undertakings (parent company's balance sheet only),
- amounts owed to associated undertakings,
- other creditors,
- corporation tax,
- other taxation and social security,
- accrued expenses and deferred income,
- proposed dividend.

Most of these are fairly self-explanatory; deferred income is probably the exception. Deferred income is money that has either been received by the company, or is due to them, but has yet to be earned. The matching principle means that it cannot show on the profit and loss account. Any advance payments for sales, or government grants, would show as part of deferred income. These could show in both creditors due in a year and creditors due in more than a year. For example a company might receive a grant of £5,000 for the purchase of a tangible asset that is expected to last for five years. The company would bring the grant into the profit and loss account over the life of the asset – £1,000 per year. The balance, not yet credited to the profit and loss account, would show on the balance sheet as deferred income, split between that deferred for a year and more than a year.

However, if you look at the notes to a set of public company accounts you will find a large variety of different types of debt. Company treasurers have become increasingly sophisticated and will raise funds from the cheapest market that matches their needs. They are innovative in their use of short-term debt instruments, often tailoring them to attract a specific investor.

Companies' short-term loans fall into two broad categories:

- overdrafts and short-term loans from banks and other financial institutions,
- issues of promissory notes (IOUs) and bills of exchange that can be held by anyone and are bought and sold.

We are all familiar with bank overdrafts but may be less familiar with the second category of short-term debt instruments. Some of the more common ones found in company accounts are:

- bills of exchange,
- notes,
- commercial paper.

These are discussed in detail below.

(a) **Bills of exchange**. We have probably all written a post-dated cheque at some time or another. Companies' post-dated cheques are called bills of exchange. Bills of exchange differ from our post-dated cheques in two respects.

- They are written by the supplier, and signed by the customer in an acknowledgement of the debt.
- They can be sold. Bills of exchange are what lawyers call 'negotiable instruments'; this simply means that you can sell them!

Bills of exchange normally have a maturity of three months. If the supplier wants the cash today, rather than in three months' time, he sells the bill. They are bought by discount houses. Discount houses are specialist banks who borrow short-term money from commercial banks, and use the cash to buy various forms of short-term IOUs like bills of exchange. If the buyer of the bill is going to have to wait three months for his money, he won't pay £100 today for a bill that will give him £100 in three months' time. He will be losing three months' interest. Bills of exchange are 'discounted', effectively interest is paid in advance – the discount reflecting the three months' interest lost. This type of bill is called a trade bill; there is another kind called a bank acceptance.

An acceptance is basically the same as a post-dated cheque, with a cheque card number on the back – the bank has guaranteed payment. The real difference is that, unlike our cheques, the acceptance can be sold. A bank puts its name on the bill, in so doing the bank is guaranteeing payment, even if the company issuing the bill defaults. The top tier of merchant banks were historically the banks who 'accepted' the bills and were known as the accepting houses. An acceptance sells at the lowest interest rates because the payment of the bill is certain.

Bills of exchange have been around for centuries, and have always been part of the normal trade practice in import and export businesses. However treasurers often use acceptances as part of their short-term financing programmes, and a marked increase in acceptances may indicate a cash shortage.

(b) **Notes.** Notes are unsecured IOUs. They are negotiable instruments and can have a maturity of up to ten years, although most have a much shorter maturity and a number of notes are repayable at the option of the holders.

(c) **Commercial paper**. Commercial paper has been widely used internationally since it started in America in the nineteenth century. The commercial paper market started in the UK in 1986 and represents another form of short-term unsecured borrowing in the form of a negotiable instrument. It is only available to high quality borrowers and in some markets (for example US) companies must have their commercial paper credit-rated. Commercial paper is only an option for large companies, as, in order to have an issue the company should have net assets over £25 million. Whilst commercial paper can have a maturity as long as five years, most issues tend to be very short-dated. (It is not unusual for commercial paper to have a maturity of three weeks.) Large companies use commercial paper as an alternative to bank overdrafts, as they are very cheap to establish. (It can cost as little as £15,000 to set up a £50 million commercial paper programme!)

Commercial paper is issued at a discount to the face value, and is often 'rolled over' – with one tranche being repaid by the issue of another.

Creditors falling due in more than a year

Any money owed by the business, that has to be repaid after more than a year will be found under this heading. This includes:

- bank loans,
- finance leases,
- payments on account,
- trade creditors,
- amounts owed to group undertakings (parent company's balance sheet only),
- amounts owed to associated undertakings,
- other creditors,
- accrued expenses and deferred income.

Most of the long-term creditors will be debt of one sort or another. The loans are analysed in the notes to the accounts and will be shown as a total and analysed in detail. The notes will detail each specific loan, the repayment date, the currency, and the rate of interest, if fixed. They will also specify how much of the loans are secured, and there will be a loan repayment schedule identifying how much has to be repaid:

- in one to two years,
- in two to five years,
- after five years.

Companies' long-term loans fall into two broad categories, similar to short-term debt:

- loans from banks and other financial institutions;
- issues of debentures and other forms of loan stock which are offered to investors, and therefore can be held by the general public. They are bought and sold in the same way as shares.

In looking at long-term borrowings we will consider in more detail:

- the type of security offered for loans,
- traditional long-term loans,
- debentures and bonds,
- Eurobonds.

(a) **Security for loans**. Any borrowings can be secured in one of two ways:

- **A fixed charge**: when we take out a mortgage on our house the building society or the bank has a fixed charge. They have a legal right to our house if we don't pay our mortgage, and we cannot sell our house without the lender's permission. Fixed charges on company's assets work in exactly the same way. The lender has the legal right to specified assets and the company cannot dispose of these assets without the lender's permission. Fixed charges tend to be given on long-term fixed assets like land, properties and ships.

  If the company falls into arrears or defaults on the agreement the lender can either:
  - repossess and sell the assets, giving any surplus to the company. This is sometimes called foreclosure,
  - appoint a receiver to receive any income from the asset (e.g. property rents).
- **A floating charge**: this is a general charge on the company's assets. Floating charges usually relate to short-term fixed assets (plant and machinery and vehicles) and current assets. Whilst the lender has the legal right to a group of assets, the company may continue to manage those assets in the normal course of business. The company has to be able to sell its stock, otherwise it will be unable to trade!

Some loans may be secured, but they rank after all the other borrowings in the event of a liquidation. These are called 'subordinated loans'.

It is also common for a lending bank to require a company to seek the bank's permission before giving security to anyone else – this is called a negative pledge.

(b) **Long-term loans**. A traditional long-term loan is rather like an endowment mortgage, but without the endowment policy. All the company has to do on a day-to-day basis is pay interest, the loan is repaid either in full at the end of the term, or in stages. It is also possible to take the loan in stages; if the company doesn't want all the money at once, they can draw it down in specified tranches. The loan could either be with one bank or syndicated amongst a number of banks.

(c) **Debentures and bonds**. There is no real difference between a debenture and a bond, both are sold to the general public and may be secured or unsecured.

A debenture is a negotiable instrument that is usually, but not always, secured and is covered by either a debenture deed or a trust deed.

- **A debenture deed**: this places a fixed or floating charge on the company's assets.
- **A trust deed**: this contains all the details of the debenture and may include clauses that restrict the operations of the company.

Bonds are also negotiable instruments offered to the general public that may, or may not, be secured on the company's assets. They are covered by a trust deed. A bondholder is entitled to receive a stream of interest payments, and the repayment of the principal at maturity. Before a company has a bond issue it will have the debt credit rated. There are two types of rating agencies looking at companies.

- Agencies who look at the company from a supplier's point of view (e.g. Dun and Bradstreet) and help to answer the question 'Will I get paid if I supply goods to this company?'.
- Agencies who look at the company from the investor's point of view (e.g. Standard and Poor, Moody) to help answer the question 'Will I lose all my money if I invest in this company?'.

It is the latter who rate corporate debt and the best quality corporate debt is rated triple A. The rating is very important as it affects both the ability to sell the bonds and the rate of interest that the company will have to pay. The higher the rating, the lower the risk; the lower the risk, the lower the interest! Bond interest is called the 'coupon' and is expressed as a percentage of the face value of the bond. The face value of the bond may not be the same as the current bond price. Bond prices are influenced by two things:

- relative interest rates, if current interest rates are 6 per cent and the bond is paying 10 per cent investors will be prepared to pay a premium to buy the bond.

- The current credit rating of the company, if the credit rating has fallen the interest rate will not reflect the current level of risk and the bond price will fall.

There are many different types of bonds found in company accounts. Banks and companies have been very innovative, custom designing bonds to attract specific investors. They have been an ideal vehicle for financial innovation as there are four variables which can be modified.

- **The security given for the bond**: for example, banks issue bonds that have our mortgages and credit card balances as collateral.
- **The coupon paid**: for example, some bonds (called 'Zeroes') are issued. that don't pay interest. They are issued at a discount, so for instance a £10 million five-year bond may be issued for £6.209 million. This has an implied interest rate of 10 per cent and the value of the bond would increase by 10 per cent a year. All other things being equal, at the end of the first year the bond would be worth £6.83 million, at the end of the second £7.513 million, and so on until the end of the fifth year when the investors would receive the £10 million.

   Some bonds increase the interest over the life of the bond (called step-up bonds), others reduce it (step-down bonds).

- **The repayment of the principal amount borrowed**: for example, the repayment of the principal in some bond issues is index-linked. In others, the bond may be issued in one currency and repaid in another (these are called dual currency bonds).
- **The bond maturity**: for example, a bond may have two options on maturity – it might have a maturity of thirty years, with an option to reduce this to ten years (a retractable bond). Alternatively it could have a maturity of ten years with an option to extend it to thirty years (an extendable bond).

(d) **Eurobonds**. Large companies often issue Eurobonds. If we are to understand a Eurobond we must understand what the term 'Euro' is. A currency goes 'Euro' when it is traded outside of the country of origin, and its banking regulations. Japanese yen on deposit in London are Euroyen, American dollars deposited in Tokyo are Eurodollars. Euro does not mean European.

A Eurobond is simply a bond that is issued outside the country of its currency and has few restrictions on its issue and trading. The company does not keep a register of Eurobond holders (it may for a domestic or foreign bond). The bond is sold in 'bearer' form (whoever holds the bond claims the interest and repayment of the principal). As Eurobond interest has no tax deducted at source, they are very attractive to investors who wish to keep their affairs secret from the tax authorities!

Eurobonds are issued by large, internationally known, high-quality borrowers.

Provisions for liabilities and charges

We discussed provisions in Chapter 2 and saw how bad debt and obsolete stock provisions reduced the value of debtors and stock. Not all provisions are concerned with the reduction in value of an asset. Some provisions are set up to cover a potential liability or loss where the outcome, or timing of the loss, is uncertain. It is these provisions that would be shown on the balance sheet under this heading. They would include:

- deferred tax provisions,
- unfunded pension obligations (unfunded pension schemes are normal in some other countries),
- rationalisation provisions,
- litigation settlement provisions.

These may be simply shown as 'deferred tax' and 'other provisions'; the degree of detail will be determined by the need for the accounts to show a true and fair view.

Capital and reserves

This represents the owners' stake in the business, and shows the businesses' share capital and the reserves. Reserves can come from a variety of sources:

- the cumulative retained profit, less any losses, since the business started – this reserve is called the profit and loss account and is the only distributable reserve;
- the extra premium paid, over the nominal value, for the shares that have been issued by the company – this is called the share premium account;
- the revaluation of the businesses' assets – this is called the revaluation reserve.

The capital and reserves on the balance sheet usually comprise:

- share capital,
- profit and loss account,
- revaluation reserve,
- share premium account.

It is possible to find other reserves on the balance sheet in addition to the reserves shown above, especially in foreign accounts.

(a) **Share capital**. In this section we will look at:

- authorised and issued share capital,
- share issues,
- the different types of shares found in company accounts.

(i) *Authorised and issued share capital.* There will be two share capital numbers in the notes to the accounts; the authorised share capital and the issued share capital. The authorised share capital represents the amount that the company can issue. If the directors of the company wish to issue more shares than have been authorised they will have to seek shareholder approval, normally this just requires the passing of a resolution by a majority of the shareholders.

The issued share capital shown on the balance sheet is the total number of shares currently in issue at their original value (this is called the nominal or the par value). All UK shares must have a par value, which is determined when the company is started. Shares cannot be issued at a discount to this value. This is not always true overseas, for example in America it is possible to have shares with no par value and to issue shares at any price. The notes to the accounts usually describe the issued shares as 'allotted (the company has decided who is going to hold the shares), called up (they have asked for the money) and fully paid'.

(ii) *Share issues*. The company's ability to issue further shares is determined by two things:

- the authorised share capital,
- the Stock Exchange rules. These limit the amount of shares that can be placed with new investors, forcing listed companies to have major new issues in the form of a 'rights issue'.

In a rights issue, the company offers its existing shareholders the opportunity to buy new shares at a discounted price. The shareholder then has three alternatives.

- They can exercise their right to buy the share.
- They can sell their rights to buy the share (in practice this option is only available to large shareholders, the smaller shareholders' profit will be wiped out by dealing fees).
- They can do nothing.

Most share issues are 'underwritten'. This is a form of insurance, provided by banks and institutions, where the underwriters agree to buy the shares if no one else wants to buy them. This ensures that the company will receive some cash from the rights issue. The underwriters were forced to buy the shares in the BP privatisation in 1987. The stock market crash put the offer price above the market price, so that most of the shares were left with the underwriters.

There are other forms of share issues that do not involve any cash coming into the business. Companies can have scrip, bonus, or capitalisation issues (they all mean the same thing!). In these issues the company converts some of the reserves into share capital. The share price will fall after the issue, reflecting that the market value of the company hasn't changed and there is an increased number of shares in issue. Companies often do this when they believe that the market price for their shares is too high.

Another way of reducing the share price, without capitalising reserves, is to have a share split. This reduces the nominal value of each share in issue. For example, if the share has a nominal value of £1.00, the company could split each share into four 25p shares.

Both bonus issues and share splits reduce the market value of the shares. In a bonus issue the shareholder would receive additional shares. In a share split the shareholder would receive new shares in place of the old share.

(iii) *Classes of share*. There are a number of different types of shares found in company accounts:

- deferred shares,
- ordinary shares,
- preference shares.

Companies may also issue warrants to allow people to subscribe for shares at some future date.

Deferred shares

These are often the founders' shares and are rarely seen now in company accounts. They either:

- do not receive a dividend until some future date, usually several years after issue,
- only receive a dividend after ordinary shareholders' dividends have reached a pre-determined level.

Ordinary shares

These are the most common form of shares. It is possible for companies to have more than one type of ordinary share; with differences in voting rights, entitlement to dividend, entitlements and ranking in the event of liquidation.

Preference shares

Preference shares have a fixed dividend that must be paid *before* other dividends can be paid. There are a number of different types of preference shares; they can include one, or more, of the features outlined below.

- **Cumulative preference shares**: if the company does not pay a preference dividend on a cumulative preference share, it is only postponing the payment, which accumulates. The preference dividend is known as 'in arrears' (which must be noted in the accounts) and no other dividend can be paid until all the preference dividend arrears have been paid.
- **Redeemable preference shares**: these have to be redeemed (repaid) at a fixed date. This makes them fundamentally the same as debt, but with the dividend being paid out of after-tax profits. They are common in two situations; management buy-outs and bank rescues (the bank undertakes

a debt equity conversion, turning loans into redeemable preference shares).

- **Participating preference shares**: shareholders may receive two dividends: the fixed dividend, and a variable dividend (usually a proportion of the ordinary dividend).
- **Convertible preference shares**: these are becoming increasingly common. Preference shareholders have the right to convert into ordinary shares at a predetermined rate, at some future date.

You may find reference in some accounts to American Depository Receipts (ADRs). These are not another type of share. They are a mechanism used in the USA to simplify the procedures for holding shares in foreign companies. The shares are bought, on behalf of the American investor, and deposited in a bank outside of the USA. An American bank then issues ADR certificates to the American shareholder. The custodian bank then processes the payment of dividends, rights issues etc. ADRs may be traded on American stock exchanges (they are then called sponsored ADRs) if the company is registered with the Securities Exchange Commission and complies with their requirements.

(b) **Profit and loss account**. This is the accumulated profits and losses made since the company started adjusted by two factors: goodwill and currency adjustments. It is the only reserve that is distributable and can be used to pay dividends. In some countries this is called a revenue reserve.

(c) **Revaluation reserve**. This represents the accumulated revaluations of fixed assets. When previously revalued assets are sold, and the revaluation is realised, the revaluation is transferred between reserves. It will be transferred from the revaluation reserve to the profit and loss account.

The revaluation reserve is not a distributable reserve, but can be used for a bonus issue.

(d) **Share premium account**. When shares are issued at a premium to their nominal value, the premium should be shown in the share premium account. The only exception to this is where shares are issued for an acquisition. The company may then qualify for statutory share premium relief under Section 131 of the Companies Act. This allows companies to write off any goodwill arising on consolidation through the share premium account, via a merger reserve.

Once a share premium has been created it is legally treated as part of the share capital of the company, and is not a distributable reserve. It may however be used for:

- writing off any expenses, commissions, or discounts relating to share or debenture issues,
- writing off the company's preliminary expenses,

- providing for any premium repayable on the redemption of debentures,
- a bonus issue.

(e) **Debt equity hybrids**. There are an increasing number of instruments which are bridging debt and equity. The three discussed below are typical examples.

(i) *Convertible bonds*. Convertible bonds give the holders the option to convert into ordinary shares, rather than take the repayment of the bond. They have two advantages, firstly the interest rate is lower because of the conversion option. Secondly, the company may not have to repay the loan, just issue additional shares (they will need shareholder permission to do this in the UK). These bonds will now show as part of the company's liabilities, disclosed separately from the other debts FRS 4 requires that the debt conversion should not be anticipated.

(ii) *Redeemable preference shares*. Redeemable preference shares are a form of equity that is repaid at a fixed date, normally at their nominal value. FRS 4 requires that these should be included in the shareholders' funds classified as 'non-equity shares'. These are shares that have any of the following characteristics:

- the dividend is fixed, and does not depend on the financial performance of the company, or the dividends paid to other shareholders,
- there are limited rights to share any 'winding up surplus' surplus if the company is liquidated,
- the shares are redeemable.

The company should also disclose:

- the dividends attributable to non-equity shares,
- the dividend rights,
- the redemption date, and the amount to be paid on redemption,
- their priority, and the amounts receivable, on a winding up of the company,
- their voting rights.

(iii) *Mezzanine finance*. Mezzanine finance is another example of a debt equity hybrid. It tends to be used in young companies or management buy-outs and buy-ins. In these situations there is a limited amount of debt that can be raised and/or a limited amount of cash available for a share issue.

Mezzanine finance is a subordinated loan (it ranks behind the other loans) that has a higher rate of interest than the other debt (to reflect the increased risk) and is convertible into shares via:

- an option to convert all, or part, of the loan into equity,
- a warrant to subscribe for equity (a warrant gives the holder the right to subscribe at some future date for shares at a fixed price).

BALANCE SHEET FORMATS

Just as it is possible to take a picture from a number of different perspectives, it is possible to prepare the balance sheet in a number of different ways. The balance sheet content is broadly the same, no matter how it is presented. The degree of detail and the basis for valuations may vary from one country to another but the information presented in the balance sheet remains similar.

The Companies Act has two formats for the balance sheet, whilst the layout is different the content of each balance sheet is identical. Most UK companies prepare the balance sheet from the shareholders' point of view, others total assets and liabilities, looking at the business from the point of view of anyone who has put money into the business. This asset and liabilities style is the most commonly used way of preparing the balance sheet in the rest of the world.

Examples of the two formats are shown on the following pages.

FORMAT 1

	£000
FIXED ASSETS	
Tangible assets	200
Intangible assets	50
Investments	75
	325
CURRENT ASSETS	
Stocks	80
Debtors	270
Investments	40
Cash	10
	400
CREDITORS: AMOUNTS FALLING DUE WITHIN ONE YEAR	
	(300)
Net current assets	100
Total assets less current liabilities	425
CREDITORS: AMOUNTS FALLING DUE AFTER MORE THAN ONE YEAR	
	(100)
PROVISIONS FOR LIABILITIES AND CHARGES	(15)
MINORITY INTERESTS	(25)
	285
CAPITAL AND RESERVES	
Share capital	50
Profit and loss account	175
Revaluation reserve	40
Share premium account	20
	285

FORMAT 2

	£000
FIXED ASSETS	
Tangible assets	200
Intangible assets	50
Investments	75
	325
CURRENT ASSETS	
Stocks	80
Debtors	270
Investments	40
Cash	10
	400
	725
CAPITAL AND RESERVES	
Share capital	50
Profit and loss account	175
Revaluation reserve	40
Share premium account	20
	285
MINORITY INTERESTS	25
PROVISIONS FOR LIABILITIES AND CHARGES	15
CREDITORS*	
	400
	725

* A Format 2 balance sheet shows creditors as a single item. In the notes, each component of the creditors must be analysed between those falling due within a year and in more than a year. The totals should also be shown.

IMI's BALANCE SHEETS

A copy of both the group and the company balance sheets are shown on the following pages.

You will notice that goodwill is disclosed in the group's balance sheet within the capital and reserves. This represents the accumulated goodwill on acquisitions since 31st December 1987.

The company does not have any tangible assets, only investments. These investments are shares in, and loans to, subsidiaries and associates. The investments in subsidiaries are not reflected in the group accounts, as they are eliminated on consolidation.

IMI plc
Group balance sheet
AT 31 DECEMBER 1993

	Notes	**1993** **£m**	1992 £m
Fixed assets			
Tangible assets	13	**277.6**	267.4
Investments	14	**12.3**	1.8
		289.9	269.2
Current assets			
Stocks	15	**253.2**	262.9
Debtors	16	**187.0**	200.7
Investments		**1.2**	9.3
Cash and deposits		**101.3**	159.4
		542.7	632.3
Creditors:			
amounts falling due within one year			
Loans and overdrafts	17	**(109.1)**	(168.8)
Other creditors	18	**(207.9)**	(225.3)
Net current assets		**225.7**	238.2
Total assets less current liabilities		**515.6**	507.4
Creditors:			
amounts falling due after more than one year			
Loans	19	**(89.5)**	(91.0)
Other creditors	20	**(10.4)**	(11.7)
Provisions for liabilities and charges	21	**(29.8)**	(26.3)
		385.9	378.4
Capital and reserves			
Called up share capital	22	**81.2**	81.0
Share premium account	23	**68.8**	67.4
Revaluation reserve	23	**7.9**	3.6
Other reserves	23	**15.0**	15.0
Profit and loss account	23	**327.7**	323.6
Goodwill arising on acquisitions	24	**(114.7)**	(112.2)
		385.9	378.4

The Accounts were approved by the Board of Directors on 7 March 1994 and signed on its behalf by:

Eric Pountain   Gary Allen
Directors

IMI plc
Company balance sheet
AT 31 DECEMBER 1993

	Notes	1993 £m	1992 £m
Fixed assets			
Investments	14	**241.9**	307.4
Current assets			
Debtors	16	**241.7**	226.7
Investments		**–**	5.7
Cash and deposits		**24.3**	6.8
		266.0	239.2
Creditors:			
amounts falling due within one year			
Loans and overdrafts	17	**(62.7)**	(100.8)
Other creditors	18	**(29.1)**	(30.0)
Net current assets		**174.2**	108.4
Total assets less current liabilities		**416.1**	415.8
Creditors:			
amounts falling due after more than one year			
Loans	19	**(83.1)**	(82.4)
Other creditors	20	**(50.8)**	(52.9)
		282.2	280.5
Capital and reserves			
Called up share capital	22	**81.2**	81.0
Share premium account	23	**68.8**	67.4
Capital redemption reserve	23	**1.6**	1.6
Profit and loss account	23	**130.6**	130.5
		282.2	280.5

The Accounts were approved by the Board of Directors on 7 March
1994 and signed on its behalf by:

Eric Pountain   Gary Allen
Directors

4

THE CASH FLOW STATEMENT

INTRODUCTION

The accounting standard (FRS 1) requires most companies (small private companies are exempted from the standard) to publish a cash flow statement in the accounts showing the movement of cash in the business. It replaces the source and application of funds statement and more clearly identifies the cash flows in the business, and is easier to understand and interpret. At the time of writing, this standard is under review and the format may well change in the future.

The cash flow statement is perhaps the most important statement found in the accounts as cash is the one thing that cannot be created! By showing the movement of cash in a business we get a clearer idea of the company's financial stability and viability. We will also see, later in the book, that the cash flow statement is often a useful starting point in financial analysis.

It shows a summary of the cash flows in and out of the company during the year, identifying where the company has got its money from and what it has spent the money on. The cash flows are shown functionally and are grouped into cash flows from:

- **trading**: called 'cash flows from operating activities',
- **interest and dividends**: called 'cash flows from returns on investment and servicing of finance',
- **tax**: called 'cash flows from taxation',
- **buying and selling fixed assets**: called 'cash flows from investing activities'.

These cash flows are totalled, identifying whether the company has generated a surplus or has a deficit. This cash flow total is called 'cash flows before financing'. Having identified whether the company is living within its means, the statement then identifies where the company has applied the surplus or, alternatively, how it has funded the deficit.

This is classified as:

- **long-term funds (shares and long-term loans)**: called 'cash flows from financing',
- **short-term funds (short-term deposits and borrowings)**: called 'cash and cash equivalents'. Sadly, real people do not talk about cash equivalents, this is accounting jargon for something that has an original maturity of

three months or less. Money placed on deposit for ten weeks is a cash equivalent, a bank overdraft is a negative cash equivalent, as it must be repaid on demand.

DETERMINING THE OPERATIONAL CASH FLOW

The cash flow statement starts by looking at the cash flows from operating activities. There are two different ways that this can be shown on the statement; the accounting standard refers to these as the direct method, and the indirect method. They only differ in the *way* they identify the operating cash flow. The direct method shows the cash receipts and payments, whereas the indirect method reconciles the operating profit to the operating cash flow. All companies must show the reconciliation to the operating profit in the notes to the accounts.

The direct method

The direct method is easier for non-accountants to understand, but is less commonly found in the accounts:

CASH FLOW FROM OPERATING ACTIVITIES:

	£000
Cash received from customers	910
Cash paid to suppliers	(530)
Cash paid to, and on behalf of, employees	(200)
Other cash paid	(100)
Net cash inflow from operating activities	80

The indirect method

If the company uses the direct method to calculate the operating cash flow it will still have to show the reconciliation to operating profit – the indirect method. This starts with the operating profit and then adds back any paper charges (primarily depreciation) that have been made in arriving at the profit to show the cash that *will* be generated from this period's trading. This is then adjusted for any changes in the working capital, to arrive at the cash that has been generated from operations during the year:

CASH FLOW FROM OPERATING ACTIVITIES:

		£000
	Operating profit	10
	Depreciation	40
Less:	Increase in debtors	(90)
Plus:	Decrease in stocks	50
	Increase in creditors	70
	Net cash inflow from operating activities	80

In the above example, the company will only generate £50,000 (£10,000 + £40,000) from the year's sales but has managed to generate £80,000 during the year – the balance coming from the working capital. Although debtors have increased, this has been more than offset by the reduction in stock and the increase in creditors.

UNDERSTANDING THE CASH FLOW STATEMENT

All companies will then follow the same format for the cash flow statement. This identifies the cash inflows and outflows over the period. A simple example is shown below.

CASH FLOW STATEMENT

	£000
OPERATING ACTIVITIES:	
Net cash inflow from operating activities	80
RETURNS ON INVESTMENT AND SERVICING OF FINANCE:	
Dividends paid	(100)
Interest paid	(40)
Net cash outflow from returns on investment and servicing of finance	(140)
TAXATION:	
Tax paid	(60)
Net cash outflow from taxation	(60)
INVESTING ACTIVITIES:	
Purchase of tangible fixed assets	(80)
Net cash outflow from investing activities	(80)
NET CASH OUTFLOW BEFORE FINANCING	(200)
FINANCING:	
Share issue	130
Loan repayment	(100)
Net cash inflow from financing	30
Decrease in cash and cash equivalents	170

This shows a company that is generating enough cash to service the interest bill, but not the dividends and the tax. There is a shortfall of £120,000 before investing activities. They then purchased tangible assets and consequently had a net cash outflow before financing of £200,000. The share issue only generated £30,000 after repaying the loan, the balance of £170,000 came from a reduction in cash and cash equivalents. At this point we don't know whether the company used cash or was forced to increase overdrafts.

The notes to the cash flow statement will help us identify how the shortfall was funded, and whether the company used its cash balances or increased its overdrafts.

	£000
Decrease in cash and cash equivalents:	
Decrease in cash balances	120
Increase in bank overdraft	50
	170

We can see that the company used some of its cash balances to fund the shortfall, but these were insufficient and the company needed to increase its overdraft by £50,000.

IMI's CASH FLOW STATEMENT

IMI's cash flow statement is shown on the following page. You will notice that the statement follows the format shown previously up to the net cash flow before financing. Thereafter it follows a slightly different format for the financing and cash equivalents. The cash inflow from financing of £19.2 million is shown in brackets, and the increase in cash and cash equivalents is not.

You will find that some companies will follow IMI's approach, showing sources of funds bracketed (and applications unbracketed) below the financing line. Other companies will follow the practice of the earlier example, continuing the practice of showing all inflows as positive and all outflows as negative.

IMI plc
Group cash flow statement
FOR THE YEAR ENDED 31 DECEMBER 1993

	1993		1992	
	£m	£m	£m	£m
Net cash flow from operating activities (Note 26)		119.4		132.7
Net cash flow from return on investments and servicing of finance				
Interest received	6.3		11.7	
Interest paid	(16.5)		(20.1)	
Dividends received	0.8		0.8	
Dividends paid	(32.4)		(32.4)	
	——	(41.8)	——	(40.0)
Taxation		(25.4)		(21.5)
Net cash flow before investing and finance		52.2		71.2
Net cash flow from investing activities				
Purchase of fixed assets	(47.7)		(53.9)	
Acquisitions (Note 25)	(6.7)		(20.4)	
Sale of fixed assets	2.0		2.5	
	——	(52.4)	——	(71.8)
Net cash flow before financing		(0.2)		(0.6)
Net cash flow from financing				
Issue of ordinary shares	(1.6)		(1.4)	
Drawdown of long term borrowings	(17.6)		(41.8)	
	——	(19.2)	——	(43.2)
Increase in cash and cash equivalents		19.0		42.6
		(0.2)		(0.6)

Reconciliation of net borrowings:

	1993			1992		
	Cash & cash equivalents	Other borrowings	Net borrowings	Cash & cash equivalents	Other borrowings	Net borrowings
	£m	£m	£m	£m	£m	£m
Balances at 1 January	28.0	(128.4)	(100.4)	(13.3)	(68.6)	(81.9)
Cash flow	19.0	(17.6)	1.4	42.6	(41.8)	(0.8)
Exchange rate changes	1.8	(0.1)	1.7	(1.3)	(18.0)	(19.3)
Balances at 31 December	48.0	(146.1)	(97.3)	28.0	(128.4)	(100.4)

5

THE STATEMENT OF TOTAL RECOGNISED GAINS AND LOSSES

INTRODUCTION

This new primary statement was introduced in June 1993, as part of FRS 3. The Accounting Standards Board felt that the statement of total recognised gains and losses was necessary, as not all of the components of a company's financial performance are reflected in the profit and loss account. Unrealised gains must be taken directly to reserves and are not shown in the profit and loss account. Therefore, the profit and loss account does not show all the gains and losses that are recorded in the period. This statement plugs that gap by showing the extent to which the shareholders' funds have increased from any gains that the company has included in the accounts, and therefore have been recognised, in the period. This is regardless of whether they have been realised and included in the profit and loss account.

Although the statement itself is new, the information contained within it has always been found in the accounts. It was always shown in the note on the reserves, but I wonder how many of us read it? The ASB felt that most non-professional readers would be unlikely to have read this note in detail, and introduced this statement to enable us to see at a glance the gains and losses recognised during the year. It bridges the profit and loss account and the balance sheet, taking information from both statements. It is intended to be used with the profit and loss account to measure the company's financial performance during the period.

The statement of total recognised gains and losses shows us:

- The profit for the financial year.
- Any revaluations of assets during the year.
- Any currency translation differences on the company's net investments.

As this statement will not be a familiar one for most readers of this book, we will construct a statement in this chapter. This will illustrate what the statement does and doesn't tell us.

CONSTRUCTING A STATEMENT OF TOTAL RECOGNISED GAINS AND LOSSES

The important thing to remember is that this statement is concerned with the gains, and losses, that have been recognised in the period. Consequently it will not include all increases and decreases in the shareholders' funds, as some of these will relate to other items. They could include an increase in the share capital or the write off of goodwill, which are clearly neither gains, nor losses, but do affect the shareholders' funds. To reflect this, companies are required to show a reconciliation to the movements in the shareholders' funds in addition to the statement of total recognised gains and losses.

We will derive a statement using the profit and loss account and balance sheets shown in the following pages. During the year our illustrative company has:

- had a major change in accounting policies, following the introduction of a new accounting standard. Conforming to this new standard will reduce the previously reported profits by £20 million,
- revalued properties upward by £10 million,
- sold fixed assets, that had previously been revalued from the cost of £3 million to £4 million, for £5 million. Consequently they reported a profit on sale of fixed assets of £1 million,
- written £2 million off an investment, to reflect a fall in the market value following a recent valuation. The value of the investment is still above the original cost,
- issued shares with a nominal value of £5 million for £7 million,
- purchased a company with net assets of £20 million for £25 million, thus purchasing £5 million goodwill. Their accounting policy is to write off goodwill through reserves,
- written off a £6 million exchange loss on overseas net investments.

These transactions are reflected in the following accounts:

Profit and loss account

	This Year £ million
Turnover	1,000
Cost of sales	(650)
Gross profit	350
Administration expenses	(100)
Distribution costs	(150)
Operating profit	100
Profit on sale of fixed assets	1
Net interest payable	(11)
Profit before tax	90
Tax	(30)
Profit for the financial year	60
Dividends	(20)
Retained profits	40

Balance Sheets

	This year £ million	Last year £ million
FIXED ASSETS		
Tangible assets	520	500
Investments	8	10
	528	510
CURRENT ASSETS		
Stock	200	150
Debtors	300	200
Cash	36	100
	536	450
CREDITORS: AMOUNTS FALLING DUE WITHIN A YEAR		
Creditors	(350)	(300)
Net current assets	186	150
Total assets less current liabilities	714	660
CREDITORS: AMOUNTS FALLING DUE IN MORE THAN A YEAR		
Borrowings	(200)	(200)
PROVISIONS FOR LIABILITIES AND CHARGES		
	(70)	(60)
	444	400

	This year	*Last year*
CAPITAL AND RESERVES		
Share capital	55	50
Profit and loss account	280	250
Share premium account	52	50
Revaluation reserve	57	50
	444	400

Note on reserves extracted from the balance sheet notes:

	Share premium account £ million	Revaluation reserve £ million	Profit and loss account £ million	Total £ million
At beginning of year as previously stated	50	50	270	370
Prior year adjustment			(20)	
At beginning of year as restated	50	50	250	350
Premium on issue of shares	2			2
Goodwill written off			(5)	(5)
Transfer from profit and loss account of the year			40	40
Transfer of realised profits		(1)	1	0
Decrease in value of investment		(2)		(2)
Currency translation differences on foreign currency net investments			(6)	(6)
Surplus on property revaluations		10		10
At the end of the year	52	57	280	389

We will use the accounts and the note on the reserves to construct a statement of total recognised gains and losses, that will reflect the transactions previously outlined.

The statement follows a standard format. It takes the profit for the financial year and adds to it any revaluations of assets to arrive at the recognised gains and losses before currency adjustments. Currency adjustments are then deducted to show the recognised gains and losses for the year. In our example the statement would be as follows:

Statement of total recognised gains and losses

	£ million
Profit for the financial year	60
Unrealised surplus on revaluation of properties	10
Unrealised loss on investment	(2)
	68
Currency translation differences on foreign currency net investments	(6)
Total recognised gains and losses for the year	62
Prior year adjustment	(20)
Total gains and losses recognised since last annual report	42

The statement clearly shows the relative importance of profit, revaluations, and currency adjustments on the company. It also highlights the fact that the company has adjusted its previously reported profits. We will look at each of the items on the statement in more detail:

- Profit for the financial year. You will notice that this is the profit before dividends, not the retained profits that are transferred to the reserves. The proposed dividends may, or may not, be approved at the Annual General Meeting after the publication of the accounts.
- The revaluations are not netted off, with surpluses and deficits separately disclosed. We can see that the recognised gains are different to those revealed by a casual glance at the movement on the revaluation reserve (the way most non-professional readers would have spotted a revaluation). The revaluation reserve has increased by seven million, not the net eight million that has been recognised. This is because one million was transferred from the revaluation reserve to the profit and loss account on sale of assets (as the gain is now realised).
- Currency translation differences are clearly shown in the body of the accounts for the first time. Whilst they have always been disclosed in the note to the reserves, the average reader of accounts would have been unaware how exposed the company's net worth was to exchange rate movements.
- Prior year adjustments. A prior year adjustment is made for a major change in accounting polices or a fundamental error in the accounts. These could be critical in our analysis of the accounts. Highlighting them in the statement (again, they were always disclosed in the notes) is an important improvement for the less informed reader.

The profit and loss accounts and the statement of total recognised gains and losses are important measures of the company's financial performance during the year. However it is important that we understand why this may not reflect the changes in the shareholders' funds, the net worth.

This is shown in the 'reconciliation of movements in shareholders' funds', which may be found either in the notes, or following the statement of total recognised gains and losses. There are two ways that this can be prepared:

	£ million
Total recognised gains	62
Dividends	(20)
New share capital subscribed	7
Goodwill written off	(5)
Net addition to shareholders' funds	44
Opening shareholders funds (originally £420 million before deducting prior year adjustment of £20 million)	400
Closing shareholders' funds	444

The other alternative starts with the profit for the financial year, not the recognised gains and losses:

	£ million
Profit for the financial year	60
Dividends	(20)
	40
Other recognised gains and losses relating to the year (net)	2
New share capital subscribed	7
Goodwill written off	(5)
Net addition to shareholders' funds	44
Opening shareholders funds (originally £420 million before deducting prior year adjustment of £20 million)	400
Closing shareholders' funds	444

This is the format illustrated in the accounting standard, but is less 'user friendly' as it is more difficult to identify the total recognised gains. To do this we have to add the profit for the financial year of £60 million to the other recognised gains and losses of £2 million. This gives us the £62 million gains recognised during the year.

IMI's STATEMENT OF TOTAL RECOGNISED GAINS AND LOSSES

A copy of IMI's statement of total recognised gains and losses, together with the reconciliation of movements in shareholders' funds, is shown below.

You will see that they have a prior year adjustment. This arises from the new requirement that the cost of providing US post-retirement benefits (primarily healthcare benefits for pensioners) should be accounted for on an accruals basis. This means that they will be charged to the profit and loss account in the same way as pension costs.

The revaluation surplus relates primarily to their investment properties. Only £0.5 million relates to the revaluation of other land and buildings in an overseas subsidiary.

Statement of total recognised gains and losses
FOR THE YEAR ENDED 31 DECEMBER 1993

	1993 £m	1992 £m
Profit for the financial year	44.9	44.1
Prior year adjustment – US post-retirement benefits	(0.9)	–
Surplus on revaluation of properties	4.3	–
Currency translation differences on foreign currency net investments	(7.4)	13.9
Total recognised gains and losses for the financial year	40.9	58.0

Reconciliation of movements in shareholders' funds
FOR THE YEAR ENDED 31 DECEMBER 1993

	1993 £m	1992 £m
Profit for the financial year	44.9	44.1
Dividends	(32.5)	(32.4)
	12.4	11.7
Other recognised gains and losses relating to the financial year	(4.0)	13.9
New ordinary share capital issued	1.6	1.4
Goodwill on acquisitions during the year deducted from reserves	(5.0)	(13.0)
Previously acquired goodwill transferred to the profit and loss account on the disposal of a business	2.5	–
Net increase in shareholders' funds for the year	7.5	14.0
Shareholders' funds at 1 January	378.4	364.4
Shareholders' funds 31 December	385.9	378.4

Historical cost profits and losses
There is no material difference between the profit before taxation and the retained profit for the year as shown in the Group profit and loss account and their historical cost equivalent.

6

NOTE OF HISTORICAL COST PROFITS AND LOSSES

INTRODUCTION

If a company has sold assets that have previously been revalued, the profit and loss account will be followed by a note of historical cost profits and losses. Following the implementation of FRS 3, companies are required to calculate profits, and losses, on sale of fixed assets from the book value of these assets. This means that the profit is determined by the value of the assets shown in the balance sheet. Therefore the profits are influenced by the company's depreciation and revaluation policies. The note of historical cost profits and losses was introduced to improve the comparability of reported profits. It tells you what the profit would have been had there been no revaluations of assets. It eliminates the distortions in reported profit that can arise from different revaluation policies. It does not consider the effect of different depreciation policies.

The impact that revaluations can have on reported profits are clearly illustrated by the following example.

Two people buy identical plots of land for £100,000; one revalues the land to £120,000 at the end of the first year. Both sell the land for £150,000 at the end of the second year. What is the profit? The cash profit for both of them is £50,000, but the reported profit will be very different. One will show £50,000 but the other, who revalued, will only show £30,000 profit.

The note of historical cost profits and losses will bring both back to £50,000.

THE NOTE OF HISTORICAL COST PROFITS AND LOSSES

The note of historical cost profits and losses shows what the profit would have been if we had not revalued the assets. Sadly, it is not quite as simple as the example shown above as depreciation provides a small complication.

As this note is not one that will be familiar to all readers, we shall illustrate the way the note can be prepared in the following example.

Two companies, A and B, buy fixed assets for £1,000 at the start of the first year, and sell them for £750 on the last day of the third year.

Both companies have identical profits, before depreciation, and depreciate 20 per cent per annum on a straight line basis.

Company B revalues the assets to £1,200 at the start of the second year, Company B doesn't.

The profit and loss accounts and balance sheets for Company A are shown below.

If we look at the profit and loss account first. Profit after depreciation is constant at £3,800. In Year 3 the fixed assets have a book value of £400 (£1,000 − (3 × £200)) and are sold for £750, generating a profit on sale of fixed assets of £350.

On the balance sheet fixed asset values decline by the depreciation charge of £200 and are sold at the end of the third year. The working capital represents total of the stocks, debtors and cash less the creditors. Logically this must reflect the cumulative profit before depreciation, plus the cash received from the sale of assets.

Company A – Profit and loss accounts

	Year 1 £	Year 2 £	Year 3 £
Turnover	10,000	10,000	10,000
Profit before depreciation	4,000	4,000	4,000
Depreciation	(200)	(200)	(200)
Profit after depreciation	3,800	3,800	3,800
Profit on sale of fixed assets	–	–	350
Retained profit	3,800	3,800	4,150

Company A – Balance sheets

	Year 1 £	Year 2 £	Year 3 £
Fixed assets	800	600	–
Working capital	4,000	8,000	12,750
	4,800	8,600	12,750
Share capital	1,000	1,000	1,000
Profit and loss account	3,800	7,600	11,750
	4,800	8,600	12,750

Company B's accounts will be different because they have revalued their fixed assets; they are illustrated on the following page.

The profit and loss account works in the same way as our earlier example. The depreciation charge changes in Year 2 when the company revalues the assets to £1,200, the depreciation charge of £240 being 20 per cent of 1,200. In Year 3 the assets are worth £720 (the revalued assets of £1,200 less the increased annual depreciation charge of £240 made in Years 2 and 3) and are sold for £750, generating a £30 profit. This compares with Company A's profit of £350.

The balance sheet is more complicated, as it involves a movement between reserves.

- In Year 2 we revalue assets worth £800 to £1,200, creating a revaluation reserve at the start of the year of £400.
- During Year 2 we depreciate these assets by £240, £40 more than we would have depreciated them by had we not revalued. This £40 reduces our profits for the year, but should not reduce our distributable reserves (the retained profits). It is illogical that the two companies should have different distributable reserves following a revaluation. Consequently each year Company B transfers the extra depreciation (£40) from the revaluation reserve to the profit and loss account. This ensures that although the retained profits are different, the reserve remains the same for the two companies.
- In Year 3 we sell the revalued assets, and the balance on the revaluation reserve (£320) is transferred to the profit and loss account. At this point the net worth of the two companies is the same, for the first time since the assets were revalued.

Company B – Profit and loss accounts

	Year 1 £	Year 2 £	Year 3 £
Turnover	10,000	10,000	10,000
Profit before depreciation	4,000	4,000	4,000
Depreciation	(200)	(240)	(240)
Profit after depreciation	3,800	3,760	3,760
Profit on sale of fixed assets	–	–	30
Retained profit	3,800	3,760	3,790

Company B – Balance sheets

	Year 1 £	Year 2 £	Year 3 £
Fixed assets	800	960	–
Working capital	4,000	8,000	12,750
	4,800	8,960	12,750
Share capital	1,000	1,000	1,000
Profit and loss account	3,800	7,600	11,750
Revaluation reserve	–	360	–
	4,800	8,960	12,750

If we just looked at the accounts as reported above we would think that Company A is far more profitable than Company B. If we compare the two companies' profit margins based on the reported results in the third year:

	Company A		Company B	
Operating margin	$\dfrac{3,800}{10,000}$	= 38%	$\dfrac{3,760}{10,000}$	= 37.6%
Overall profit margin	$\dfrac{4,150}{10,000}$	= 41.5%	$\dfrac{3,790}{10,000}$	= 37.9%
Return on capital	$\dfrac{4,150}{12,750}$	= 32.6%	$\dfrac{3,790}{12,750}$	= 29.7%

On every measure that an analyst might use Company A outperforms Company B, even though we know that both businesses are, in reality, identical! To bring the numbers back to a common base Company B would follow its profit and loss account with a note of historical cost profits and losses:

Note of historical cost profits and losses Company B – Year 3

Reported profit	3,790
Realisation of revaluation gains of previous years	320
Difference between the historical cost depreciation charge and the actual depreciation charge of the year calculated on the revalued amount	40
Historical cost profit	4,150

This shows us that the two companies' profits are identical, and we have a basis for comparing their profits.

The reported profit is adjusted for the transfer from the revaluation reserve to the profit and loss account (the reserve) and the additional depreciation that has been charged in the third year on the revalued assets.

This note is useful if you want to compare the profits of two companies in the same sector, who have different policies on revaluation. In some sectors where property profits may be a significant component of reported profit (for example retailers) and there is a variety of revaluation policies, the note becomes an integral part of the analysis.

A published note of historical cost profits and losses will show both historical cost profit before taxation and historical cost retained profits.

IMI's NOTE OF HISTORICAL COST PROFITS AND LOSSES

IMI does not publish a note of historical cost profits and losses. They state 'there is no material difference between the profit before taxation and the retained profit for the year as shown in the Group profit and loss account and their historical cost equivalent'.

7

OTHER INFORMATION DISCLOSED IN THE ACCOUNTS

INTRODUCTION

The notes disclose other information which is useful to read when we are assessing a company's financial performance. Turnover, operating profit and operating assets will be analysed between different businesses and geographical locations. The way that the company has accounted for pensions, contingent liabilities, commitments and post-balance sheet events will also be disclosed in the notes to the accounts.

All of this is useful information that increases our understanding of the company's financial performance. It enables us to look at the company's performance in specific areas, identify any potential future problems and see if the company has changed between the date of the accounts and publication.

This chapter discusses this other information that is disclosed in the accounting notes.

SEGMENTAL ANALYSIS

When we are looking at multinational diverse companies the group accounts often don't give us the detailed information that we need. We want to know where the company is trading and where it is making its profits. Unless we know where the profits are being made and the assets are located it is difficult to make a realistic assessment of the risks facing a company and its long-term prospects. We must have more detailed information about the company's activities and the different markets the company trades in before we can assess a company's performance. We should be able to understand how changes in the political and economic climate will affect the company's performance. Analysing performance and assets by different activities and markets is called segmental reporting.

All companies are required by the Companies Act to disclose the turnover and profit, or loss, before tax for each class of business and geographical market which differ substantially from one another. There is, however, an exception that is often used by smaller companies – if 'in the opinion of the directors the disclosure of any information would be seriously prejudicial, that information need not be disclosed'.

The Stock Exchange has additional requirements and public and large private companies are required to comply with additional provisions in SSAP 25. (For the purpose of segmental reporting, a large company is defined as one that has ten times the medium-sized company criteria. Currently they would need to exceed two out of the following three criteria: turnover £112 million, total assets £56 million, 2,500 employees.)

Companies have to report their performance by different business segments and classes of business. The accounting standard provides some guidelines for identifying these. Business segments are those with different:

- returns on investment,
- degrees of risk,
- rates of growth,
- levels of potential.

Whereas classes of business are those where part of the company provides different products or services.

The accounting standard requires disclosure by both different classes of business and geographical segments where the turnover, or the profit and loss, or the net assets are 10 per cent, or more, of the total. (The rules are slightly different for associated undertakings: they would be separately disclosed where the profit and loss or net assets are 20 per cent, or more, of the total.)

Disclosure requirements of SSAP 25

Companies are required to disclose turnover, profits (or losses) before tax, and operating assets by class of business and geographical segment.

(a) **Turnover**. There are two ways that we can establish geographical segments. We can either look at where the company's operations are located, or where the goods and services are sold. The standard refers to these as 'origin' and 'destination'.

The accounting standard requires that the disclosure of turnover should be by origin, unless the company exports a significant proportion of its goods where both must be disclosed. The basic measure for turnover has to be one based on the location of the sales, as this is the basis used for determining the profits and the operating assets.

(b) **Profit**. This is usually the profit before interest, tax, minority interests and extraordinary items. Interest is the one area where companies may differ. The accounting standard requires the exclusion of interest unless 'all, or part, of the entity's business is to earn and/or incur interest . . . or where interest income/expense is central to the business'.

(c) **Operating assets**. These are the assets and liabilities used by the business. They represent the non-interest-bearing assets less the non-interest-bearing liabilities.

ACCOUNTING FOR PENSIONS

Whilst pensions accounting can appear very esoteric, the way a UK company accounts for pensions can have a significant impact on its apparent financial performance. Consequently it is important to understand some of the more important principles of pension accounting if we want to be able to interpret a set of accounts.

Types of company pension scheme

Pension schemes may be either unfunded (often found overseas, for example in Greece) or funded (UK practice). In an unfunded scheme the company pays the pensions of its employees, therefore there is likely to be a large provision shown in the accounts. In a funded scheme the company will make a payment to the pension fund. These schemes may be in the form of:

- **a defined contributions scheme**: the contributions are invested and the employee's pension will be determined by the investment performance of the scheme. The accounting treatment for these schemes is simple, the contributions relating to the period will be charged to the profit and loss account.
- **a defined benefits scheme**: in this type of scheme the employee is entitled to receive a proportion of his salary on retirement. This is totally unrelated to the investment performance of the scheme. If the scheme under-performs, the company will have to make additional contributions to honour its obligations. The cost of providing the pension is spread over the working lives of the employees.

The way that a company accounts for pension costs is likely to differ fundamentally from the way that it makes contributions into the scheme. It is primarily defined benefit schemes that create the accounting problems and these are discussed in detail below.

In order to calculate the pension costs charged to the period's profit and loss account the company must:

- determine the size of the fund required to meet its obligations,
- identify whether the fund is in surplus or deficit,
- account for the surplus/deficit in calculating the pension cost for the period,
- identify the contribution rate for the scheme.

The size of the fund

Determining the fund required is complicated, as it is based on a number of assumptions based on the following questions:

- how many of us will stay with the scheme until we retire?
- when will we retire?
- what will we be earning when we retire?
- how will the fund perform until we retire?
- will it generate a return sufficient to cover its liabilities?

Actuaries will carry out valuations, usually every three years, to identify the size of the fund the company needs to meet its pension liabilities. The accounts will disclose their actuarial assumptions, which are usually very conservative (they tend to overestimate salary increases and underestimate fund performance). They will also disclose whether the fund is in surplus or deficit. A surplus arises when the fund's value is greater than the amount needed to satisfy its liabilities. Given the conservatism of the actuarial assumptions, it is easy for a pension fund to be in surplus. This was particularly true during the 1980s when returns from shares easily outpaced wage inflation. The 1990s have seen this trend continuing, but now coupled with staff reduction. Redundancies have the effect of increasing the surplus by reducing the fund's liabilities. (Although if people elect for early retirement it can increase the fund's liabilities; this is illustrated later.)

Historically the way that companies were accounting for these surpluses (charging the actual cost, often nothing, to the profit and loss account) worried accountants as it was not consistent with the matching principle. Costs were not being matched to revenues. It was felt that the cost of providing a pension should be matched to the time that the company was benefiting from the employees services. Consequently in 1988 SSAP 24 was issued. This requires companies to match the pension costs charged to the profit and loss account to the working lives of employees. This means that the profit and loss account is being charged with the cost of providing pensions over the period that the company is benefiting from the employees' services. Consequently the accounting charge for pensions can be very different from the cash cost of funding pension schemes. The charges to the profit and loss account will probably not reflect the cash flows to the fund.

Accounting for a surplus

The accounting standard states that companies should spread a surplus over the remaining service life of employees. The surplus relating to the current year could exceed the normal cost of the company's contributions. This can give rise to a 'negative cost' (effectively a credit) to the profit and loss account that will be reflected by a prepayment asset in the balance sheet. For example the normal cost of providing the future pension (called the regular cost) could be £10 million, the surplus allocated to this period could be £12 million. The profit and loss account would not be charged with any pension cost, instead it will be credited with £2 million. A £2 million prepayment would be shown on the balance sheet to reflect this credit. The accounting treatment for pensions poses two problems for financial analysis.

- If the fund moves out of surplus, the company's profits will appear to collapse as the company has to charge the normal costs. The comparative profits will fall by £12 million!
- The current assets will be overstated, as the pension fund prepayment is not a liquid asset of the company. A small number of companies have recognised this and show the surplus separately, outside of their current assets (for example Coats Viyella plc).

Today's surplus is tomorrow's deficit. A good example of this is British Telecom. In their 1990 accounts they stated that their pension fund assets were sufficient to cover 118 per cent of the liabilities. The fund was in surplus. On 1st January 1993 it merged its two pension funds, without affecting the benefits of the members. The pension fund was valued on that date, using the same actuarial assumptions as had been used for the previous valuation. The valuation identified a deficit of £750 million, with the assets only covering 95 per cent of the liabilities. The company believed the deficit derived from a combination of three factors:

- the cost of providing pensions to people who had elected to take early retirement,
- the impact of the recession on the investment returns of the fund,
- the reduction in the ACT credit from 25 per cent to 20 per cent.

As the pension fund was now in deficit BT felt it prudent to charge to the profit and loss account £550 million to cover the costs of early retirement. The effect on the future annual charge is also dramatic. In its 1993 accounts the company says that the annual charge will increase by £90 million, from £160 million to an estimated £250 million in 1994. It also announced that during the year to 31st March 1994 it was likely to have to make a contribution to the scheme of £800 million.

The size of the surplus is a matter of judgement. There are a number of different ways of spreading the surplus; different methods will have different impacts on reported profits, over time. We cannot identify whether the fund would be in surplus if a different actuarial valuation basis were used. Perhaps the important thing for us to understand is that any surplus apportioned to a year will reduce the charge to the profit and loss account. This could have a significant impact on reported earnings.

It is further complicated by the fact that the accounting standard allows the company to charge a notional interest, where an asset arises from the difference between the charge to the profit and loss account and the cash cost. (This is to reflect the money that the prepayment is earning as part of the fund.) The logic may be sound, but there is no cash flowing into the company. It just represents the interest that may be earned on the surplus. Companies can use the notional interest either to further reduce the pension charge to the profit and loss account, or to reduce the interest charge. Most companies do not disclose whether they are taking interest into account and where the notional interest is being credited.

We have seen how a prepayment can be created when the normal cost is less than the proportion of the surplus relating to the year. However pension prepayment assets may not be accumulated 'negative costs', they may reflect the pension fund surplus. When the standard was issued in 1988, companies were allowed either to:

- spread the surplus as outlined above, or
- incorporate the pension fund surplus, or deficit onto the balance sheet by a prior year adjustment. A prior year adjustment was used to create a pension prepayment reflecting the surplus (if there is a deficit an accrual was created).

We can see the combination of the two in Williams Holdings. They disclose in their 1993 accounts 'The pension fund prepayment of £129.3 million (1992 £123.5 million), which substantially arose in respect of acquisitions, has been included in debtors. This amount represents the surplus arising on implementation of SSAP 24, adjusted for acquisitions and disposals, and subsequent credits to the profit and loss account'.

Pension accounting and financial analysis

It is always worth referring to the notes on pensions. Whilst the technicalities of pension accounting are important to accountants, it is their implications that are important for financial analysis. There are a number of points to check when looking at a set of company accounts.

- Is the fund in surplus or deficit?
- How has this been accounted for?

If there is a surplus:

- How much of the debtors' figure is pension fund prepayments? (In Williams Holdings 1993 accounts the pension fund prepayment represented nearly 33 per cent of their total debtors.)
- Has notional interest been charged on the prepayment? (In Williams Holdings 1993 accounts they disclosed 'In previous years a net pension credit has arisen in the profit and loss account since the interest accrued on the surplus, and the spread forward of the further surplus arising from the actuarial valuation in 1991 exceeded the regular cost of providing pension benefits'.
- Where?

CONTINGENT LIABILITIES

A contingency is a potential gain or liability which has not materialised by the date of the balance sheet. The accounting standard (SSAP 18) identifies the accounting treatment for contingent gains and contingent losses:

Probability	Gain	Loss
Probable (prudence applies).	Note in the financial statements, but do not anticipate the gain.	Include in costs, does not usually have to be disclosed separately.
Possible.	Ignore.	Does not have to be included in the accounts, but should be noted.
Unlikely.	Ignore.	Ignore.

Some contingencies are regularly disclosed by companies (e.g. bank guarantees, discounted bills, performance bonds). Whereas others are only reluctantly disclosed. Most companies do not like disclosing contingent liabilities arising from court cases, as they feel that disclosure may jeopardise their position. Few companies identify their foreign exchange exposure risks as a contingent liability.

CAPITAL COMMITMENTS

The note on capital commitments discloses the capital expenditure for the next year that has already been approved by the directors. It is sorted out into two categories:

- expenditure where the contracts have been placed,
- expenditure that has been approved, but contracts have not been placed at the date of the balance sheet.

This is often a useful note to refer to as it gives some indication of the company's expansion plans and future cash flows.

POST BALANCE SHEET EVENTS

The accounts give a snapshot of the company at the balance sheet date, but the company could have changed significantly in the three months between taking the snapshot and publishing the accounts. The accounting standard (SSAP 17) recognises this and divides post balance sheet events into two types:

- **adjusting events**. These give you extra information about conditions you knew about at the time of the balance sheet. The extra information allows you to adjust the figures. For example, you could have been worried about a customer and felt it prudent to make a provision for doubtful debts. The customer has subsequently gone into liquidation, confirming your view. The amount would need to be written off, but would not have to be disclosed separately unless the amount was so large that separate disclosure was felt to be necessary for the true and fair view.
- **non-adjusting events.** These did not exist at the balance sheet date. examples of non-adjusting events could be acquisitions, disposals, resignation of directors and share issues. These would have to be separately disclosed in the notes to the accounts and an estimation of the financial impact should be provided, where possible.

8

ACCOUNTS IN OTHER COUNTRIES

INTRODUCTION

There are a number of pressures for the standardisation of accounting practices and presentation.

- The activities of various international bodies, including the United Nations, the Organisation for Economic Cooperation and Development, the European Commission, and the International Accounting Standards Board. This was originally established in 1973 by the accounting bodies of nine countries. The membership has subsequently increased nearly ninefold, and they have issued over thirty International Accounting Standards. These standards are taken more seriously in some countries than in others, as there is no requirement to comply to them.

- The globalisation of capital markets. Large companies raise finance in the cheapest market, therefore the users of accounts want to have comparable accounting formats and practices.

- The inter-relationships between international economies.

- The increasing desire for political union.

Despite these pressures, both accounting formats and practices vary widely across the world. These differences are inevitable and are likely to continue for the foreseeable future as the accounting practices and formats are shaped by a number of factors which include:

- **the legal system**: legal systems can be categorised into two major groups: the Roman legal system and a common law system. The two systems have generated different levels of government intervention. Roman law usually involves extensive governmental prescription, whereas common law survives on limited government intervention. It is inevitable that these different legal frameworks will lead to the development of different accounting systems. Countries adopting Roman law have a strong legal framework, with accounting rules enshrined in law, accounting plans, or commercial codes.

- **corporate ownership**: in some countries the ownership of most companies is still in the hands of the board of directors, whereas in others ownership is separated from the management of the company. Where the ownership is separated there is an increased demand for financial reports and external audit. Consequently both the quality and the quantity of accounting information will inevitably vary from one country to another with disclosure increasing as the ownership of the company becomes separated from its management.

- **the taxation system**: the taxation rules will influence many day-to-day financial decisions such as provisioning and the valuation of assets. Some tax systems require that the figures in the financial accounts should be the same as those shown on the tax accounts. This means that the accounting numbers will be largely determined by the tax rules. Other countries are bedevilled with the problems of deferred tax, as the tax rules are substantially different from the accounting rules. In these countries two sets of accounts will be prepared: the ones reporting performance to the shareholders, and the ones complying with the tax rules.
- **political and historical factors**:
  - Commonwealth countries have a legacy of UK accounting practices, prior to the 1981 Companies Act,
  - French accounting has been strongly influenced by the German occupation, with the *Plan Comptable* largely reflecting the ideas proposed by professor Eugen Schmalenbach and adapted by the Vichy government in 1942. This has subsequently been modified but still clearly reflects the original proposals,
  - Japanese accounting is a hybrid that has been influenced by American practices,
  - entry into the EEC has affected the accounting practices of all member countries, and will continue to do so for the foreseeable future.

These factors interact to provide us with a wide variety of accounting practices. Despite the attempts at standardisation embodied in the Fourth Directive, the formats of accounts within the EEC are still different. The accounting practices are even more varied. This presents analysts with difficulties when making international comparisons – it becomes essential to know the detail of each country's accounting regulations. For the non-professional, an awareness of the major differences is probably sufficient.

This chapter is not intended to be exhaustive, and will not cover some of the more esoteric differences – like accounting for deferred tax. It summarises the main differences in both practices and presentation of USA, France, Germany and Japan.

Public companies in these countries will prepare a profit and loss account and balance sheet, whereas private companies often have more limited disclosure requirements than those found in the UK. Most public companies will prepare some form of cash flow statement, although the format of this statement is not uniform and is subject to wide variation. As there is no standard format for cash flow statements, there are no examples given in this chapter. It will only detail the formats for the profit and loss account and the balance sheet.

The profit and loss accounts and balance sheets of the European countries will bear some similarity to our own as they will be covered by the European Community directives. But even within EEC countries there are considerable and fundamental differences. There were two balance sheet formats and four profit and loss account formats in the fourth directive. The way that these formats have been adhered to varies widely across Europe.

This chapter will discuss the major accounting differences and will give an example of the format used for the profit and loss account and balance sheet.

UNITED STATES OF AMERICA

Introduction

America and Britain have the reputation of being separated by a common language. It is as true in accounting as in any other area of life. The terms you will see in a set of American accounts may not be familiar and a 'translation' of the main terms is given below:

UK	*USA*
Financial year	Fiscal year
Profit and loss account	Income statement
	Statement of earnings
Turnover	Revenue/sales
Associated company	Affiliated enterprise
Earnings per share	Net income per share
	Net earnings per share
Scrip dividend	Stock dividend
Balance sheet	Balance sheet
	Statement of financial position
Tangible fixed assets	Property, plant and equipment
Stock	Inventory
Own shares	Treasury stock
Debtors	Receivables
	Accounts receivable
Credit ɔrs	Payables
	Accounts payable
Provisions	Accounting for loss contingencies
Shares	Stock
Profit and loss account reserve	Retained earnings
Share premium account	Paid in surplus
Operating review	Management's discussion of operations
Financial review	Management's discussion of financial resources and liquidity

It is important to understand the American accounting jargon, as overseas accounts are often translated into American English (for example Japanese accounts).

American companies will publish a profit and loss account, a balance sheet and a cash flow statement. Public companies will publish interim statements, which tend to be more detailed than the ones prepared in the UK.

The income statement/statement of earnings

The profit and loss account is known as the Income Statement, or Statement of Earnings. They are similar to a UK Format 1 Profit and Loss Account. They will show the sources of income on the face of the profit and loss account, showing a number of income figures.

Some of the major differences are:

(a) **capitalisation of interest**. Interest must be capitalised if:

- the assets have been built by the company for its own use,
- the assets are constructed in distinct projects and are intended to be sold or leased (e.g. ships),
- the company has to spend additional money to start operations in an investment in order to start trading. This investment must be accounted for using the equity method.

(b) **extraordinary items**. Extraordinary items are still common in American accounts. Extraordinary items are defined as transactions distinguished by the unusual nature and infrequency of their occurrence.

(c) **dividends**. Dividends do not relate to any accounting period's earnings and are not shown on the accounts until they are formally declared. Then they are shown as a liability and a deduction from retained earnings. The only dividends shown on the profit and loss account are those paid during the year.

(d) **earnings per share**. A number of earnings per share figures are required for all public companies. They are calculated on:

- profit before extraordinary items,
- profit from continuing operations,
- profit from discontinued operations,
- any cumulative effect of a change in accounting policies.

(e) **comparatives**. There will be three years' profit and loss accounts shown in the accounts.

The balance sheet/statement of financial position

Balance sheets are prepared using an assets and liabilities format and they will generally show assets and liabilities in order of liquidity (i.e. cash will be the first asset shown, and fixed assets the last). (This compares with the UK practice of showing assets and liabilities in reverse order of liquidity.)

(a) **Goodwill**. Goodwill is capitalised, and must be amortised over its useful life, which should not exceed forty years.

(b) **Fixed assets**. Property, plant and equipment must be shown at historical cost and depreciated. Acquisitions are the only exception to this, as assets are required to be restated to fair values.

(c) **Debtors**. Debtors due after a year are shown separately and must be shown as non-current.

(d) **Shares**. State laws govern the issue of shares. They may be issued with or without a par value.

The cash flow statement

The cash flow statement is similar to that found in the UK, although cash flows are categorised slightly differently. They comprise:

- operating activities. These include cash flows from interest and taxation,
- investing activities,
- financing activities,
- cash and cash equivalents.

American accounts

Examples of the layout for the profit and loss account and balance sheet used by American companies are given in the following pages.

CONSOLIDATED STATEMENT OF INCOME/STATEMENT OF EARNINGS

REVENUES
    Sale of goods
    Sale of services
    Other income

    Total revenues

COSTS AND EXPENSES:
    Cost of goods sold
    Cost of services sold
    Interest and other financial charges
    Other costs and expenses
    Minority interest in net earnings of consolidated affiliates

    Total costs and expenses

EARNINGS FROM CONTINUING OPERATIONS BEFORE INCOME TAXES
Provision for income taxes

EARNINGS FROM CONTINUING OPERATIONS
Earnings from discontinued operations net of taxes

NET EARNINGS

NET EARNINGS PER SHARE (in dollars)
Continuing operations
Discontinued operations

Net earnings per share

DIVIDENDS DECLARED PER SHARE (in dollars)

BALANCE SHEET/STATEMENT OF FINANCIAL POSITION

ASSETS
    Cash and equivalents
    Marketable securities
    Securities purchased under agreements to resell
    Current receivables
    Inventories
    Other receivables
    Property plant and equipment
    Intangible assets
    All other assets
    Net assets of discontinued operations

TOTAL ASSETS

LIABILITIES
    Short-term borrowings
    Accounts payable
    Securities sold under options to repurchase
    Dividends payable
    All other current costs and expenses accrued
    Long-term borrowings
    All other liabilities
    Deferred income taxes
    Total liabilities

    Minority interests in equity of consolidated affiliates

    Common stock
    Other capital
    Retained earnings

      Total share owners' equity

TOTAL LIABILITIES AND EQUITY

FRANCE

French accounting is largely encapsulated in the accounting plan (*Plan Comptable Général*). This is prepared by a government committee and has the force of law. It is very prescriptive, making French accounts very easy to read, as everything is shown in the same place in the accounts and calculated in a similar manner. French accounts are strongly influenced by the tax rules. Fiscal considerations appear to override the need for a true and fair view, although the true and fair view is supposed to be the overriding principle in law.

Small- and medium-sized companies are allowed to prepare abbreviated accounts. These accounts would disclose similar information to those prepared by UK companies, with medium-sized companies benefiting from slightly less disclosure in the accounting notes.

The profit and loss account (*Compte de résultat*)

The law provides for the profit and loss account to be prepared either horizontally or vertically. The format used reflects our Format 2, identifying what the company has spent its money on, rather than why it has spent it.

Individual companies prepare a two-sided profit and loss account. Expenses and profit are shown on the left, and income and losses, on the right. Consolidated accounts are normally prepared vertically, and then often follow UK Format 2. (The two-sided version is given as an example in this chapter, as this is an unfamiliar layout for UK readers of accounts.)

The grouping of expenses with profits and income with losses in the profit and loss account will seem strange to any British readers who are unfamiliar with the principles of double-entry bookkeeping, whether it is presented vertically or horizontally. In the vertical format expenses and profits are followed by income and losses, in the horizontal format expenses are shown on the left, and the income and profits on the right.

The expenses are categorised into:

- operating expenses,
- financial expenses,
- exceptional expenses,
- taxation.

The income follows a similar grouping:

- operating income,
- financial income,
- exceptional income.

Only the profit, or loss, from joint ventures and the overall profit, or loss, are disclosed separately on the profit and loss account – the reader has to calculate the familiar categories of profit. For example, operating expenses would have to be deducted from operating income to arrive at operating profit.

Whilst the appearance of the profit and loss account, grouping expenses and income, may at first sight appear confusing, it actually contains more information than its British counterpart. However, given the tax-related basis of French accounting it gives us little useful additional insight into the operations of the company.

(a) **Depreciation**. Depreciation is determined by the tax rules. The usual asset lives are:

- buildings   20 – 30 years,
- plant and machinery   10 years,
- vehicles   5 years.

(b) **Provisions**. Large French companies disclose more information about their provisions than their UK counterparts. They show the different types of provisions; analysing those relating to asset writedowns (with provisions relating to fixed assets and current assets disclosed separately) and those relating to potential liabilities and losses. However, many provisions are tax-deductable, and the provisions often bear little resemblance to the commercial reality that would seem to be consistent with the true and fair view. The provisions that have been made for tax purposes are 'corrected' in the consolidated accounts, which consequently show deferred tax provisions.

(c) **Extraordinary items**. Extraordinary items are called '*exceptionnel*' in France. They cover items that would be considered both extraordinary and exceptional in the UK. They include all items outside normal trading activities, and would include things like profits or losses from the sale of fixed assets.

(d) **Research and development**. Research and development costs are usually written off as incurred, but the company can make exceptions if the project is technically feasible and commercially viable. Once it has been capitalised it should be written off as soon as possible, usually within five years. If the project proves to be unviable, the costs should be written off immediately. Whilst the research and development is capitalised, dividends can only be paid if there are sufficient reserves to cover the research and development asset.

Balance sheet (*Bilan*)

Balance sheets are prepared on an assets and liabilities (*actif et passif*) format, with assets and liabilities being shown in reverse order of liquidity. They are usually prepared horizontally, although consolidated accounts are allowed to be prepared in a vertical format.

At first glance the French balance sheet appears more detailed than a UK balance sheet. However, the degree of detail shown in both countries is similar, the difference lies in where the detail can be found. It is customary in France for detailed information to be presented in the balance sheet itself, rather than the notes.

(a) **Goodwill**. Goodwill may, in exceptional cases, be written off through reserves. However this is unusual and goodwill would normally be capitalised and amortised over its useful life. There is no maximum period for amortising goodwill, most companies would amortise goodwill between twenty and thirty years.

(b) **Fixed assets**. Balance sheet valuations are unlikely to reflect market values. Fixed assets are largely shown at historical costs, with revaluations occasionally allowed by the Ministry of the Economy and Finance. Fixed assets were revalued as a result of the 1978 fiscal laws in accordance with certain inflation-based ratios, previous revaluations were conducted in 1959 and 1945. Any other revaluations are subject to tax, and consequently are rarely made. The revaluations must not exceed the market values of the assets.

Assets held on finance leases may be capitalised in the consolidated accounts. However, there is no explicit definition of what a finance lease is.

(c) **Legal reserves**. Public companies must establish a reserve equivalent to 10 per cent of issued share capital. This is designed to increase the undistributable capital base of the company and provide more protection for creditors.

Cash flow statement (*Ressources et emplois des fonds, Tableau de financement*)

A cash flow statement is recommended by the *plan comptable*, and is prepared by listed companies.

French accounts

Examples of the layout of the two-sided profit and loss account and a horizontal balance sheet are shown on the following pages.

PROFIT AND LOSS ACCOUNT – FRANCE (TWO-SIDED VERSION)

EXPENSES

INCOME

OPERATING EXPENSES:
Purchases of goods for resale
Variation in stocks
Purchases of raw materials and consumables
Variation in stocks

Other purchases and external charges

Taxes and similar payments
Wages and salaries
Social security costs
Valuation adjustments:
  On fixed assets: depreciation
  On fixed assets: other amounts written off
  On current assets: amounts written off
  Relating to provisions for liabilities and
    charges
Other operating expenses

TOTAL OPERATING EXPENSES

SHARE OF LOSS ON JOINT VENTURES

FINANCIAL EXPENSES
Value adjustments
Interest and similar expenses

Losses on foreign exchange
Net loss on transfers of short-term securities

TOTAL FINANCIAL EXPENSES

EXCEPTIONAL EXPENSES
Operating
Non-operating
Depreciation and other amounts written off

TOTAL EXCEPTIONAL EXPENSES

Profit share of employees

Tax on profit

TOTAL EXPENSES

  Balance – Profit

SUM TOTAL

OPERATING INCOME:
Sales of goods bought for resale
Sales of goods and services produced
Net turnover (including exports)
Variation in stock of finished goods
  and work in progress
Work performed for own purposes
  and capitalised
Operating subsidies
Provisions written back
Other operating income

TOTAL OPERATING INCOME

SHARE OF PROFIT ON JOINT
  VENTURES

FINANCIAL INCOME
From participating interests
From other investments and loans
  forming part of the fixed assets

Other interest receivable and similar
  income
Provisions written back
Gains on foreign exchange
Net gain from transfers of short-term
  securities

TOTAL FINANCIAL INCOME

EXCEPTIONAL INCOME
Operating
Non-operating
Provisions written back

TOTAL EXCEPTIONAL INCOME

TOTAL INCOME

  Balance – Loss

SUM TOTAL

BALANCE SHEET – FRANCE

ASSETS

Issued share capital not called

FIXED ASSETS:
Intangible fixed assets:
    Formation costs
    Research and development costs
    Concessions, patents, licences, trademarks
      and similar rights and assets

Goodwill

Other intangible fixed assets
Payments on account

Tangible fixed assets:
    Land
    Buildings
    Plant, machinery, tools
    Other tangible fixed assets
    Tangible fixed assets in the course of
      construction
    Payments on account

Investments:
    Shares in group and related companies
Amount owed by group and related
    companies
Other fixed asset investments
Other loans
Other investments

CURRENT ASSETS:
Stocks and work in progress:
    Raw materials and consumables
    Work in progress (goods and services)
    Goods for resale
Payments on account and deposits
Debtors:
    Trade debtors
    Other debtors
    Called up share capital not paid
Investments:
    Own shares
    Other investments
Cash at bank and in hand

PREPAYMENTS AND ACCRUED INCOME
Prepayments
Accrued income

Debenture redemption premiums

Translation differences

CAPITAL AND LIABILITIES

CAPITAL AND RESERVES:
Share capital (of which paid up . . .)
Share premiums
Revaluation reserves
Reserves:

    Legal reserve
    Reserves required by articles or
      contract
    Reserves required by regulations
    Other (optional) reserves
Carry forward from the profit and loss
    account:
    (credit or debit balance)
Profit/loss for the accounting period
Sub-total: net worth
Investment subsidies
Provisions required by regulations
PROVISIONS FOR LIABILITIES
AND CHARGES:
Provisions for liabilities
Provisions for charges

CREDITORS:
Convertible debenture loans
Other debenture loans
Loans and sundry creditors
Payments received on account
Trade creditors
Debts relating to fixed assets

Taxation and social security
Other creditors
Accruals and deferred income

Translation differences

GERMANY

German accounting is noted for its uniformity and is based on the historical accounting rules found in the commercial code. German accounts tend to be determined by the tax rules, one of the major elements of German accounting law is '*Massgeblichkeitsprinzip*' (the principle of bindingness). This aims to have tax accounts prepared on the same basis as the accounts prepared for the shareholders. This means that they are unlikely to reflect the same definition of a 'true and fair view' that a British reader would understand.

When looking at German accounts it is important to remember five things:

- German companies have supervisory boards which have both share-holders and employee representatives as members of the board. This means that they are involved in the decision-making and have access to the management accounts. Consequently they are less reliant on the published accounts than their British counterparts.
- Bankers can also have access to the management accounts.
- Tax allowances can only be taken if they are reflected in the accounts.
- Shareholders can claim up to half the profits of a public company, and all of the profits of a private company.
- German companies tend not to have the same degree of separation of the management of the company from the ownership of the company that you would find in their British counterparts. Banks, rather than individual shareholders, are the major providers of capital. Therefore there is less requirement for disclosure. (The requirements for detailed disclosure and that accounts should reflect a 'true and fair view' tend to mirror this separation of ownership from management.)

The accounts reflect the interaction of these five factors. The European Community Fourth Directive required that accounts within the Community should show a true and fair view. Whilst Germany has included this requirement, it operates a different interpretation of the term to that under-stood in Britain. German accounting sticks to the strict letter of the law and does not reflect the accounting principle of 'substance over form'.

Profit and loss account (*Gewinn – und Verlustrechnung*)

The profit and loss account must be presented vertically, in a similar way to the UK formats.

(a) **Depreciation**. Depreciation is based on tax tables for a particular asset in a particular location.

(b) **Provisions**. Provisions are used to smooth out the profit figures, and are often found under 'other accruals'. Even general provisions are allowed for tax purposes, consequently the level of provisioning rarely reflects the commercial position.

(c) **Capitalisation of interest**. This is only allowed where there is a recognisable relationship between the loan and the asset.

(d) **Dividends**. The dividends shown on the profit and loss account are the interim dividends paid during the year. The final dividend will not have been approved at the year end, and will only be shown in the appropriation account.

(e) **Research and development**. Research and development expenses may not be capitalised unless the research has been purchased from a third party.

(f) **Long-term contracts**. The 'percentage of completion' method can only be used in exceptional circumstances, therefore most long-term contracts are not shown in the profit and loss account until they are finished.

Balance sheet (*Bilanz*)

Balance sheets are prepared on an assets and liabilities format; with assets and liabilities being shown in reverse order of liquidity. They must be prepared in a horizontal format.

(a) **Goodwill**. Goodwill may be either written off against reserves, or capitalised. The law mentions an amortisation period of four years for goodwill, but periods of forty years are not uncommon.

(b) **Fixed assets**. The revaluation of assets is not allowed. Leases must not be capitalised.

(c) **Stocks**. Long-term contract work in progress must be valued at cost, not the percentage of completion basis.

(d) **Reserves**. To protect creditors, companies are required to build up a legal reserve of 10 per cent of share capital. Five per cent of the annual profits are transferred to the reserve until it has reached the required size.

Cash flow statement (*Kapitalflussrechnung Bewegungsbilanz*)

A cash flow statement is not required, although some large companies prepare one.

German accounts

Examples of the layout of the two formats for the profit and loss account and the balance sheet are shown on the following pages.

PROFIT AND LOSS ACCOUNT – GERMANY (FIRST FORMAT)

Sales

Increase/decrease in finished goods inventories and work in progress

Own work capitalised

Other operating income

Cost of materials:

Cost of raw materials, consumables and supplies of purchased merchandise

Cost of purchased services

Personnel expenses:

Wages and salaries

Social security and other pension costs, of which in respect of old-age pensions:

Depreciation:

On intangible fixed assets and tangible assets as well as on capitalised start up and business expansion expenses

On current assets to the extent that it exceeds depreciation which is normal for the company

Other operating expenses

Income from participations, of which from affiliated enterprises:

Income from other investments and long-term loans, of which relating to affiliated enterprises

Other interest and similar income, of which from affiliated enterprises:

Amortisation of financial assets and investments classified as current assets

Interest and similar expenses, of which to affiliated enterprises:

Results from ordinary activities

Extraordinary income

Extraordinary expense

Extraordinary results

Taxes on income

Other taxes

Net income/loss for the year

PROFIT AND LOSS ACCOUNT – GERMANY (SECOND FORMAT)

Sales
Cost of sales
Gross profit on sales
Selling expenses
General administration expenses
Other operating income
Other operating expenses
Income from participations, of which from affiliated enterprises:
Income from other investments and long-term loans, of which from affiliated enterprises:
Other interest and similar income, of which from affiliated enterprises:
Amortisation of financial assets and investments classified as current assets
Interest and similar expenses, of which to affiliated enterprises:

Results from ordinary activities
Extraordinary income
Extraordinary expense

Extraordinary results
Taxes on income
Other taxes

Net income/loss for the year

BALANCE SHEET – GERMANY

FIXED ASSETS

Intangible assets:
  Concessions, industrial and similar
  rights and assets and licences in such
  rights and assets
  Goodwill
  Payments on account

Tangible assets:
  Land, land rights and buildings,
  including buildings on third party land
  Technical equipment and machines
  Other equipment, factory and office
  equipment
  Payments on account and assets under
  construction
Financial assets:

  Shares in affiliated enterprises
  Loans to affiliated enterprises
  Participations
  Loans to enterprises in which
  participations are held
  Long-term investments
  Other loans

CURRENT ASSETS

Inventories:
  Raw materials and supplies

  Work in process
  Finished goods and merchandise
  Payment on account

Receivables and other assets:
  Trade receivables
  Receivables from affiliated enterprises
  Receivables from enterprises in which
participations are held
  Other assets
Securities:
  Shares in affiliated enterprises
  Own shares
  Other securities
Cheques, cash in hand, central bank and
postal giro balances, bank balances

PREPAYMENTS

EQUITY

Subscribed capital
Capital reserves
Revenue reserves:
Legal reserve
Reserve for own shares
Statutory reserves
Other revenue reserves

Retained profits/accumulated losses
brought forward
Net income/loss for the year

ACCRUALS

Accruals for pensions and similar
obligations
Tax accruals
Other accruals

LIABILITIES

Loans, of which convertible:
Liabilities to banks
Payments received on account of orders
Trade payables
Liabilities on bills accepted and drawn
Payable to affiliated enterprises
Payable to enterprises in which
participations are held
Other liabilities;
  of which taxes:
  of which relating to social security and
  similar obligations

DEFERRED INCOME

JAPAN

Japanese accounting has been subject to three influences:

- a local, medieval tradition of double entry bookkeeping,
- the adoption of the Prussian commercial legal code in the 19th century. This is reflected in the Commercial Code,
- the post-war influence of American practices reflected in the Securities and Exchange Law.

The form and content of accounts are determined by these two accounting laws.

- **The Commercial Code**: this is based on German law and affects all companies regardless of size. The commercial code determines the form and content of the information that should be sent to shareholders. In 1963 it established legally binding accounting and reporting. An independent audit is only required for large companies.
- **The Securities and Exchange Law**: this is based on the US 1934 Securities Act and details the form of accounts required for listed companies. Japanese companies tend to use American accounting terms. Listed companies must have an independent audit and complete a more detailed report that is sent to the Ministry of Finance.

Tax laws also have a big impact on published accounts, as they must be followed regardless of whether this gives a true and fair view. Japanese accounts are more concerned with the tax position and the legal form than a true and fair view.

The practical effect of this is that most public companies prepare two sets of accounting information, which for large or listed companies, must be audited by an independent, professional auditor. Some companies also produce a third set of accounts, which are translated for the overseas investor. These may or may not be in the same amount of detail as the statutory accounts.

Japan does not have a tradition of accounting disclosure, largely as a result of the structure of their share ownership. Both suppliers and customers are likely to be shareholders in Japanese companies, with the investment decision being more influenced by the possibility of long-term sales growth than short-term profit maximisation. This cross-ownership of companies and resulting emphasis on long-term decision-making further complicates the interpretation of Japanese accounts.

Profit and loss account

The Statement of Income is similar, but more detailed than the UK Format 1 Profit and Loss Account. Costs are shown in more detail than a UK company would disclose. The level of detail is more like that usually found in the management accounts in Britain.

(a) **Depreciation**. Depreciation is determined by tax law.

(b) **Provisions**. Many provisions are set at the maximum allowable for tax purposes, which may not reflect the commercial reality.

(c) **Extraordinary items**. These are shown pre-tax and include both exceptional and extraordinary items, some of which would not be regarded as material in the UK.

(d) **Earnings per share**. These are calculated before extraordinary items and are therefore not comparable with UK figures. It is impossible to determine the split between exceptional and extraordinary items.

(e) **Dividends**. The dividends shown on the profit and loss account are the interim dividends paid during the year. Proposed dividends are not accrued. The final dividend will not have been approved at the year end, and will only be shown in the appropriation account.

Balance sheet

Balance sheets are prepared using the assets and liabilities format, showing both in order of liquidity.

(a) **Goodwill**. Goodwill may be written off immediately through the profit and loss account (*not* the reserve), or may be capitalised and written off, usually within five years as required by the Commercial Code.

(b) **Fixed assets**. Fixed assets are shown at historical cost as the revaluation of assets is not allowed. Leases may be capitalised, but this is very rare because of the tax implications. Leased assets are disclosed in the notes to the accounts.

(c) **Intangible assets**. Specific research and development projects may be capitalised. The research costs may also be capitalised. Research and development must be amortised within five years.

(d) **Stocks**. Stocks are generally shown at cost, not the lower of cost and net realisable value. The Commercial Code does not require provisioning for any falls in value.

(e) **Share capital**. Shares do not have to have a nominal value in Japan.

(f) **Reserves**. There are three types of reserves shown in Japanese accounts:

- **Capital reserve**: this includes the share premium account.

- **Legal earned reserve**: this is designed to protect creditors. Companies must build up the legal reserve of 25 per cent of share capital, by allocating at least 10 per cent of dividends until the required amount is reached.
- **Other surpluses**: this is undistributed profits and proposed dividends.

Cash flow statement

An unaudited cash flow statement is provided by listed companies as supplementary information in the annual report.

Japanese accounts

A profit and loss account and balance sheet, following the format recommended for public companies by the Ministry of Finance, are shown on the following pages. You will notice that they are very detailed, and it is unlikely that companies will have entries for all the items. The example has been included to illustrate the detail of disclosure required by the Ministry of Finance.

PROFIT AND LOSS ACCOUNT – JAPAN

TURNOVER
Turnover in affiliates
Turnover to other customers

COST OF SALES
Opening stock
Purchases
Sub total
Closing Stock

GROSS PROFIT

DISTRIBUTION COSTS AND ADMINISTRATIVE EXPENSES
Packing and freight
Commission
Warehouse
Advertising
Directors' remuneration
Payroll
Bonuses
Welfare benefits
Travelling
Postage, telephone and telex
Utilities
Insurance and maintenance
Taxes and dues
Provision for accrued enterprise tax
Depreciation
Provision for allowance for doubtful accounts
Research and development
Others

OPERATING PROFIT

NON-OPERATING INCOME
Interest income and dividends
Interest income from affiliates
Interest income on securities
Dividend income
Dividend income from affiliates
Gain on sale of marketable securities
Others

NON-OPERATING EXPENSES
Interest and discounts
Interest on bonds payable
Amortisation of deferred charges
Valuation loss on marketable securities
Exchange loss
Others

ORDINARY INCOME

EXTRAORDINARY GAINS
Gain from sale of fixed assets
Recovery of bad debts written off
Gain on sale of shares in subsidiary
Gain from sale of investment securities

EXTRAORDINARY LOSSES
Adjustment of depreciation provided in previous years
Fire loss
Loss on sale of fixed assets

Income before income taxes
Corporate income and inhabitants tax
Net profit
Unappropriated retained earnings brought forward
Reversal of reserve for self insurance
Interim dividends
Legal earned reserve appropriated in relation to interim dividend
Unappropriated retained earnings as at the end of the year

BALANCE SHEET – JAPAN

ASSETS

CURRENT ASSETS:
Cash in hand and at bank
Trade notes payable
   Allowance for bad debts
Trade accounts receivable
   Allowance for bad debts
Trade notes and accounts receivable
from affiliates
   Allowance for bad debts
Marketable securities
Treasury stock
Merchandises
Finished goods
Semifinished goods
Work in progress
Raw materials and consumables
Supplies
Advance payments
Prepaid expenses
Other accounts receivable
Other accounts receivable from affiliates
Short-term loans
   Allowance for bad debts
Short-term loans to affiliates
   Allowance for bad debts
Other current assets
   Total current assets

FIXED ASSETS:
Tangible fixed assets:
Buildings
   Accumulated depreciation
Structures
   Accumulated depreciation
Machinery and equipment
   Accumulated depreciation
Vehicles
   Accumulated depreciation
Tools, fixtures and fittings
   Accumulated depreciation
Land
Construction in Progress
   Total tangible fixed assets
Intangible Assets:

LIABILITIES

CURRENT LIABILITIES:
Trade notes receivable
Trade accounts payable
Trade notes and accounts payable to
affiliates
Short-term borrowings
Current portion of long-term
borrowings
Other accounts payable
Accrued corporation and inhabitants tax
Accrued enterprise tax
Accrued expenses
Deposits received
Deferred income
Allowances:
   Allowance for bonus payments
   Allowance for damages
   Allowance for repairs
   Allowance for warranty
Other current liabilities
   Total current liabilities

LONG-TERM LIABILITIES:
Bonds payable
Bonds with warrants
Convertible bonds
Long-term borrowings
Long-term borrowings from
shareholders, officers and employees
Long-term borrowings from affiliates
Allowances:
   Allowance for severance payments
   Allowance for special repair
Other
   Total long-term liabilities
   Total liabilities

CAPITAL

SHARE CAPITAL
CAPITAL RESERVE
LEGAL EARNED RESERVE
OTHER SURPLUSES

Mining rights
Land rights
Trade mark rights
Patents
Telephone rights
Goodwill
   Total intangible fixed assets
Investment and other assets:
Long-term cash at bank
Investment in securities
Investment in subsidiaries
Long-term loans
   Allowance for bad debts
Long-term loans to shareholders, officers
and employees
   Allowance for bad debts
Long-term loans to affiliates
   Allowance for bad debts
Doubtful receivables
Long-term prepaid expenses
Other
      Total investment and other assets
      Total fixed assets

DEFERRED CHARGES
Organisation expenses
Pre-operating costs
Experimental research costs
Development costs
Stock issuing costs
Bond discounts
Interest during constructions
      Total deferred charges
      Total assets

Other capital surpluses
   Reserves for government grants
   Reserves for gain on insurance
   claims
Voluntary reserves
   Reserve for overseas investment
   losses
   Reserve for dividend equalisation
   Reserve for business extension
   Reserve for additional equipment
   Reserve for sinking fund
   General reserve
Investment in affiliates
   Unappropriated
Investment in partnerships
   Total capital
   Total liabilities and capital

Part II

HOW DO I ANALYSE
THE ACCOUNTS?

9

INTRODUCTION

Welcome to the world of the amateur detective! We are now moving on to the section in this book where we start to understand what the accounts do (and don't) tell us about the financial performance of a company. Like any good detective, we will probably have as many questions as answers, but we should be able to make sense of what is going on in the company. It is only after we have understood the wealth of information found in the accounts, that we can start to analyse and interpret it.

This section shows you how to do this in a structured way. It looks at the accounts, the components of business financial performance, shows you how to complete a financial analysis and then interpret it. It identifies the main elements of measuring a business's performance and will provide you with a structured approach for analysing any company's accounts. The subsequent interpretation involves taking this analysis of isolated factors and tying them together into a coherent whole. All the factors interact with one another to reveal the company's financial performance.

The section starts by looking at creative accounting and subsequently identifies the ways that we can measure the financial performance of a company. However, the most important tool in financial analysis is not found in this book. It is one you already have – your common sense! Your common sense will help you identify creative accounting, and will help you assess the company's financial performance. Financial performance is often measured by using financial ratios. Most ratios only quantify what you can already see. They measure it to six decimal places, and give you a feeling of comfort as they demonstrate to you that you were right in the first place! Ratios are reassuring; but there is a tendency for people, who are not familiar with financial analysis, to become overly obsessed with them. They often lose sight of what the ratios actually mean.

There is no need to calculate every ratio illustrated in this book, the ratios you use will be determined by your objective and the things you spotted when you read through the accounts. When you are analysing a company's accounts you will find that ratios are not as easy to calculate as you first thought. Most people want to see nice standard formulas that they can program into a spreadsheet, input the accounts, press the return key, and get the ratios. Sadly it isn't quite that simple. (If it was, you wouldn't need financial analysts in the city, computers would do the job for less money!)

You need to engage your brain to work out what numbers should be included in the ratios.

Take the return on capital (sometimes called the return on assets), a ratio that most managers have heard of. This tells us what return the company is making on the capital it uses to generate the profit. This is an important measure as it allows us to rank companies' financial performance, and identify whether they are achieving a better return than we could get elsewhere. For reasons explored in detail in Chapter 12, this is calculated by using the following formula:

$$\frac{\text{Profit before tax and interest paid on long-term loans}}{\text{Capital employed}}$$

It would appear, on first sight, that the only problem we are going to have is identifying the capital employed. This is the long-term capital tied up in the business – the capital and reserves and any long-term loans. Should we include provisions for liabilities and charges? It would certainly make calculating the ratios easier, on UK accounts we could just lift the number off the balance sheet from the total assets less current liabilities line. Some of the provisions will have been made to 'smooth' profits. If they hadn't been made the profits would have been larger and that would be reflected in the capital and reserves. Should we take account of the different policies that different companies have in accounting for goodwill and revaluation of assets? You'll need to read Chapter 12 to find the resolution to this debate!

But identifying the capital is only one half of the story; identifying the profit can be equally problematic. The profit before tax includes operating profit, profit (or losses) on sale of fixed assets, and profit (or losses) on sale of subsidiaries. If the company has sold a sizeable subsidiary during the year it could have a considerable impact on the profits reported for the year. Should this be included? Should we only include profit made on continuing businesses?

We have to decide what should be included in the ratios, different people will have different views. These views about how to calculate the ratios could generate different opinions about the financial performance of the company. Therefore the ratios are not always what they appear to be. Most managers like ratios because they think they are an objective measure of the company's performance. Unfortunately, they aren't. Reporting ratios to six decimal places is confusing precision with accuracy. We have to decide how to calculate them, and we must always remember that they are based on numbers that represent the 'best' picture that the company could present. Ratios give us a feel for what is going on in the company. In isolation they are meaningless, we always need to look at trends. Ideally we would need to look at the company's performance over a number of years, and within the context of its sector.

Despite their attendant problems, it is important that we do understand how to calculate ratios. This section of the book will show you how. Firstly we will calculate the ratios using a simple example, then we will look at how to calculate them from published accounts. To illustrate this we will use IMI's accounts for 1993. We will learn where we can find the data we need to use in the ratios and how to calculate them. Then we will look at how to use them to assess a company's financial performance.

In this section of the book we will cover:

Creative accounting – do we believe the numbers in the accounts?

Published accounts are a marketing brochure, designed to market the company to banks, investors and customers. The Companies Act says that they must be true and fair, and they undoubtedly are – but they will be a version of the truth that reinforces the company's successes and minimises its failures! We always tell the truth, but the whole truth?

Companies have long discussions with auditors about the amount of information disclosed in their accounts. The people who advocate full disclosure, for investor protection, are never the people who run companies! You need to check for signs of creative accounting for two reasons:

- it's pointless working out ratios based on numbers you don't believe in the first place!
- creative accounting is often the first sign of business failure. We only need to dress up the numbers if we have something to hide!

The accounting notes are always the first place to start in any financial analysis. They will disclose the accounting policies and help to identify how the numbers in the accounts have been determined. It is always useful to look at the extra information found in company accounts, this is the information that the auditors insisted on including to ensure that the accounts give that all important true and fair view.

Solvency – can the business pay its debts when they fall due?

This is obviously the crucial question; it is insolvent businesses that go bust, not unprofitable ones. We need to be able to identify whether the company is likely to have any problems with either its bank or its suppliers. If they do have problems, are they likely to be able to resolve them? This chapter will help you identify if the company has any current, or potential, solvency problems.

Profitability – is the business profitable?

This chapter helps you identify if the profitability of the company has changed, what caused that change, and whether any improvement is likely to be sustainable. The profitability of the company needs to be considered in detail to find out:

- whether the company is more or less profitable than it used to be,
- whether the company is more or less profitable than its competitors,
- why the company is more or less profitable.

Cash – is the business managing its cash in the most effective way?

The cash flow statement is our starting point for looking at the way that a company manages its cash. We need to identify where the company is getting its money from and what the company is spending its money on. Is it tapping the right sources of funds, considering the type of expenditure? Is it living within its means? What is the company's approach to managing its cash resources? Is it conservative or innovative? There will be different risks and opportunities associated with different strategies.

Investment performance – are they satisfying their shareholders?

In most financial analyses we will need to look at the business from the investors' point of view. This will give us information about the company's ability to have a rights issue, or to make an acquisition. We will be able to see whether they are underperforming the market and are a possible takeover target. Understanding the stock market perspective is an important management skill. Sometimes the market undervalues companies – why? Does it matter?

Interpreting the data – what does it all mean?

Analysing the information is only the first step in conducting the analysis. We must tie all the information together to understand what is really going on in the company. This chapter will integrate the analysis to form a view of the financial performance of IMI, over the last five years.

IMI is an international engineering company. In 1993 nearly 61 per cent of its profit, and over 53 per cent of its turnover, came from overseas. Most of us will have seen and used some of IMI's products – when we run a bath, use our central heating at home, or when we have a drink in our local pub. IMI makes the copper tubing, valves and fittings used in central heating and water systems. It also makes the machines that dispense soft drinks in pubs, fast-food restaurants and canteens. In addition to these everyday products that we use, IMI makes a range of specialised products for industry. It makes titanium for use in aircraft engines, heat exchangers, miniature valves and air lines used in industrial robots.

It is organised into four main divisions.

- **Building products**. This division produces a range of copper tubes, valves and fittings for central heating, water and air conditioning systems.
- **Drinks dispense**.This division produces the machines that dispense the soft drinks that we buy in pubs and restaurants.
- **Fluid power**. This division produces components for the compressed air technology that is used in most factories.
- **Special engineering**. This division produces a wide range of products. Their products include titanium for aircraft engines, coins, shotgun cartridges and special-purpose valves.

They also have two computer companies and a property company.

In each chapter we will identify the key issues, the principal ratios, and what they tell us. By the time you have read this section of the book you will be able to analyse and interpret a set of company accounts. You will have seen how ratios can be calculated from a set of published accounts and how they can be used to assess a company's performance.

10

CREATIVE ACCOUNTING

INTRODUCTION

Although there are always steps being taken to eliminate it, creative accounting is probably here to stay. Consequently it is important that we are aware of the possibility of creative accounting when we are analysing companies' accounts. Whilst there has always been some element of 'window dressing' in the accounts, this was primarily companies trying to 'smooth' out their profits. However in the 1980s things started to get out of hand. Companies were:

- taking their debt off the balance sheet,
- improving post-acquisition profits with the use of acquisition provisions, which increased the amount of goodwill written off to reserves, and reduced the rationalisation costs charged to the profit and loss account,
- manipulating earnings per share by classifying exceptional items as extraordinary,
- showing profits on disposal of subsidiaries, by calculating the profit from the net asset value, not what they had originally paid for the subsidiary.

Creative accounting is largely a child of the 1980s. It probably started when companies got into difficulties in the recession of the early 1980s. There was pressure to produce better profits, when profits of any description were hard to find. Then companies discovered that the rules only told you what you can't do, not what you can! If you couldn't earn profits you could at least create them!

In that recession creative accounting bought companies time. The latest recession went on too long and many companies reporting 'creative' profits were forced into liquidation. In fact this is probably the only recession where many large, apparently profitable companies have gone bust. By the end of the 1980s it was difficult to believe that accounts were supposed to be true and fair! The ability to read and understand the notes became an integral part of financial analysis. You usually started with the notes if you wanted to understand what was really happening in the company.

Since its inception in 1990 the Accounting Standards Board has reduced the amount of large-scale creative accounting. It has:

- standardised the format for the cash flow statement and made it much more 'user friendly',
- reduced the scope for 'off balance sheet' funding with FRS 2 and further reduced it with FRS 5, which applies to accounts relating to accounting periods ending on, or after, 22nd September 1994,
- introduced a more detailed profit and loss account. This now enables us to see how much profit has come from acquisitions, and how much will be disappearing next year as it was generated by businesses sold, or discontinued, during the year,
- revised the definitions for operating profit, profit on sale of fixed assets and subsidiaries, and earnings per share,
- encouraged the usage of multiple earnings per share calculations, and tightened the definition of extraordinary items to make the standard earnings per share figures more comparable,
- compiled another draft rule (FRED 7) that will reduce the scope for creativity when accounting for acquisitions.

So although many of the opportunities for large-scale creative accounting have gone or will disappear there is still some scope for manipulating the numbers and we must be aware of these before we embark on our analysis.

Large, public companies manipulate their numbers in a different way to small, private companies. Large companies tend to want to improve their profits, often at the expense of the balance sheet (but to the enhancement of many of the ratios). Small, private companies tend to be more concerned with improving their net worth, often enhancing their profits at the same time. They have different concerns and different objectives. A public company wants to show nice steady profit growth. That is the one thing that will be guaranteed to keep their shareholders happy. A private company's shareholders are usually the directors, so the shareholders tend not to be the problem. Their main problem is usually the bank. To keep the bank happy they need to show a reasonable profit, but more importantly they need to have a lot of assets. The bank won't lend to them on the strength of their good name!

In this chapter we will identify some of the ways that a company can flatter profits and assets. Some of the techniques are very visible, some are hidden. We have already touched on many of the issues, in other parts of the book, but need to review them in the context of the opportunities they offer for creative accounting.

IMPROVING REPORTED PROFITS

In the profit and loss account we talk about different levels of profit, deducting costs in a standard way.

- Operating costs to arrive at operating profit.
- Losses on sale of assets (or adding profits), and interest to arrive at

profit before tax.
- Tax, to arrive at profit after tax.

Each one of these is important, for different aspects of our analysis. Operating profit is the key component of profit, as it is sustainable and generates 'quality' earnings. Profit before tax is the base figure for the return on capital employed calculation. Profit after tax is used for calculating earnings per share and other investment ratios. Each one can be 'managed'. Let's look at how.

Operating profit

Operating profit can be improved in one of two ways; either you increase the sales, or you reduce the costs. Increasing the sales is an obvious option for the company, but more difficult for the reader of accounts to spot. It is much easier to spot companies trying to reduce their costs.

(a) **The problems of revenue recognition**. In a cash business determining the turnover is very straightforward. It's the cash that has gone through the till. In most manufacturing businesses it is the delivery of the goods, or the transfer of title, that determines turnover. That has led some companies, for example Fisons until 1994, to practise 'trade loading'. Some of next year's despatches are pulled forward into the last period of the current year. Most managers are aware of this practice, and goods and invoices are often despatched, or delayed, at the end of the financial year. Over a period of time it probably doesn't matter, as this sort of manipulation cancels out.

Turnover becomes more difficult to identify when the revenue bridges different accounting periods, for example in long-term contracts. Companies must then determine the accounting period in which they will be recognising the revenue. It is not unusual for companies involved in long-term contracts to have agreed stage payments, but the inclusion of turnover doesn't necessarily reflect the cash flow. When should the turnover be recognised on the company's profit and loss account? In Chapter 2 we considered the problems associated with accounting for long-term contracts. In the UK turnover from long-term contracts is generally included in the profit and loss account on a percentage of completion basis. But this is only easy to determine if the contract is divided into readily identifiable parts, or where the contract is structured on a 'cost plus' basis. If not, the contract turnover can be included in a number of different ways. It could be determined by:

- a valuation by an independent surveyor,
- a valuation by the management,
- a cost basis. There are a number of different formulas that can be used, based on different costs: for example labour costs, or total costs.

It almost goes without saying that different ways of calculating the percentage of contract completion will give different turnover figures.

The important thing to spot here is consistency. If the turnover has been calculated on the same basis from one year to the next, the numbers are roughly comparable. Bringing turnover forward into this year, will make next year's profit figures harder to achieve. If the company has changed its definition of turnover, the comparability of the numbers will be affected.

(b) **Reducing the costs**. In reality most costs can't be changed, what can be changed is where they are charged. Every invoice has to show up somewhere in the accounts, but is it the profit and loss account or the balance sheet? That's fine for the costs that have been invoiced, but not all costs can be traced in this way. Some are 'paper' charges that we include to ensure that the profit and loss account reflects the costs that relate to the sales made in the period. These adjustments are paper transactions to cover things like probable bad debts. They are based on judgements, and judgements can be changed. Consequently there are two possibilities for creative accounting to reduce the costs.

- Charging costs to the balance sheet. This would include transferring costs to stock and capitalising interest.
- Reducing the 'paper charges' made to the profit and loss account. This would include provisions, exchange differences and depreciation.

(i) *Valuing stock*. The valuation of stock is important. The costs of stock are excluded from the profit and loss account, as they do not relate to the sales made in the period. In Chapter 2 we looked at the valuation of stock in detail. We saw that there were two aspects to stock valuation:

- identifying the volume of the closing stock,
- calculating the value of stock.

Measuring the amount of stock in the warehouse should be simple, but anyone who has been involved in stocktaking will know how difficult it is in practice! Errors in stocktaking are not usually deliberate in large companies, after all the auditors will do a physical stocktake. (Smaller companies have been known to overstate the volume of stock. Beware of accounts where the auditors feel unhappy about the cut-off level for stock!) Some degree of error will be built into the system, and shouldn't affect the company's performance over time. It is the stock valuation that gives most scope for creative accounting. There are three possible options for the creative accountant.

- Change the method of valuing stock.
- Increase the level of overheads charged to stock.
- Overstate the net realisable value.

Stock valuation
In Chapter 2 we discussed the different methods of valuing stock. A change in the method used could have a significant impact on the reported profits.

Let's consider a very small business selling widgets for £2.00 each. Last year they sold 9,700, generating revenues of £19,400. Salaries were £5,000 and other costs £2,000. They bought widgets at different prices during the year:

		Units	Unit cost £	Total £
1st January	Opening stock	1,500	1.00	1,500
28th February	Purchases	2,000	1.05	2,100
1st April	Purchases	1,500	1.06	1,590
30th June	Purchases	2,000	1.08	2,160
31st August	Purchases	2,200	1.10	2,420
30th November	Purchases	1,500	1.13	1,695
		10,700		11,465
31st December	Closing stock	1,000		

There are three recognised ways of calculating the costs to be included in cost of sales.

- First in first out.
- Weighted average cost.
- Last in first out.

These will give us different charges to the profit and loss account and different stock values shown on the balance sheet:

	Cost of sales £	Stock values £
First in first out	10,335.00	1,130.00
Weighted average	10,393.50	1,071.50
Last in first out	10,465.00	1,000.00

If we consider the effect on the profit and loss account:

	FIFO £	Average £	LIFO £
Turnover	19,400.00	19,400.00	19,400.00
Materials	(10,335.00)	(10,393.50)	(10,465.00)
Staff costs	(5,000.00)	(5,000.00)	(5,000.00)
Other costs	(2,000.00)	(2,000.00)	(2,000.00)
Operating profit	2,065.00	2,006.50	1,935.00

Last in first out gives us the smallest profit, but is unlikely to be seen in a UK company, as LIFO should only be used if it is the only method that would show a true and fair view. However, the method used by the company is less important than a change in the method. It is only by changing the method that we can 'grow' profits. (In our example a move from average cost to FIFO would add nearly 3 per cent to the operating profit.) The percentage improvement in profits would increase as the materials cost percentage increases.

Inclusion of overheads

Our example was very simple, as it showed stock valuation based purely on the materials cost. Direct labour costs, direct manufacturing expenses and manufacturing overheads also have to be included in the valuation of stocks. The accounting standard (SSAP 9) defines the cost of stock as the 'cost of purchase . . . such costs of conversion . . . as are appropriate to that location and condition'. The definition of the cost of conversion is sufficiently loose to allow companies some latitude in their stock valuation.

According to the accounting standard 'cost of conversion' comprises:

(a) costs which are specifically attributable to units of production, e.g., direct labour, direct expenses and sub-contracted work;

(b) production overheads*;

(c) other overheads, if any, attributable in the particular circumstances of the business to bringing the product or the service to its present location and condition.

* These are subsequently defined to be those 'overheads incurred in respect of materials, labour, or services for production, based on the normal level of activity, taking one year with another'.

Therefore the cost of stock must include the direct costs, a proportion of production overheads relating to normal activities, and may include a proportion of other overheads as well! The accounting standard argues that the principle of prudence should be applied through the requirement to show stock at the lower of cost and net realisable value, not through the exclusion of relevant costs. This is a logical argument that relies on the auditor's ability to verify net realisable value, and to find his way through the minefield of cost apportionment.

Any manager who has worked in a manufacturing company understands the difficulties involved in allocating overheads. It is an area fraught with difficulties, and involving many, often arbitrary, judgements. If you asked four accountants how a cost should be apportioned, you would probably have five different views! Consequently the allocation of overheads to stock involves judgement and therefore gives scope for creativity.

The next problem lies in defining 'the normal level of activity'. The accounting standard gives some guidance in the appendix. It says that companies should consider the plant capacity, the budgeted level of activity, and current and previous year's performance. The problems start when the company has a fall in sales. They then have to determine whether this is a short-term problem, or a continuing one.

Consider the following example:

A company has a production facility that has been designed to produce 100,000 units a year. In the first year it produced 94,000 units, in the second 95,000 units, in the third 96,000 units, and this year only produced 80,000 units, 10,000 of which are still in stock. Budgeted production for this year was 95,000 units and the company was operating close to budget until the last quarter, when sales fell off dramatically. The production overheads for the period were £2 million.

The plant has never operated at maximum capacity, although 100 per cent efficiency is probably an impossible dream! Average production over the period is 95,000 units, the same as the budgeted production for this year. If the overheads were apportioned across 95,000 units there would be a charge to stock of £210,526. This would be appropriate if it was believed that the fall in sales was only temporary (for example, customers could have been destocking towards the year end). If the fall in sales is thought to be permanent then the 80,000 units produced would be a more appropriate basis for apportioning the overheads. This would give a charge to stock of £250,000, an increase of nearly 19 per cent. The more overhead that is included in the stock value the higher the profit for the year (but the lower the profit for the next year, unless the company can have a price increase to reflect the increased 'costs'). Whilst the auditors would want to see some consistency, the company would argue that it was taking a prudent view!

Net realisable value

We have been looking at what costs should be assigned to stock, but we mustn't forget that stock should be shown at the lower of cost or net realisable value. Charging all these costs to stock, doesn't help if the 'cost' then exceeds the net realisable value! But what is net realisable value? The definition, in the accounting standard, has been given in Chapter 2. However, trying to ascertain whether the stock has fallen below its market value, in its current state, is an area for discussion. Small companies, in particular, are loath to make provisions for obsolete stock. Provisioning reduces both profits and net worth.

Summary

Charging costs to stock and having an optimistic view of net realisable value flatters both profits and net worth. Unfortunately the information given by companies about their stock valuation is somewhat limited. The note on stocks for IMI is fairly typical:

Stocks

Stocks are valued at the lower of cost and net realisable value. In respect of work in progress and finished goods cost includes all direct costs of production and the appropriate proportion of production overheads.

Companies would have to disclose a change in the valuation method, but provisions are only disclosed separately if that is necessary to show a true and fair view. Therefore we are forced to rely on our common sense. Is the stock number believable when we look at the company's history of managing stock and the performance of other companies in the industry?

(ii) *Provisions*. Provisions have always been used by companies to 'smooth' profits. The stock market likes to see a steady growth in profits; unfortunately life isn't like that – you have bumper years and bum years. Reporting a bumper profit always gives companies problems. If the market expects a profit of £100 million and it looks like being £120 million, should the company report £120 million? The stock market behaves very much like bosses, it moves the goalposts! If the company reported £120 million profit, they would expect £130 million next year. For a public company, disclosing profits in one year creates an expectation for the next. Consequently there has always been a tendency to make large provisions in good years (taking a prudent view) and smaller provisions in bad years. The only exception to this rule is when new management take over, or the market expects a bad year, then the company will always make large provisions to depress profits. Then the following year, the new management have turned the business around!

Provisions are only disclosed separately in the accounts, if disclosure is necessary to give a true and fair view. Then they will be shown as exceptional items. They will be detailed in the notes, but will only be disclosed separately on the face of the profit and loss account if they are so material that separate disclosure is necessary for the true and fair view. Consequently most provisions are not disclosed separately, thus becoming an ideal vehicle for 'smoothing'.

Provisions that relate to the reduction in value of an asset are deducted from that asset. Therefore bad debt provisions are deducted from debtors, and obsolete stock provisions reduce the value of stock shown on the balance sheet. Other provisions relate to potential losses, or liabilities, and are charged to the profit and loss account and shown on the balance sheet as part of provisions for liabilities and charges.

The draft accounting standard, FRED 7, is concerned with 'Fair values in acquisition accounting'. It is an important draft standard as it proposes to disallow acquisition provisions, which have been a useful way of improving post-acquisition profits. These provisions are different to the provisions that we have discussed so far. All the previous provisions have been charged to the profit and loss account, and have affected reported profits. These are charged to the reserves, and haven't affected reported profits.

It is probably worth talking about them, in spite of the proposal to disallow them, for two reasons. Firstly the comments on the exposure draft may generate a need for modification. (It is not a popular proposal, 'with only a small majority in favour of the proposed treatment'.) Secondly the draft allows a transitional period and consequently acquisition provisions are likely to be found in accounts for some time.

Acquisition provisions work very simply. I buy a company for £5 million with a book value of £4 million. I know that I will need to spend £1 million rationalising the acquisition. I have two options, either I charge the acquisition costs to my profit and loss account as they are incurred, or I create an acquisition provision. When accounting for the acquisition I will have to make two other adjustments to arrive at the acquisition's net assets.

- **Fair value adjustments**: in simple terms these restate asset values to their market values, in their current state, and liabilities to what is expected to be paid. This does involve a degree of judgement and can be used to enhance future profits. For example stocks and debtors could be written down. When the stocks are sold and the debtors collected the old balance sheet values may be realised, not the reduced, restated values. The stock writedown will go straight through to the operating profit. The collection of the debtors will help operating profit indirectly. It will reduce the need to make a charge for bad debt provisions in the current year.
- **Accounting policy alignment**: the accounting policies of the acquisition should be the same as the ones used in the rest of the company. When the new accounting policies are applied, adjustments are likely to be made to the values of the assets and the liabilities.

To illustrate the impact, on the accounts, of an acquisition provision we will assume that the assets and liabilities are already at fair values and there are no accounting policy alignments.

The notes found in the accounts will analyse the acquisition into its component assets and liabilities, but a summary of the information is as follows:

	Book value £m	Reorganisation/ acquisition provisions £m	Fair value to the group £m
	4	(1)	3
Goodwill			2
Consideration			5

By making the acquisition provision we increase the goodwill. As most goodwill is written off through reserves, we reduce the past profits, rather than the future ones. (This will also improve some of our ratios.) When I spend the money rationalising my acquisition all I will do is reduce the provision shown on the balance sheet. It will only impact on my profit and loss account if I spend more than £1 million. (Then I could have the option of writing off more goodwill, and increasing the provision.) Therefore if I spent £700,000 in the first year, the provision would reduce to £300,000. The rationalisation costs won't show in the profit and loss account, but will affect the cash flow. As £700,000 has been spent the operating cash flow would be reduced. This would be shown under the heading of 'provisions utilised'.

There are many prestigious supporters of acquisition provisions, for example in their 1993 accounts Tomkins set up a provision of £90.4 million to cover the reorganisation of Rank Hovis McDougall. During the year £8.8 million was charged against the provision, leaving a balance on the provision of £81.2 million after exchange adjustments.

In 1991 Grand Metropolitan set up disposal provisions of £308 million when it sold its brewing operations to Inntrapreneur Estates (a joint venture between Courage and Grand Metropolitan) and added 330 former Courage pubs to the Chef and Brewer managed estate (subsequently sold to Scottish and Newcastle). In their 1992 accounts the notes to their disposal provisions (by now reduced to £213 million) gave more detail about the original provision.

- £115 million was a 'beer discount provision' (in March, when the deal was agreed, the initial provision was £130 million). Their deal with Courage included a four-year beer supply agreement. Grand Met's managed pubs were committed to buy beer from Courage at a premium to the market price. The provision was established to cover the excess cost element of the agreement, ensuring the excess cost was charged to the provision rather than the current year's profit and loss account. During 1992 £27 million was utilised, and credited to the profit and loss account. In 1993 another £29 million was utilised.
- £148 million was set aside to cover commitments relating to businesses sold during the year. In 1992 £76 million was utilised, and £21 million was utilised in 1993.
- £45 million to cover losses made on disposal of businesses subsequent to the year end. By 1992 this provision had increased to £53 million, reducing to zero in 1993.

The advocates of acquisition and disposal provisions tend to be the preparers of accounts, rather than the readers of accounts. They argue that these are costs that were taken into account as part of the acquisition, or disposal, decision. (In my simple example I knew that buying the company was going to cost me £6 million, not the £5 million that I paid for the company. When deciding whether it was a worthwhile acquisition, I would have needed to consider the total cost, not just the purchase cost.) The Accounting Standards Board took the view that there is adequate 'facility for proper disclosure and explanation of the resulting volatility in the reported results', as FRS 3 would require these to be shown as exceptional items. They believe that:

- only purchased goodwill should be shown in the accounts. The increase in goodwill following these provisions should not be reflected as such in the accounts, as it is generated by the acquirer,
- although rationalisation costs would be part of the investment decision, they should not be used to increase the liabilities of the acquired company.

There are strong arguments on both sides, and it is difficult to predict the outcome. From our point of view acquisition and disposal provisions increase post-acquisition, or disposal, profits. Like all provisions, they are based on judgements and can be used to 'manage' profits. Not every company uses this technique, and we need to be aware of it when we analyse company accounts. If we are looking at the performance of a single company, we would normally do our analysis both with and without the acquisition provisions. It is useful to exclude the acquisition provisions and to charge the costs directly to the profit and loss account. This enables us to have a better understanding of the success, or otherwise, of the acquisition. If we are comparing companies with different acquisition policies, we would need to exclude the impact of acquisition provisions to make their numbers comparable.

Summary
Provisions are not normally detailed in UK accounts (the main exception is banks' accounts where bad debt provisions are required to be disclosed). Any disclosure is to ensure that the accounts show a true and fair view.

Most provisions have the effect of moving profit from one year to the next. Acquisition provisions are different, as they have not been charged to the profit and loss account. They show only as a liability on the balance sheet, with the goodwill charged to reserves having been increased or decreased by the amount of the provision.

When analysing accounts we need to read the notes to see if any provisions have been disclosed, and determine their impact on the financial performance of the company.

(iii) *Depreciation*. Depreciation was discussed in detail in Chapter 2. As a paper charge, depreciation offers considerable scope for creative accounting. There are a number of different elements in the decision.

- **Asset lives**: in its last set of accounts, published in 1993, British Rail changed its asset lives on locomotives from 20 years to 20–30 years. A similar extension was applied to most of the lives, on assets that they had always depreciated. They also included, for the first time, their infrastructure assets (track, signals etc.) as fixed assets.

    In 1990 British Airports Authority changed its runway life from 40 years to 100 years, and terminals from 30 years to 50 years.
- **Change in method**: in Chapter 2 we saw how a change in the method used to calculate the depreciation charge would impact on the reported profit and asset values.
- **Change in net residual value**.

To spot any changes in the depreciation policy you need to read the notes carefully and compare the accounting policies and profits declared from one year to the next. If the company declares a profit in 1993, is the same profit figure shown for comparative purposes in 1994? If not, has the fixed asset number changed on the balance sheet? If it has, there has been a change in the depreciation policy.

We cannot comment on whether the company was right or wrong to change its depreciation policy, we are only concerned with trends in performance. We are looking for any changes in the accounting policies of the company that make the numbers less comparable. We need to exclude these changes from our analysis, to establish a trend.

Summary

Before embarking on a financial analysis we need to read the notes to the accounts carefully to see if there has been a change in the depreciation policy. Depreciation is an easy number for companies to change. It is a paper charge and if they keep the assets for long enough they will have appreciated, not depreciated! The accounting policies will disclose some information about depreciation, although it tends to be somewhat limited as the notes for IMI reveal:

Fixed assets

Freehold land, and assets in the course of construction are not depreciated. Depreciation is calculated so as to write off the cost of other tangible assets to residual values over the period of their estimated useful lives within the following ranges:

Freehold buildings	25 to 50 years
Leasehold land & buildings	period of lease
Plant & machinery	3 to 20 years

Expenditure on patents purchased by the group is charged against profits in the year in which it is incurred.

(iv) *Exchange rates*. Exchange rates were discussed in detail in Chapter 2. They offer companies two opportunities to engage in creative accounting:

- change the method of calculating exchange rates,
- the treatment of exchange differences for borrowings and deposits.

Changing the method

The methods used to account for exchange rates have slightly different rules for individual companies and groups. They are detailed in Chapter 2 and are summarised below:

Individual companies:

- **profit and loss account items**: the exchange rate prevailing at the time of the transaction or the average rate,
- **balance sheet items**: the closing rate.

Group accounts:

- **profit and loss account items**: the average rate or the closing rate, unless the foreign enterprise is not independent, where the temporal method should be used,
- **balance sheet items**: the closing rate.

Any change in the method would have an impact on the reported profitability of the company. The effect on profits would have to be disclosed if it was material.

The accounting treatment for exchange differences in borrowings and deposits

The general rule is that exchange gains and losses on monetary items should be taken into the profit and loss account. Whether it is prudent to take unrealised gains on foreign currency borrowings as part of profits is a matter of debate (the Companies Act says that only realised gains should be taken into the profit and loss account). However, this treatment is required under SSAP 20, unless the exchange gains should be excluded on the grounds of prudence, or there are doubts about the convertibility and marketability of the currency.

The exception to this rule is where foreign currency borrowings have been used to hedge against, or finance, foreign equity investments. In this case, the exchange differences are written off through reserves. This is a development of the principle of matching assets to liabilities.

The problems arise when we are looking at a multinational company with a diverse loan portfolio. This is becoming increasingly common as treasurers use the international capital markets and take advantage of the extensive range of funding instruments that are now widely available. How do you identify which loans have been used to finance, or hedge, the investments? There is considerable scope for creativity. The accounting standard tries to minimise this by insisting on consistency of accounting treatment from one year to the next, but there is still scope for improving the reported results.

A company could borrow in a currency where interest rates are low (improving profit before tax), and take exchange differences to reserves arguing that the loan is a hedging or financing instrument.

To illustrate this, a company borrows $100 million, for five years at 4 per cent when exchange rates were $1.50 to £1.00. UK interest rates were 6 per cent at the time, making the US a cheaper place to borrow money. If we assume that the loan was converted immediately into sterling the company would receive £66.67 million. The dollar loan could impact on the profit and loss account in two ways.

- The interest bill could be reduced. The cost of borrowing dollars is lower than the cost of borrowing sterling.
- The interest bill could be eliminated if the company had placed the proceeds of the loan on deposit.

To illustrate this we will assume that the money had been put on deposit, in the UK, at 5 per cent. The interest would be:

		£m
Interest received	(£66.67 × 5%)	3.33
Interest paid	(($100 × 4%)/1.50)	2.67
Net interest received		0.66

The company has generated £660,000 profit by investing someone else's money! If it was that simple we would all be doing it.

The problem is that a relatively low interest rate reflects a stronger currency, that will probably appreciate. In five years' time, when the loan has to be repaid, the dollar is likely to have strengthened against the pound. If we assume that the exchange rate, at the time of repayment, is $1.20 to £1.00, the company has to exchange £83.88 million to repay the $100 million loan. This gives the company a capital loss of £17.21 million. This would normally be reflected in the profit and loss account during the loan period. As the dollar strengthened against the pound the exchange loss would be taken into the profit and loss account, unless the company argued that the loan was being used to hedge a US investment. (It could hardly argue that it was being used to finance a US investment if the loan has been converted into sterling!) If this argument was accepted by their auditors, the profit and loss account would benefit from the interest income and they could defer the capital loss until the loan has to be repaid. Then they incur the loss, in cash terms, but it would not show on the profit and loss account.

Summary

Reported profits will reflect exchange gains and losses on monetary items, unless these have been used to finance, or hedge, investments. The accounting policies will disclose whether the company is doing this. The note for IMI on foreign currency translation is:

Foreign currencies

Assets and liabilities denominated in foreign currencies have been translated into sterling at the rate of exchange ruling on 31 December 1993. The profit and loss accounts of overseas subsidiary undertakings are translated at the appropriate average exchange rates for the year and the adjustment to year end rates is taken directly to reserves. Exchange differences arising on the retranslation of opening net assets in foreign currencies and foreign currency loans used for overseas investment are taken directly to reserves. Differences arising on trading transactions in the year are reflected in profit before taxation.

The notes to the reserves will disclose if the company has any material unrealised gains and losses.

(a) **Profit before tax**. The profit before tax can be improved by:

- improving the profit on sale of fixed assets,
- reducing the interest charged to the profit and loss account.

(i) *Profit on sale of fixed assets*. Since the implementation of FRS 3, profit on sale of fixed assets is calculated by reference to the book value of the assets. If the assets cost £100,000, and have been depreciated by £70,000, they will have a book value of £30,000. If they are subsequently sold for £40,000, the company will show a profit on sale of assets of £10,000. This represents an overdepreciation of the assets and is shown separately on the profit and loss account, after operating profit. The profit on sale of assets is determined by the book value of the assets. This is influenced by two things:

- The depreciation policy of the company.
- The revaluation policy of the company. If the asset is a building that the company has held for a number of years, it will probably have increased in value. This increase in value may or may not have been recognised in the accounts. If the company has not revalued its assets, it is almost certain to make a profit on disposal. It is interesting to note that following the implementation of FRS 3 a number of companies' *directors* (in conjunction with their own professional qualified staff) felt it prudent to *devalue* their properties.

Summary
Profit on sale of assets is dependant upon the book value of the assets, a low book value is more likely to generate a profit. The book value of the asset will be determined by the depreciation and revaluation policy of the company.

(ii) *Capitalisation of interest*. Companies have always capitalised costs. Any costs associated with the improvement or construction of assets have always been charged to the balance sheet, as they are capital costs that do not relate to the sales in the period. If you look at any company that has major capital projects, you will find that a significant proportion of their staff costs are capitalised. (In 1993 Severn Trent Water capitalised just over 24 per cent of their total staff costs, SWEB just under 19 per cent.)

The capitalisation of interest in property development, and other areas, is a more recent phenomenon. The argument for capitalising interest is that interest is as much a part of the cost as the bricks and mortar, and, if the asset had been purchased from someone else, interest would be included in the costs that were recovered in the selling price. The capitalisation of interest, like any other cost, has the effect of improving the profits and the asset values on the balance sheet. One of the problems is deciding how much interest should be capitalised. It is straightforward if there is a specific loan taken out to fund the development of the asset. Problems arise when the development of the asset is funded from the general borrowings of the company. Then the amount to be capitalised can be either:

- the cost of funding the incremental borrowings required to finance the asset,

or

- an average of the interest on the total borrowings of the company, applied to the cost of the asset.

Therefore there is scope for companies to manipulate profit, and there have been occasions where the book value of properties (including the capitalised interest) has exceeded the market value.

When we are analysing the accounts we need to understand that when a company starts to capitalise interest, it will affect both their reported profits and asset values. It will also affect some of the ratios that we calculate. One important ratio is interest cover, which is concerned with a company's ability to service its debt.

Summary

The capitalisation of interest costs reduces the comparability of companies' reported profits and asset values. There is scope for manipulating the amount of interest that can be capitalised; therefore it may be prudent to ignore it when analysing a company's accounts.

(b) **Profit after tax**. The tax charge that is reported in the profit and loss account is critical to a public company as it affects the earnings per share. The lower the tax charge the greater the profit available to shareholders and vice versa. Companies have two pressures on them when calculating the tax charge. The need to minimise their tax bill (this is real cash out of the business) and the need to satisfy the shareholders by reporting a growth in earnings per share. The tax planning considerations are probably more important than manipulating profits for shareholders, as no one likes paying tax. Consequently most manipulation of the tax charge occurs through deferred taxation. This is a paper adjustment that will not affect the money handed over to the tax authorities, only the profit declared to the shareholders.

We know that in the UK taxable profits are calculated on a different basis to published profits. Two types of difference were discussed in Chapter 2 – permanent differences and timing differences. Deferred tax tries to take account of the timing differences, to the extent that they are likely to crystallise in the future. It brings the tax charge to what it would have been had the tax been based on the profits declared in the accounts. Any potential liability is then carried forward on the balance sheet, as part of provisions for liabilities and charges.

Deferred tax gives companies the opportunity to engage in creative accounting as they have to make a decision about whether the timing differences are expected to reverse and generate a future liability. To do this they have to consider their future plans in order to assess the probable future tax liabilities, taking account of both the company's strategic intent and the budgeted capital expenditure. The accounting standard suggests that a projection over three to five years would be appropriate where there is a regular pattern to the timing differences, a longer period would be appropriate if there was no uniform pattern. Like all plans the longer the timescale, the less reliable the plan (reflect on the corporate plan of your own company)! Like all other provisions charged to the profit and loss account, an overcharge in one year can be written back in subsequent years. It would be argued that the deferred tax provision is no longer needed in the light of the company's revised plans.

Summary

Deferred tax can be used for short-term 'smoothing' of reported profits. The deferred tax charge is based on a number of assumptions. We are not in a position to know whether these assumptions are realistic or not. The effect of deferred tax can only be short-term, as the auditors will be in a position to see whether the proposed plans materialise.

IMPROVING THE VALUE OF ASSETS

This has been discussed indirectly in the preceding part of this chapter. Fixed asset values are influenced by depreciation and revaluation policies, stock by valuation methods and provisioning, debtors by provisioning. The capitalisation of interest will increase asset values. Most capitalised interest relates to fixed assets, but it could also affect stock values. All of the creative accounting tools affect the balance sheet, most improve the asset values.

SUMMARY

The starting-point for any financial analysis has to be the auditors' report, closely followed by the accounting policies and the notes to the accounts. These will determine the numbers that we will use for the ratios.

Do the auditors believe the accounts are 'true and fair'? If not, what type of qualification do they give? (The types of qualification and their relative importance was discussed in Chapter 1.)

The auditors may have stated that, in their opinion, the accounts are a true and fair view, but in arriving at that opinion they will have asked the company to make specific disclosures in the notes to the accounts. These disclosures are one of the most important things to be found in the accounts.

If the accounting policies have changed, try to identify the effect of the change on profits and net assets. Is it significant? Will it be more significant next year? (A change in the depreciation policy this year could have a big impact on next year's profits if there are a lot of assets in the course of construction. Companies usually change their accounting policy a year earlier than they want to, in the hope that you think that it will not have a big impact on their profitability!) Try to have at least two sets of accounts, this year's and last year's. This enables you to see if the company has changed some of the accounting policies that do not require disclosure. The notes to the accounts tell you how the company has arrived at the numbers shown in the accounts. They also tell you useful things like contingent liabilities and guarantees given by the company. Reading the notes is an important part of financial analysis.

Unfortunately, looking at the notes and the accounting policies will not always tell you whether the company is engaging in creative accounting. What may help you to spot it is if you look at:

- the cash flow,
- the profit margins.

(a) **The cash flow statement**. A company can create profits, but, as we know from personal experience, we either have cash or we don't. Unlike profits, cash can't be created. If you are looking at a profitable company that is skint, ask yourself 'why'? There are only four possibilities:

- a major capital expenditure programme,
- a credit control problem,
- a build-up in stock,
- creative accounting.

If none of the first three apply, then the profit is probably coming from creative accounting, rather than operating performance.

(b) **Profit margins**. Another thing to look for is a company making much larger profit margins than other companies in the sector. It is almost impossible for one company to make 10 per cent operating profit margin, when everyone else is making 3 per cent (although it's very easy to make 3 per cent when everyone else is making 10 per cent)! Either they have a wonder product that has rendered everyone else's obsolete, or they have entered a new market, or they have found a new way of making the product. Either way their competitive advantage will only be short-term. Everyone else will follow. The more likely explanation for continued higher profit margins is creative accounting.

11

SOLVENCY

INTRODUCTION

When we are looking at a company, one of our first concerns may well be whether the company is likely to go bust in the near future. If it is, doing any further analysis would seem largely irrelevant! Consequently we are always interested in finding out how solvent a company is, as this gives us some idea of whether the company has a long-term future.

A business is solvent when:

- its assets exceed its total liabilities (i.e. it has a positive net worth),
- it can pay its debts when they fall due.

We can look at solvency on three timescales.

- Will the company be able to meet its long- and medium-term obligations?
- Will the company be able to meet its short-term obligations?
- Could the company pay all its short-term liabilities immediately?

When we are looking at solvency we are primarily using information from the balance sheet, as it is this snapshot that shows us the business's assets and liabilities.

LONG- AND MEDIUM-TERM SOLVENCY

There are a number of different indicators of a company's long-term solvency:

- positive net worth,
- gearing,
- interest cover,
- the loan repayment schedule.

Net worth

The first thing that we must check is that the company's total assets exceed its total liabilities, and by how much. The bottom line on the balance sheet in a UK company will show us this instantly. But sadly it is not quite that simple, as the net worth shown on the balance sheet can be influenced by a number of things.

- Net worth can be increased by revaluation of assets. Revaluation is an imprecise science, or maybe art would be a better description! If the revaluation reserve is the only thing giving the company a positive net worth, check the following:
    - what assets have been revalued?
    - what was the basis of this revaluation?
    - who carried out the revaluation?
    - when were the assets revalued?

    We need to consider these as it is possible that the assets were revalued to make the company look as though it had a positive net worth. (This is not uncommon in smaller companies' accounts.)
- Net worth can be reduced by the way we account for goodwill. If the company has a low net worth, check whether they have had a sizeable acquisition, and their accounting policy for goodwill. If they are writing goodwill off through reserves, the net worth will be adversely affected. If the company you are analysing is a public company, they will disclose how much goodwill has been written off through reserves in the notes on the reserves.

Gearing

Gearing is a measure of the amount of debt a company has. To illustrate this we will consider two companies in the same sector with identical profits, but with different capital structures:

	Company A	Company B
	BALANCE SHEETS	
	£	£
Fixed assets	100,000	100,000
Current assets:		
Stock	10,000	10,000
Debtors	25,000	25,000
Cash	5,000	5,000
	40,000	40,000
Creditors: due in a year:		
Trade creditors	(15,000)	(15,000)
Other creditors	(5,000)	(5,000)
Bank overdraft	(10,000)	(10,000)
	(30,000)	(30,000)
Net current assets	10,000	10,000
Total assets less current liabilities	110,000	110,000
Creditors: due in more than a year		
Loans @ 10%, repayable in 20 years	–	(60,000)
Net assets	110,000	50,000
Capital and reserves:		
Share capital (£1 nominal value)	80,000	20,000
Profit and loss account	30,000	30,000
	110,000	50,000

The capital available to both companies on a long-term basis is identical at £110,000, but the mix of capital is very different. Company A's funding is exclusively from shareholders, whereas Company B has a mixture of long-term debt and shareholders' funds. Company A would be a safer company in times of falling profits. Dividends don't have to be paid unless the company chooses to do so. Whereas for Company B the situation is different – interest has to be paid regardless of the level of profitability. If the profits fell, the company could experience difficulties in paying their interest bill. However, in times of profit growth Company B would look more attractive. Their share capital is a quarter of Company A's, and the shareholders are likely to receive a higher dividend per share.

To illustrate this if we assume that both companies had identical profits before interest and tax of £10,000, were taxed at 33 per cent and paid £1,000 interest on their overdraft. Their profits for the financial year attributable to shareholders, from which dividends are paid, would be:

	Company A	Company B
	£	£
Profit before interest	10,000	10,000
Interest on overdraft	(1,000)	(1,000)
Interest on long-term loans	–	(6,000)
Profit before tax	9,000	3,000
Tax @ 33%	(2,970)	(990)
Profit for the financial year	6,030	2,010

This profit is attributable to 80,000 shareholders in Company A and 20,000 shareholders in Company B. The profit for each share would be 7.54 pence in Company A and 10.05 pence in Company B. (This measure is called the earnings per share and is discussed in detail in Chapter 14.) Company B's shareholders are better off than Company A's. But if we consider what happens if profits fall by 20 per cent, we will see that this position reverses:

	Company A	Company B
	£	£
Profit before interest	8,000	8,000
Interest on overdraft	(1,000)	(1,000)
Interest on long-term loans	–	(6,000)
Profit before tax	7,000	1,000
Tax @ 33%	(2,310)	(330)
Profit for the financial year	4,690	670

The profit per share in Company A is now 5.86 pence per share, whereas Company B's is 3.35 pence per share. Borrowing money is good for shareholders when the company is expanding, and bad when the company is contracting.

It is obvious that Company B has borrowed more than Company A; we need to find a way of measuring this. Accountants use the gearing ratios to quantify the proportion of borrowed capital. Gearing measures the proportion of borrowed money, either to the total capital (the old UK accountant's approach), or to the shareholders' stake in the business (the city and banking approach). Always remember that the gearing ratios you calculate are subject to the same problems we discussed in net worth. The revaluation of assets could either increase or decrease the reserves shown on the balance sheet, writing off goodwill will reduce the value of reserves. If you were trying to make some international comparisons you would need to:

- exclude the revaluation reserve. Revaluation of assets is not allowed in some countries, whilst in others it is done for fiscal reasons,
- add back goodwill. Public companies disclose, in the notes to the

reserves, the amount of goodwill that has been written off through reserves. Most countries would show goodwill on the balance sheet, as an intangible asset. They would also amortise it, so whichever way you go you will have a technical comparative error.

The nature of your analysis will determine whether it is appropriate to make these technical adjustments. For most purposes it is just worth bearing in mind that:

- a recent revaluation will impact on most ratios,
- an acquisition will also have an impact on the ratios, the size of the impact being determined by the significance of the goodwill written off through the reserves.

To illustrate how the gearing ratios are calculated we will use Company B's balance sheet. The two different ways of calculating gearing will show us variants of the same thing.

(a) **Accounting gearing**. The traditional way of calculating gearing measured long-term loans as a percentage of the long-term capital available to the business. This shows us what percentage of the total long-term capital has been borrowed:

$$\frac{\text{Long-term loans}}{\text{Capital employed}} = \frac{60,000}{110,000} = 54.55\%$$

Gearing calculated in this way will always generate a percentage below one hundred; the city's method of calculating gearing can generate percentages above a hundred.

(b) **City gearing**. This looks at the relationship between long-term debt and the equity (the shareholders' stake in the business). There are a number of different ways that this can be calculated, using:

- long-term debt,
- all debt,
- net debt.

We shall look at all three.

(i) *Long-term debt*.

$$\frac{\text{Long-term loans}}{\text{Capital and reserves}} = \frac{60,000}{50,000} = 120\%$$

The company's long-term loans are 20 per cent greater than its equity.

(ii) *All debt*. This is a measure that is often used by banks and credit rating agencies. It may also be a more appropriate measure when looking at smaller private companies, who have limited access to long-term loans.

$$\frac{\text{All debt}}{\text{Capital and reserves}}$$

We can now calculate a gearing figure on this basis for both of the companies, as Company A has a bank overdraft:

Company A:

$$\frac{10,000}{110,000} \quad = \quad 9.1\%$$

Company B:

$$\frac{70,000}{50,000} \quad = \quad 140\%$$

Company A's total debt is just over 9 per cent of its equity, whereas Company B's debt is 40 per cent greater than its equity.

(iii) *Net debt*. This is the commonest way of calculating gearing in the city. It deducts any cash and short-term deposits from the debt. The total debt is usually the figure used. This tends to be a better measure when looking at multinational companies who may have both cash balances and bank over-drafts. These are often in different countries, with the cash balances in one country and bank overdrafts in another. There are two reasons why this may occur.

- It is very difficult to take cash out of some countries. Consequently companies may have an overall cash surplus but are reluctant to use it in a country with these remittance restrictions, so they will borrow money in these countries instead of transferring the cash.
- Some companies take advantage of interest rate differentials, borrowing money in countries with low interest rates and depositing in countries with high interest rates. As we saw in Chapter 10, whilst this may flatter profits in the short term, it can create problems in the long term. Countries paying higher interest rates aren't doing so because they feel generous towards investors! Their economy is viewed as being a less attractive one to invest in, so they have to pay higher rates to attract investors. Companies doing this always run the risk of incurring future exchange losses. If the economy does not perform well the relative value of the currency will fall.

To return to the gearing calculation, gearing on this basis would be:

$$\frac{\text{All debt} - \text{cash and short-term deposits}}{\text{Capital and reserves}}$$

We can calculate the gearing for both of the companies in our example:

Company A:

$$\frac{5,000}{110,000} \qquad = \qquad 4.5\%$$

Company B:

$$\frac{65,000}{50,000} \qquad = \qquad 130\%$$

Net debt is probably the most common way of calculating gearing today, but we should choose the definition of gearing that seems most appropriate for the company that we are analysing.

The way we choose to calculate gearing is largely irrelevant, as long as we are consistent in the way that we calculate it – we should still see the same trends. It is important to calculate our own gearing figures, and not to rely on the ones chosen in the company accounts. Finance directors will always pick the most flattering definition, which may change from one set of accounts to the next!

We have seen that there are a number of different ways of calculating gearing, but does it matter? The answer is . . . maybe, or may be not – it all depends! There are two factors we would need to consider in answering the question.

- Are profits increasing or declining? Company B has to pay £6,000 a year interest (10 per cent of £60,000) regardless of its level of profitability. If profits are increasing the interest bill will become an increasingly smaller proportion of the profits, but if profits are falling the interest could wipe out any profits that the company made.
- Can the company afford to service and repay the debt? To do this we must look at interest cover and the loan repayment schedule.

Servicing the debt – interest cover

Repaying the debt is not a problem that Company B has to consider in the short term, and we would need to look at the cash being generated by the company to be able to take a view on its ability to repay the loan. Servicing the debt may, however, be a more immediate problem. To see if the company is having any difficulties in paying the interest we need to look at both the profit and loss account and the cash flow statement.

Profit and loss account

	£
Sales	100,000
Cost of sales	(60,000)
Gross profit	40,000
Administration expenses	(20,000)
Distribution costs	(10,000)
Operating profit	10,000
Interest	(7,000)*
Profit before tax	3,000

* This is interest on the long-term loan and the overdraft

The interest charge is 70 per cent of the available profit! Fortunately the long-term loan is at a fixed rate so the company is only exposed to rises in interest rates on its short-term borrowings. However, it could easily be exposed to falls in profits! It is obvious that the company could have problems with servicing the debt. As soon as there is something that is obvious we must have a ratio to quantify it!

This ratio is called interest cover. Interest cover divides the interest bill into the available profit to identify how many times the company could pay the interest bill:

$$\frac{\text{Profit before interest}}{\text{Interest payable}} = \frac{10,000}{7,000} = 1.43 \text{ times}$$

This is too low: we would want to see an interest cover falling between four and six times, depending on the risk profile of the company. The riskier the company the more cover we would want to see. Most interest cover ratios are prepared from the profit and loss account, but interest is paid from cash and it is also useful to look at the cash interest cover. To do this we need to look at the cash flow statement:

Cash flow statement

Operating activities

Operating profit	10,000
Depreciation	1,000
Increase in stock	(2,000)
Increase in debtors	(5,000)
Increase in creditors	3,000

Net cash inflow from operating activities	7,000

Returns on investment and servicing of finance:

Interest paid	(7,000)

The operational cash flow only just covers the interest charge, giving a cash interest cover of:

$$\frac{\text{Operational cash flow}}{\text{Interest paid}} = \frac{7,000}{7,000} = 1.00 \text{ times!}$$

All of the operational cash flow is going to pay the interest bill! It wouldn't take much of a fall in profits, or poor control of the working capital before the company would be unable to pay the interest to the bank! If the long-term loan had been at variable interest rates, the company would be even more vulnerable, as it would be exposed to rises in interest rates on all its debt.

High levels of borrowing and poor interest cover is an indication of possible future solvency problems. Looking at companies is just the same as the real life. In the 1980s banks and building societies were prepared to lend up to four times joint salary to enable us to buy a house, and lots of us took out enormous mortgages. We were highly geared. Had we borrowed less our gearing would have been irrelevant. Our mortgage would have been a smaller percentage of our 'take home' salary. But many people borrowed the maximum amount that they could, believing that 'there's nowt as safe as houses'. For them, being highly geared became *the* problem. They had a poor interest cover. Real people experienced exactly the same problems as companies. Our 'profits' fell; we lost bonuses (and some of us lost jobs), just at the time when interest rates doubled. And there was a limit to the number of lodgers we could fit into our house! For a lot of people it was even worse! People in the south of England had the same problems that the property companies had. Their mortgage payments were larger than their salary, but they couldn't sell their house as they wouldn't get enough money back from the sale to repay the loan! Negative equity is not just a domestic problem, it is a corporate problem.

Interest cover is crucial; if you look at the large companies who went into liquidation in the last recession, they were highly geared companies with low interest cover. In fact you probably don't even need to be highly geared, your borrowings could be relatively low, but you could still have poor interest cover. The important thing is can the company afford to service its debt?

When calculating interest cover you need to remember that the interest figure shown on the face of the profit and loss account is the *net* interest figure. To illustrate this we will consider a different example:

	£
Operating profit	70,000
Net interest payable	(20,000)
Profit after interest	50,000

There will be a note in the accounts detailing the calculation of the net interest payable figure, a summary of this note for the above example is shown below:

Interest payable	60,000
Interest receivable	(15,000)
Interest capitalised	(25,000)
Net interest payable	20,000

What is the interest cover? A lot of brokers' reports would say 3.5 times, but is it? We look at the interest cover ratio to identify whether the company is having difficulties in servicing its loans. Whether interest is charged to fixed assets or the profit and loss account is irrelevant. (That's why interest cover calculated from the cash flow statement is so useful, even though it is still unusual to find it included in analysis.) Consequently the total interest payable figure should be used. Whether we should include the interest receivable in the numerator is a matter of debate. If the company was a retailer, where receiving interest was a normal part of their businesses' profits, we should include it. If we are looking at a company who does not normally receive interest, but for one reason or another has managed to have cash balances generating interest this year, we should probably calculate two interest cover figures, one including it and one without. We would need to do this to see the likely trends, with the cash balance at historical levels and at the new level. Sadly, analysing company accounts is an art, not a science; we need to make judgements based on the individual company under consideration.

If we calculate interest cover in both ways:

	Including interest received		*Excluding interest received*	

$$\frac{85,000}{60,000} \quad = \quad 1.42 \text{ times} \qquad \frac{70,000}{60,000} \quad = \quad 1.17 \text{ times}$$

Either way of calculating the interest cover gives us a much poorer figure than the one we would have calculated using the net interest.

The loan repayment schedule

The loan repayment schedule is an important element of solvency analysis. If the company has to repay a large proportion of its debt in the near future, it will need to find the cash or refinance the debt. The loan repayment schedule is disclosed in the notes to the balance sheet.

If we consider the following example:

Bank loans and borrowings are repayable as follows:

	£
Between one and two years:	
Bank loans	15,000
Borrowings	10,000
Between two and five years:	
Bank loans	20,000
Borrowings	40,000
In five years or more:	
Bank loans	10,000
Borrowings	30,000
	125,000

The company has to repay £25,000 in the next two years. The notes to creditors falling due within a year will identify how much might have to be repaid in the next year:

	£
Bank loans and overdrafts	7,000
Portion of long-term loan due for repayment	5,000

We don't know how much of the bank loans and overdraft figure is overdrafts. This would be useful to know as overdrafts, although repayable on demand, are only likely to have to be repaid if either the company or the bank is in difficulties. If we took the pessimistic view (the overdraft will have to be repaid) the company would have to find £12,000 in the next year. Is it likely to be able to find this money? To answer this question we need to look at the cash flow statement together with the cash and short-term investments on the balance sheet.

A summarised cash flow statement is illustrated below:

	£
Net cash inflow from operating activities	45,000
Net cash outflow from returns on investment and servicing of finance	(30,000)
Net cash outflow from taxation	(10,000)
Net cash outflow from investing activities	(20,000)
Net cash outflow before financing	(15,000)

The cash balance for the company, at the year end, is £5,000.

It is difficult to reach any definite conclusions with only one year's cash flow – we would really need to look at cash flow trends. But if the company's cash flows remain at this level the company will experience difficulties in repaying the debt unless it:

- can repay existing loans with new loans. Would the bank view the business as a good risk, taking into account things like their relative performance, their market conditions and their interest cover?
- has sufficient cash to repay the loans. The company may be able to generate cash from the working capital, or sell some of its assets,
- can have a share issue. A number of major companies have managed to have a rights issue, getting more cash from their shareholders by highlighting the alternatives!

To summarise long-term solvency . . . when we are looking at the company's ability to meet its obligation in the long term we need to ascertain whether:

- its assets cover its liabilities,
- it has borrowed too much money,
  - it can service its borrowings,
  - it can repay the loans.

SHORT-TERM SOLVENCY

When we are looking at short-term solvency we are trying to see if the company can meet all its short-term liabilities. To identify this we need to look at the balance sheet and look at the relationship between the current assets and the creditors falling due within a year. We will be using the balance sheet shown below to illustrate the short-term solvency ratios:

	£
Fixed assets	100,000
Current assets:	
Stock	10,000
Debtors	25,000
Cash	5,000
	40,000
Creditors: due in a year:	
Trade creditors	(15,000)
Other creditors	(5,000)
Bank overdraft	(10,000)
	(30,000)
Net current assets	10,000
Total assets less current liabilities	110,000
Creditors: due in more than a year	(60,000)
Net assets	50,000
Capital and reserves:	
Share capital	20,000
Profit and loss account	30,000
	50,000

We can see that the company has £40,000 in current assets, compared to £30,000 in short-term liabilities. So it has £1.33 in short-term assets, for every £1.00 in short-term liabilities.

This is a ratio called the current ratio:

$$\frac{\text{Current assets}}{\text{Creditors falling due in a year}}$$

Whether a current ratio of 1.33:1 is good or bad depends on a number of things based on the type of company we are looking at. For example:

- **grocers**: when you look at grocers' accounts you will find that they have net current liabilities, as their short-term liabilities are greater than their short-term assets. They have very little stock, only give credit via credit cards, but have the usual credit terms with their suppliers. Buying grocery is a daily buying decision and so they feel fairly safe in not having their liabilities covered by their assets.
- **manufacturing companies**: manufacturers need more in current assets than retailers. They may be carrying the retailers' stock, give the retailers

normal corporate credit terms and have the same terms with their suppliers. Consequently we can see that a manufacturer would need more cover than a retailer. How large the current ratio needs to be depends on the type of manufacturing business. It is really dependent on the length of the production cycle. The longer it takes them to turn their raw materials back into cash the more they need in current assets to cover their creditors. A heavy engineering company, who may have nine-month production cycles, may need as much as 2.5; whereas for a confectioner a current ratio of 1.4 may be acceptable.

Consequently when we are looking at short-term solvency we need to look at it contextually.

- We need to look at the ratio over a period of time, remembering that increasing computerisation has allowed companies to reduce stock levels (a large number of companies now run on 'just in time') and so we would expect the current ratio to be falling.
- We need to look at the company's current ratio, and compare it with other companies, of a similar size, in the same sector.

IMMEDIATE SOLVENCY/LIQUIDITY

Immediate solvency is the same as liquidity; liquidity is the term used to describe the company's ability to pay its short-term liabilities. This is the most pessimistic view of solvency, as you are imagining that all the company's creditors falling due within a year ask for immediate payment. If we adopt this scenario we have to identify what assets the business could turn into cash within a day. Again this is largely dependent on the type of company that we are analysing. Most manufacturers would be unable to sell their stock in a day (particularly as part of it would be in work in progress), but retailers could. You need to look at the company and determine their 'liquid assets' – those that could be quickly sold to generate cash. Retailers would normally be able to realise all of their current assets, most manufacturers would only be able to realise debtors (remember factoring?), short-term investments and cash. No one would be able to sell fixed assets within the timescale.

If we continue with our previous example and assume that we need to exclude stock, and look at the liquid assets in relation to the creditors due in a year, we find that we have a £1.00 for every £1.00 that we owe. Therefore we are unlikely to have an immediate liquidity problem. As long as the company doesn't have a large customer go into liquidation they should have no difficulties in meeting their immediate obligations. This ratio of liquid assets to short-term liabilities is called either the quick ratio or the acid test:

$$\frac{\text{Liquid assets}}{\text{Creditors falling due in a year}}$$

This is a pessimistic measure, but is it appropriate? That largely depends on whether we think that everyone is likely to ask for their money back immediately. To find this out we need to see if the company is likely to be having difficulties with its suppliers. How long is it taking to pay its suppliers? We know that the company has trade creditors of £15,000 at the end of the year; if we knew what the purchases were we could calculate how long the company is taking to pay its suppliers.

Unfortunately, purchases are only shown on a Format 2 profit and loss account (the least popular presentation of the profit and loss account), so we are unlikely to be able to get an accurate figure. Some analysts use cost of sales as an approximation to purchases, but this can mean different things to different companies. If you want to compare companies you need to look at creditors in relation to turnover. Although it's wrong, it's consistently wrong and enables you to compare one company with another! You must remember that you are only trying to identify whether the company may have a problem. You are always going to be unable to quantify the size of the problem exactly as the balance sheet has already been managed to give you the best view. You do not need to have a Mensa-sized intellect to know that if turnover is at £3 million, and trade creditors are at £1.5 million – the company is likely to have a problem.

Whichever way you choose to calculate how long the company is taking to pay its suppliers you should still get the same trend (unless profit margins have fluctuated wildly during the period), although not the same answer!

If you wanted to calculate how many days the company was taking to pay its suppliers you would need to look at trade creditors in relationship to either turnover or cost of sales. Below is the profit and loss account for the company (which has trade creditors of £15,000) mentioned in our last example.

	£
Sales	100,000
Cost of sales	(60,000)
Gross profit	40,000
Administration expenses	(20,000)
Distribution costs	(10,000)
Operating profit	10,000
Interest	(6,000)
Profit before tax	4,000

From it we can calculate our creditor days:

Sales based   *Cost of sales based*

$$\frac{\text{Trade creditors}}{\text{Turnover}} \times 365 \qquad\qquad \frac{\text{Trade creditors}}{\text{Cost of sales}} \times 365$$

In our example:

$$\frac{15,000}{100,000} \times 365 \qquad\qquad \frac{15,000}{60,000} \times 365$$

$$\qquad = 54.75 \text{ days} \qquad\qquad\qquad = 91.25 \text{ days}$$

(We need to multiply by 365, as the creditors is the amount of money owed on a given day and the sales are the sales for the whole year.)

We can see that using sales as the denominator will have the effect of understating creditor days. Even assuming the worst view, the company is taking three months to pay its suppliers, they are unlikely to be threatening liquidation, yet!

When we are looking at liquidity, we are taking a pessimistic view. We are assuming that all the creditors falling due in a year want to be repaid today. This is only likely to happen if someone wishes to petition to have the company liquidated. The creditor days calculation is a good indicator of whether the company is experiencing difficulties in paying its trade creditors.

SOLVENCY IN IMI

In this part of the chapter we shall use the 1993 numbers from the IMI accounts to look at the three levels of solvency that have been illustrated in this book:

- long- and medium-term solvency,
- short-term solvency,
- immediate solvency.

This will show you how to calculate the ratios from a set of published accounts. An analysis of trends in IMI will be discussed in Chapter 15.

Long- and medium-term solvency

(a) **Net worth**. A quick glance at the IMI accounts shows that the company has a positive net worth of £385.9 million. This net worth shown on the balance sheet is a very conservative figure, as the revaluation reserve of £7 million relates primarily to the investment properties. The note to the fixed assets discloses 'Gross book value represents costs except for investment properties and £1.0m in respect of revaluations of land and buildings in overseas subsidiaries'. (The accounting standard requires that investment properties are revalued annually, at market value.)

Of the £277.6 million tangible assets shown on the balance sheet £99.8 million are land and buildings. At the end of 1993 £22.6 million were investment properties.

Therefore the company is worth considerably more than it discloses in the accounts.

(b) **Gearing**. We have discussed the three different ways of calculating gearing earlier in the chapter, each giving a slightly different perspective on the business's capital structure. Because the capital and reserves are an important element of the gearing equation we have to decide what to do about revaluation and goodwill. We have seen how the revaluation in IMI is relatively insignificant, but goodwill disclosed on the balance sheet has reduced the shareholder's funds by almost 23 per cent by 1993. (When all goodwill is included there is a reduction of 37 per cent.)

Goodwill becomes more significant when looking at trends. The goodwill written off through reserves has more than doubled from £54.5 million over five years. The accounting policy of writing goodwill off through reserves will have the effect of increasing the gearing ratio. It has reduced the capital and reserves. When we look at numbers in isolation, as we are doing in this chapter, it will not make any difference. The problems start when we are looking at trends and trying to interpret the data. Whether you should include or exclude goodwill is a matter of debate, it can distort the ratios but in some companies' accounts it is immaterial. However, on balance it is better to add it back to give a comparable basis for analysing the financial performance of a company. IMI disclose the goodwill written off through reserves since 1987 on the balance sheet; most companies would disclose this in the notes to the reserves. In addition to the £114.7 million disclosed on the balance sheet there is another £111.8 million that has been charged to the reserves. This is disclosed in the notes. Therefore the total goodwill in 1993 is £226.5 million.

In this chapter we will calculate the gearing ratios, both excluding, and including, goodwill.

(i) *Accounting gearing*. This tells us the proportion of the company's long-term capital that has been borrowed. It looks easy to calculate from IMI's accounts as the borrowings are disclosed separately on the face of the balance sheet; however if you wanted to reflect the true extent of long-term borrowings you would have to see whether any of the long-term debt is due for repayment within a year. Note 17 to the group balance sheet discloses:

	1993 £m	1992 £m
Bank loans and overdrafts	107.7	157.5
7¾% loan stock 1988/93	–	10.0
Net obligations under finance leases	0.5	0.7
Other loans	0.9	0.6
	109.1	168.8

Of the 109.1 million falling due within a year £1.4 million relates to repayment of long-term debt. This will not have a significant impact on the gearing figure that we calculate. Let us look at the number we would have taken from the long-term loans shown on the balance sheet:

$$\frac{\text{Long-term loans}}{\text{Capital employed}} \quad = \quad \frac{89.5}{515.6} \quad = \quad 17.36\%$$

We can now compare it with the 'technically correct' gearing figure:

$89.5 + 1.4$

$$\frac{\text{All long-term loans}}{\text{Capital employed}} \quad = \quad \frac{90.9}{515.6} \quad = \quad 17.63\%$$

When working out the gearing ratio you will have to decide how technically correct you need to be! The important thing to know is that if you use the first definition the trend on gearing can appear to be distorted when long-term loans are due for repayment within a year.

If we now consider the same ratios including goodwill in the capital and reserves we will find that gearing falls:

$$\frac{\text{Long-term loans}}{\text{Capital employed}} \quad = \quad \frac{89.5}{742.1} \quad = \quad 12.06\%$$

$$\frac{\text{All long-term loans}}{\text{Capital employed}} \quad = \quad \frac{90.9}{742.1} \quad = \quad 12.25\%$$

(ii) *City gearing.* This is just a different way of approaching the gearing calculation, this time looking at loans as a percentage of the shareholders' funds. There are three different ways of defining the loans used in this ratio:

- long-term loans,
- all loans,
- net debt.

We will calculate all three, so that you know how to calculate any gearing ratio from a set of published accounts.

Long-term loans

If we use the two different definitions of long-term loans outlined above we would have gearing ratios, excluding goodwill, of:

$$\frac{\text{Long-term loans}}{\text{Capital and reserves}} \quad = \quad \frac{89.5}{385.9} \quad = \quad 23.19\%$$

$$\frac{\text{All long-term loans}}{\text{Capital and reserves}} \quad = \quad \frac{90.9}{385.9} \quad = \quad 23.56\%$$

If we now consider the same ratios including goodwill in the capital and reserves:

$$\frac{\text{Long-term loans}}{\text{Capital and reserves}} \quad = \quad \frac{89.5}{612.4} \quad = \quad 14.62\%$$

$$\frac{\text{All long-term loans}}{\text{Capital and reserves}} \quad = \quad \frac{90.9}{612.4} \quad = \quad 14.84\%$$

All debt

This looks at the relationship of total debt to the shareholders' funds. The total debt is easily found on IMI's balance sheet as borrowings are separately disclosed on the balance sheet. (You may have to extract this from the notes to the creditors in other companies' accounts.) They have short-term debt of £109.1 million, and long-term debt of £89.5 million, giving total debt of £198.6 million. The gearing ratio calculated on this basis will be much higher as most of IMI's debt is short-term.

Let's calculate the gearing ratio excluding goodwill:

$$\frac{\text{All debt}}{\text{Capital and reserves}} \quad = \quad \frac{198.6}{385.9} \quad = \quad 51.46\%$$

Including goodwill:

$$\frac{\text{All debt}}{\text{Capital and reserves}} \quad = \quad \frac{198.6}{612.4} \quad = \quad 32.43\%$$

Net debt

This is the most widely used definition of gearing and looks at net borrowings as a percentage of shareholder's funds. IMI has cash of £101.3 million and current asset investments of £1.2 million. Unfortunately we don't know what these investments are, although they are hardly material in the context of the gearing ratio. Any investment shown as a current asset is intended to be sold in the next twelve months. We would need to know how marketable these investments are. (There have been examples of companies who have been unable to sell their investments within the year.) If they were marketable securities we would include them as part of the cash figure; if it was a subsidiary selected for disposal it would be prudent to ignore it. We will include the £1.2 million in the cash and short-term deposits figure in the calculation. This will give us net debt of £96.1 million (198.6 − 101.3 − 1.2).

Excluding goodwill:

$$\frac{\text{All debt} - \text{cash and short-term deposits}}{\text{Capital and reserves}} = \frac{96.1}{385.9} = 24.90\%$$

Including goodwill:

$$\frac{\text{All debt} - \text{cash and short-term deposits}}{\text{Capital and reserves}} = \frac{96.1}{612.4} = 15.69\%$$

(iii) *Summary*. Gearing can be calculated in many different ways. Goodwill and revaluations can distort the trends shown in the analysis. Consequently, if they have changed significantly during the period it will be necessary to rewrite the reported figures to have a basis for comparison. When we have this common base we then need to decide which gearing calculation to use. This will largely be determined by the capital structure of the company – it would be pointless using a measure based on long-term debt if all the company's borrowings are short-term! The net debt calculation offers the best basis for comparison.

(c) **Interest cover**. This looks at the company's ability to service its debt and can be calculated from both the profit and loss account and the cash flow statement. As a manufacturing business interest received is not a large component of profit. Interest received is disclosed in the notes to the accounts and has fallen from £11.7 million in 1992 to £6.3 million in 1993. This would reflect both the reduction in the reported cash balances (remember that these are year-end balances and average balances may be different) and the falls in interest rates from 1992 to 1993.

For a business like IMI it is more appropriate to calculate interest cover excluding the interest received. Let's calculate a profit-based interest cover, using the interest payable figure of £16.5 million disclosed in the notes to the accounts:

$$\frac{\text{Profit before interest}}{\text{Interest payable}} = \frac{80.4}{16.5} = 4.87 \text{ times}$$

Although IMI is not highly geared, interest is a significant cost, and the interest cover is relatively low.

On a cash basis the situation does look better:

$$\frac{\text{Operational cash flow}}{\text{Interest paid}} = \frac{119.4}{16.5} = 7.24 \text{ times}$$

The interest payable may be different from the interest paid shown on the cash flow statement, as the interest will be accrued on the profit and loss account. The cash flow statement will only be concerned with the interest that is paid during the year.

(d) **The loan repayment schedule**. The loan repayment schedule for the group is disclosed in the notes to the accounts:

	1993 £m	1992 £m
Bank Loans:		
Between one and two years	23.6	0.9
Between two and five years	42.4	65.5
In five years or more	20.3	20.0
	86.3	86.4
Loan stock and other loans:		
Between one and two years	0.3	1.4
Between two and five years	0.3	0.5
In five years or more	2.6	2.7
	3.2	4.6
	89.5	91.0

We can see that IMI has to repay £23.9 million within two years. Their cash flow before financing is negative at £200,000, following a considerable reduction in the cash spent on investing activities. Unless there is an upturn in the market, the company will probably have to repay the existing debt with new loans. This should not pose too many problems with their current solvency ratios.

Short-term solvency

When we are concerned with a company's ability to pay its debts in the short term we are interested in their current ratio. Here we are looking at the relationship between the company's current assets and their creditors falling due within a year. Unfortunately not all of the current assets may be realisable within a year. The debtors' figure in the current assets represents the total amount of money owed to the company; some may be due within a year and some may fall due in more than a year. The notes to IMI's accounts disclose that £182.3 million falls due within a year and £4.7 million in more than a year. This £4.7 million should be excluded from the current ratio, as it will not be realisable in the short term. (Pension-funded prepayments should also be excluded, as they are also not realisable.) Consequently the realisable current assets are £538 million (542.7 − 4.7).

$$\frac{\text{Current assets}}{\text{Creditors falling due in a year}} = \frac{538.0}{317.0} = 1.70$$

IMI has £1.70 in current assets for every £1.00 it owes.

Immediate solvency/liquidity

To look at the liquidity of a company we need to look at the acid test, which is sometimes called the quick ratio. This looks at the relationship between the company's liquid assets and the creditors falling due in a year. An engineering company's liquid assets are debtors falling due in a year, investments and cash. Consequently IMI's liquid assets in 1993 will be £284.8 million (182.3 + 1.2 + 101.3). The acid test will be:

(21.6 + 103.2 + 17.1

$$\frac{\text{Liquid assets}}{\text{Creditors falling due in a year}} = \frac{284.8}{317.0} = 0.90$$

If all the creditors asked for immediate repayment IMI would be able to pay 90 pence in the pound. But how likely is this? To check on the likelihood of the creditors asking for immediate repayment we need to look at who the creditors are and how long they have been waiting to be paid. Firstly, we can see from the balance sheet that over 34 per cent of their creditors are bank loans and overdrafts. From the ratios we have already calculated we can see that the bank is unlikely to be demanding immediate repayment.

We can look at how long the company is taking to pay its suppliers by calculating creditor days. We need to go to the notes to identify the trade creditors.

The notes on other creditors for the group disclose:

	1993 £m	1992 £m
Trade creditors	101.4	94.9
Bills of exchange payable	0.8	1.1
Corporation tax	3.9	9.1
Other taxation	24.3	37.9
Social security	5.1	4.7
Accruals and deferred income	50.5	56.0
Proposed dividend	18.9	18.8
Other creditors	3.0	2.8
	207.9	225.3

It is the trade creditors of £101.4 million that are used in the creditor days calculation. This calculation can be based on either sales or cost of sales. Cost of sales is shown in note 3 to the accounts. If we calculate creditor days based on turnover:

$$\frac{\text{Trade creditors}}{\text{Turnover}} \times 365 = \frac{101.4}{1,064.6} \times 365 = 34.77 \text{ days}$$

On a cost of sales basis:

$$\frac{\text{Trade creditors}}{\text{Cost of sales}} \times 365 = \frac{101.4}{772.3} \times 365 = 47.92 \text{ days}$$

On these creditor days it is highly unlikely that anyone will be demanding instant repayment.

12

PROFITABILITY

INTRODUCTION

Imagine that you have come into a lot of money . . . if you suddenly won two million pounds, what criteria would you use for your investments? You would be looking for something that gave you a good return with a minimum level of risk, after all you don't want to lose all your money and have to go back to work again! Whatever return you were offered you would automatically compare with the sort of returns you could get from a building society. For most of us, with very little money, this represents the risk-free rate (in as much as anything can be risk-free). If we had a lot of money the risk-free rate we could get would increase slightly, as we could now enter the money market.

Comparing risk and return is an everyday activity; we do it when we look for jobs (are you in the best-paid job available?) in just the same way as when we plan our investments. Most of us are risk averse: a small increase in risk means that we want to see a substantial increase in the return. Other people aren't, and embark on lifestyles (and investments) that we would find too risky even to contemplate.

In looking at a company's financial performance we need to find a way of looking at the profitability and comparing it to the risk-free rate. That way we can decide whether investing in the company is worthwhile. This is important when you remember that investing in a company isn't risk-free. The level of return that we would find acceptable is determined by two factors: our personal risk profile, and the risk inherent in the company. We would want to see a higher return from a car company than a grocer; we all have to eat every day, but we don't have to buy a car every year! The return on capital employed (sometimes called the return on assets) ratio enables you to have a basis for comparing the overall profitability of companies.

The return on capital is exactly what it says – a measure of the return being generated on the capital being used by the company. It defines the capital as the long-term capital tied up in the business. This is regardless of whether it is in the form of equity or debt. This allows you to compare companies with different capital structures, to identify who is generating the best return overall. If you were concerned purely with the return for the shareholders, you would calculate another ratio (the return on equity) which is discussed in detail in Chapter 14.

We will discover that companies can improve their return on capital in a number of different ways, and it is important to understand the determinants of return on capital. This allows us to identify whether any improvement is a 'one off', or whether it represents a sustainable growth in profits.

In this chapter we will look at the return on capital ratio in more detail and identify the factors that determine the return on capital.

THE RETURN ON CAPITAL EMPLOYED

The return on capital employed is simply:

$$\frac{\text{Profit before tax and interest on long-term loans}}{\text{Capital employed}}$$

We look at profit before tax and interest on long-term loans because we want to be able to compare a company's performance in two ways.

- **Over time**: we need to look at profit before tax as the tax rules change from one year to the next. If we are trying to look at a company's performance over time we need to ignore the factors outside its control.
- **With other companies in the same sector**: if we want to compare companies with different capital structures we have to recognise that the price that we pay to service debt, interest, comes out of before-tax profits. Dividends come out of after-tax profits. Using profit before interest on long-term loans allows us to ensure that we are comparing apples with apples!

The capital employed is the capital and reserves plus any long-term loans. However, working out what numbers to use for capital employed is not as simple as it sounds. There are two problems involved in determining the capital employed.

- Calculating the reserves.
- Provisions for liabilities and charges.

We shall look at each in turn.

Calculating the reserves

The reserves are affected by the company's policies on accounting for revaluation of assets and goodwill.

- A recent revaluation will affect the return on capital employed. A revaluation of asset values downwards would increase it (it would reduce the denominator in the equation) and revaluation upwards would reduce it (it would increase the denominator).
- An acquisition will also have an impact on the return on capital. If the

company has written the goodwill off through reserves, the return on capital will increase (it would reduce the denominator in the equation). If they show it as an intangible asset on the balance sheet, the return on capital will fall (this would increase the denominator).

Essentially we have the same problems in identifying the capital and reserves that we discussed in Chapter 11.

Provisions for liabilities and charges

We have seen that provisions for liabilities and charges fall into two categories.

- **Deferred tax**: deferred tax is an accounting adjustment to reflect the differences between the published accounts and the accounts prepared for tax purposes. It does not affect the company's cash flow. The deferred tax charge in the profit and loss account has the effect of equalising the tax charge over the life of the company's assets. Any balance on the deferred tax account is shown as part of the provisions for liabilities and charges. In Chapter 10 we discussed how the deferred tax charge could be used in short-term 'smoothing' of profits. If the company had not made a charge for deferred tax, the reported profits would be different.
- **Other provisions**: this will include all the provisions that don't relate to the reduction in value of a specific asset. We have discussed in Chapter 10 how companies may use these provisions to 'manage' their profits. Should these be included in capital employed? There are two types of other provisions shown here: provisions that have been charged to the profit and loss account, and provisions that have been charged to reserves. If the company has made the provision to manage its profits, the profits, and therefore the reserves, should be larger.

If they have already been charged to the profit and loss account logically they should be used as part of capital employed. No cash has left the business and therefore it will still be available for the company to spend in any way it likes. If other provisions are included in the capital employed, why not deferred tax? After all it's only an accounting adjustment. It is certainly easier to include the two, as the number can then be picked directly from the balance sheet. It depends largely on how technically accurate your analysis needs to be!

Calculating the return on capital employed

We will use the profit and loss account and the balance sheet shown below to calculate the return on capital, and all the subsequent ratios discussed in this chapter.

Profit and loss account

	£
Turnover	100,000
Cost of sales	(60,000)
Gross profit	40,000
Administration expenses	(20,000)
Distribution costs	(10,000)
Operating profit	10,000
Interest	(7,000)
Profit before tax	3,000
Tax	(1,000)
Profit after tax	2,000
Dividends	(1,000)
Retained profit	1,000

Balance Sheet

	£
Fixed assets	100,000
Current assets:	
Stock	10,000
Debtors	25,000
Cash	5,000
	40,000
Creditors: due in a year:	
Trade creditors	(15,000)
Other creditors	(5,000)
Bank overdraft	(10,000)
	(30,000)
Net current assets	10,000
Total assets less current liabilities	110,000
Creditors: due in more than a year:	
Loan @ 6%	(60,000)
Net assets	50,000
Capital and reserves:	
Share capital	20,000
Profit and loss account	30,000
	50,000

The return on capital employed is:

$$\frac{\text{Profit before tax and interest on long-term loans}}{\text{Capital employed}} = \frac{9,000}{110,000} \text{*} = 8.2\%$$

* The £9,000 is the £3,000 profit before tax plus the £6,000 interest on long-term loans

We now know how to calculate the return on capital, and can see that this company has a return on capital of 8.2 per cent, but what does it tell us? In isolation we don't know if this figure is good or bad. To discover this we would need to know:

- what was their return on capital in preceding years?
- what is the risk-free rate (for example building society or money market rates)?
- what returns on capital do other companies in the sector get?

All ratios need to be looked at in context, not in isolation.

Conceptually the return on capital is a simple ratio, it quantifies the return that the company is earning on the capital it uses. However, determining what should be included in the ratio is more problematic. The profit can be affected by a number of 'one off' transactions, and the capital employed is influenced by the company's accounting policies.

IMPROVING THE RETURN ON CAPITAL EMPLOYED

Improving the return on capital is a combination of improving profit margins and making the same amount of capital generate more sales:

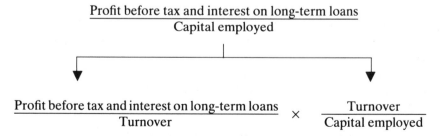

$$\frac{\text{Profit before tax and interest on long-term loans}}{\text{Capital employed}}$$

$$\frac{\text{Profit before tax and interest on long-term loans}}{\text{Turnover}} \times \frac{\text{Turnover}}{\text{Capital employed}}$$

For those of you who can remember junior school arithmetic, the return on capital is a straight multiplication of the two ratios above as the turnovers cancel one another out! Therefore the return on capital is the multiplication of the profit margin and a ratio known as the asset turn, or the asset turnover. The asset turn tells us how many pounds' worth of sales (or in this case pence) are generated for every pound of capital. It is a measure of how efficiently the company is utilising its capital. A fall in this ratio indicates the company is becoming less efficient, a rise indicates improved efficiency.

If we look at our example it would be calculated as follows:

$$\text{Profit margin:} \qquad\qquad \text{Asset turn:}$$

$$\frac{9,000}{100,000} = 9\% \qquad \frac{100,000}{110,000} = 0.91$$

$$\text{(or 91p sales per £ capital invested)}$$

And just to check that the arithmetic works: $9\% \times 0.91 = 0.082$, or 8.2%.

Therefore if the company wanted to improve the return on capital employed it has two options:

- improve its profit margins,

or

- use the assets more effectively to generate more sales per pound of capital.

Improving the profit margins

The profit margin we are considering, as the component of the return on capital formula, is the profit before tax and interest paid on long-term loans. This profit encompasses five possible elements:

- operating profit,
- profit on sale of assets,
- profit on sale of subsidiaries,
- interest received,
- Interest paid on short-term borrowings.

We should look at each of these to ascertain their effect on the return on capital. We particularly need to identify those factors which have a 'one off' impact on the ratio, so that we can exclude them from our analysis of the trends over a number of years. We will find that we often need to prepare a number of return on capital figures; our main analysis showing the trend, but with supplementary data showing the ratios calculated using the traditional definition.

(a) **Operating profit**. This is the most important component of the profit before interest and tax (PBIT) margin. It is from this profit that any sustainable improvement in the profitability side of the return on capital will be derived. Any analysis of profitability must include an operating profit margin. This is simply the operating profit expressed as a percentage of the turnover (in our example the operating profit margin is 10 per cent).

If a company wants to improve its profitability it must reduce costs or grow revenues. It can improve its operating profit margins by:

- increasing prices,
- increasing volumes,
- reducing costs,
- changing the sales and product mix. If they can increase the proportion of their sales coming from higher margin activities, they will improve profits.

We can do some analysis of the changes in the costs by looking at the company's profit and loss accounts over a number of years. But remember, we can only do this analysis within one company. We cannot compare different companies' control of costs. They will have slightly different definitions of cost of sales, administration expenses and distribution costs.

If we had the management accounts, the ones that the company prepares internally, we could identify the components of operating profit in detail. The published accounts do not contain the same quality of information to which managers have access.

(b) **Profit on sale of assets**. Profits and losses on sale of assets are shown after operating profit, and before tax. Consequently they are included in the PBIT margin used for calculating the return on capital. In essence they represent an underdepreciation, or overdepreciation of assets. For most companies, however, they would not be seen as providing an ongoing source of profits, or loss. Retailers might constitute an exception. They are always buying and selling shops to reposition themselves in the high street, and many are as much property developers as they are retailers.

(c) **Profit on sale of subsidiaries**. Profits, or losses, on disposal of subsidiaries should be seen as 'one offs'. They can give a considerable distortion to the return on capital calculation. If the company you are analysing has significant profits or losses from selling subsidiaries you would be advised to exclude them from the main analysis. You could show a second return on capital calculation, including profit, or loss, on sale of subsidiaries as a supplementary ratio.

(d) **Interest received**. Interest received may or may not be significant, and may or may not be a normal component of the company's profit. If it is insignificant, or is fairly constant, we can ignore it and calculate the return on capital in the normal way. But if it was unusually significant, it would seem sensible to do two return on capital figures, the main analysis incorporating the one which excludes interest received.

(e) **Interest paid on short-term borrowings**. If the company changes its pattern of borrowing, increasing the short-term borrowings at the expense of long-term, there will be an impact on the return on capital. It will be a matter of judgement to decide whether to exclude the impact of interest on short-term borrowings from the main analysis. In practice this is likely to be included, as it is difficult to separate the interest paid on long- and short-term loans from the information given in the accounts.

(f) **Profit from discontinued operations**. Following the implementation of FRS 3, companies will analyse their profit between continuing and discontinued operations. This gives us the opportunity to do a more detailed analysis than was previously possible. If the company has discontinued some of its operations we would want to calculate return on capital for the continuing operations, as well as for the total business. However the definition of discontinued operations may not be as helpful as it first appears. A discontinued operation is one that has been sold or terminated during the year or shortly after the year end. This is defined as the earlier of:

- three months after the date of the balance sheet,
- the approval date of the financial statements.

This means that the assets and liabilities of the discontinued operations may still be shown on the balance sheet, and included in capital employed.

Improving the asset turn

If we want to use the same amount of capital to generate more sales (or less capital to generate the same level of sales) we must look at what the company spends its capital on. A company uses the capital it raises to buy fixed assets and working capital. Improving the asset turn is a combination of doing two things: using the assets more effectively, and reducing the working capital requirements.

Sadly, this does not have the same arithmetic simplicity of our earlier example, especially when we consider the way that these derivative ratios are usually expressed. We would normally look at how many pounds' worth of sales are generated by every pound invested in fixed assets (the fixed asset turn). Working capital, on the other hand, is usually expressed as a percentage of sales, showing how many pence (usually, although sometimes it can be pounds) we would have to have tied up in the working capital to generate a pound's worth of sales. The ratios that influence the asset turn are:

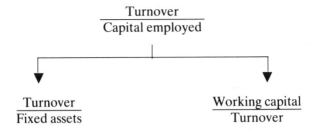

In our example they would be calculated as follows:

Fixed asset turn

$$\frac{100,000}{100,000} = 1.00$$

Working capital

$$\frac{20,000}{100,000} = 20\% \text{ or } 20\text{p/£1 sales}$$

Calculating the fixed asset turn was fairly straightforward in this example. However, the working capital ratio required more thought. The £20,000 for the working capital has been calculated as follows:

	stock	£10,000
plus	debtors	£25,000
less	trade creditors	£15,000
		£20,000

Only the trade creditors are included, as they are the only creditors that relate to sales. Bank overdrafts don't and other creditors relate to fixed assets. The same logic would apply to debtors, if there were different categories of debtors only the trade debtors would be used in the calculation.

If we had been looking at published accounts, where the fixed assets would have included investments, we would have had a similar problem. Do investments generate turnover? They generate income; either as income from associated undertakings, or dividend income. Sales from investments are not included in the turnover figure in the profit and loss account. So should investments be included in the fixed asset turn calculation? Logic says not. Should intangibles be included? If they are brand names and patents then they will generate current sales, but will goodwill or development costs? Logically we should only include those assets that make a contribution to turnover.

Improving the fixed asset turn

The fixed assets can be broken down into their component parts:

● tangible assets:
  – land and buildings,

- plant and machinery,
- motor vehicles,
- intangible assets.

If you felt that it was appropriate you could calculate ratios for these:

$$\frac{\text{Turnover}}{\text{Land and buildings}} \quad = \text{Land and buildings turn}$$

$$\frac{\text{Turnover}}{\text{Plant and machinery}} \quad = \text{Plant and machinery turn}$$

$$\frac{\text{Turnover}}{\text{Motor vehicles}} \quad = \text{Motor vehicles turn}$$

$$\frac{\text{Turnover}}{\text{Intangible assets}} \quad = \text{Intangible asset turn}$$

Clearly it would be ridiculous to do all of these: you would end up with lots of facts and no information. You need to identify the type of asset that is helping to generate the sales. So if you were analysing Tesco it may be appropriate to do the land and buildings turn, GKN the plant and machinery turn, P & O the vehicles turn and Grand Metropolitan the intangible asset turn.

Improving the working capital ratio

The working capital ratio is so important as it is a good indicator of management efficiency. An efficient management team would be trying to reduce stocks and debtors whilst managing creditors ethically. We have identified the cash that needs to be tied up to generate a pound's worth of sales. We can analyse the working capital in more detail to see how the company is managing the individual components of working capital: stocks, debtors and creditors.

(a) **Stocks**. There are two ways of looking at stocks. Either you can see how many times a year the company turns its stock over, or you can work out how many days stock the company is carrying. You should use whichever measure you find easiest to understand and are most familiar with.

(i) *Stockturn*. Companies calculate this differently in their internal accounts than we calculate it using published accounts. Stocks relate to the merchandise sold in the period for a retailer and to the materials, labour and overheads used in sales for a manufacturer. We don't have these figures available to us in the published profit and loss account. We could use cost of sales if we were only analysing one company, but not if we were comparing companies as it means different things to different companies. Most people use sales as the denominator (for the reasons we discussed in Chapter 11). Even though it is wrong it is consistently wrong, and allows us to make comparisons between companies! It would only be a problem if we were comparing companies with very different profit margins. If we look at the stockturn calculation using both sales and cost of sales as the denominator:

Sales-based	*Cost of sales-based*
$\dfrac{\text{Turnover}}{\text{Stock}}$	$\dfrac{\text{Cost of sales}}{\text{Stock}}$

In our example it would be:

$$\frac{100{,}000}{10{,}000} = 10 \text{ times} \qquad \frac{60{,}000}{10{,}000} = 6 \text{ times}$$

(ii) *Stock days*. This is the alternative way of looking at stock and is calculated in a similar way to the way we calculated creditor days in Chapter 11.

Sales-based		*Cost of sales-based*	
$\dfrac{\text{Stock}}{\text{Turnover}}$	$\times\, 365$	$\dfrac{\text{Stock}}{\text{Cost of sales}}$	$\times\, 365$

In our example it would be:

$$\frac{10{,}000}{100{,}000} \times 365 = 36.5 \text{ days} \qquad \frac{10{,}000}{60{,}000} \times 365 = 60.8 \text{ days}$$

(Remember that we are multiplying by 365 as we are looking at the sales for the year and the stock on a given day.)

You can see how using sales, rather than cost of sales, as the denominator has the effect of understating stocks. As this number is not calculated in a way that ensures its accuracy it is important that it is looked at contextually. Is the control of stocks improving, does this company have lower stocks than other companies in the sector?

(b) **Debtors**. Calculating debtor days is very simple:

$$\frac{\text{Trade debtors}}{\text{Turnover}} \times 365$$

In our example we would have debtor days of:

$$\frac{25,000}{100,000} \times 365 = 91.3 \text{ days}$$

The company is giving just over 91 days credit.

(c) **Creditors**.

Sales-based   *Cost of sales-based*

$$\frac{\text{Trade creditors}}{\text{Turnover}} \times 365 \qquad \frac{\text{Trade creditors}}{\text{Cost of sales}} \times 365$$

In our example:

$$\frac{15,000}{100,000} \times 365 \qquad \frac{15,000}{60,000} \times 365$$

$$= 54.8 \text{ days} \qquad = 91.3 \text{ days}$$

THE HIERARCHY OF RATIOS

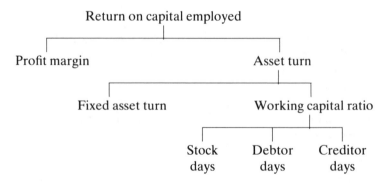

We have evolved a hierarchy of ratios, identifying the main determinants of the return on capital. This return on capital hierarchy helps us identify the profitability of the company and how effectively it is utilising its trading assets. The one area of the balance sheet that is not covered by the subsidiary ratios we have discussed in this chapter, is the return on the company's investments. Associated companies will be separately disclosed in the profit and loss account. Here we will see the percentage of the associates' profit, or loss, that is attributable to the company. In Chapter 2 we saw that this can be very different from the cash received as dividends. However the return from smaller investments, where the company does not have a participating interest, will be harder to quantify. These investments could be shown on the balance sheet as both fixed and current asset investments. The income will be included with the interest and dividends received. In a seasonal business where there will be peaks of cash and short-term deposits it will be very difficult to ascertain the return on investments. We will not be able to calculate the average cash balances, and therefore we will be unable to calculate a return on those investments.

The return on the trading assets, shown in the hierarchy of ratios, has to be a major concern for analysts. These trading assets will be generating the greater part of the profits. We can see that small changes in the subsidiary ratios will have a disproportionate effect on the return on capital. We need to identify the changes in these ratios if we want to understand the underlying performance of the company. Some change could generate 'one off' improvements, whereas others will give ongoing benefits. Companies have managed to improve their return on capital from the stock reduction benefits associated with the introduction of EDI (electronic data interchange). This movement to a 'just in time' stockholding policy only happens once. Subsequent improvements will have to come from other sources. We need to understand that companies improve the return on capital by improving the subsidiary ratios. They focus on improving profit margins, utilising their fixed assets more effectively and minimising their working capital.

We should also understand that if the company improves its return on capital by reducing the working capital, there will be solvency implications. If the company reduces stocks and debtors whilst increasing creditors the solvency ratios will be adversely affected. We would expect the current ratio and the acid test to fall.

PROFITABILITY IN IMI

We will analyse the profitability in IMI during 1993 following the hierarchy of ratios illustrated earlier in this chapter. This analysis will show you where to find the data that is used in the ratios.

The return on capital employed

We start by looking at the return on capital. You will notice in their profit and loss account that IMI have two exceptional items in their 1993 accounts:

- the loss on sale of Brook Street Computers,
- the reclassification of International Radiator Services Ltd as an associated undertaking.

If we want to look at trends in the financial performance of IMI we will have to take the profit before tax and exceptional items – £71.7 million. We now have to add back the interest payable on long-term loans, as these will relate to the long-term loans included in the capital employed.

The note on interest discloses:

Net interest payable

	1993 £m	1992 £m
Bank loans and overdrafts	15.0	18.3
Interest on finance leases	0.4	0.5
Other loans		
Wholly repayable within five years	1.0	1.2
Not wholly repayable within five years	0.1	0.1
	16.5	20.1
Interest receivable	(6.3)	(11.7)
	10.2	8.4

IMI has £89.5 million loans falling due for repayment after a year, the interest on these loans has to be included in the bank loans and overdrafts figure. Whilst it is technically correct to add back the interest only on long-term loans, it is practically impossible to determine what the figure should be! Consequently we have identified that we will have to add back the total £16.5 million interest paid. Therefore the profit that we will use for the return on capital calculation is £88.2 million (71.7 + 16.5).

Having identified the numerator for the return on capital calculation, the next step is to identify the denominator. In the last chapter we have discussed the fact that the revaluation reserve in IMI relates largely to the investment properties. it is so small that it may be immaterial for our analysis of the return on capital. However, we will do the calculations on both bases so that we can see the effect on the ratios. Goodwill, on the other hand has to be added back as it too large to be regarded as immaterial. The goodwill in 1993 was £226.5 million, the £114.7 million disclosed in the accounts plus the £111.8 million previously written off through reserves. Therefore the capital employed will be £742.1 million (515.6 + 226.5) including the revaluation reserve and £734.2 million (515.6 + 226.5 − 7.9) excluding the revaluation reserve.

The returns on capital employed will be as follows:

Including revaluation:

$$\frac{\text{Profit before interest payable and taxation}}{\text{Capital employed including revaluation}} = \frac{88.2}{742.1} = 11.89\%$$

Excluding revaluation:

$$\frac{\text{Profit before interest payable and taxation}}{\text{Capital employed excluding revaluation}} = \frac{88.2}{734.2} = 12.01\%$$

There are two components to the return on capital, the asset turn and the profit before interest and tax margin.

Calculating the asset turn

This shows us how many pounds of sales IMI is managing to generate for every pound of capital invested in the business.

The asset turn, based on capital employed including goodwill and excluding revaluation, is calculated as follows:

$$\frac{\text{Turnover}}{\text{Capital employed}} = \frac{1,064.6}{734.2} = 1.45 \text{ times}$$

Calculating the profit before interest and tax margin

This is the other element of the return on capital and identifies the profitability of the sales.

It is calculated as follows:

$$\frac{\text{Profit before interest payable and taxation}}{\text{Turnover}} = \frac{88.2}{1,064.6} = 8.28\%$$

The most important element of the PBIT margin is the operating margin and that is:

$$\frac{\text{Operating profit}}{\text{Turnover}} = \frac{79.7}{1,064.6} = 7.49\%$$

We must now look at the components of the asset turn – the tangible fixed asset turn and the working capital ratios.

The tangible asset turn

When calculating the tangible fixed asset turn we must decide whether to exclude the revaluation reserve. If we were only looking at one year's performance revaluation wouldn't matter. However, if we want to look at a company's financial performance over time we would need to exclude the revaluation reserve, otherwise revaluations would distort the trends.

Consequently the tangible asset figure that we would use is £269.7 million (277.6 – 7.9).

$$\frac{\text{Turnover}}{\text{Fixed assets}} = \frac{1{,}064.6}{269.7} = 3.95 \text{ times}$$

Every pound invested in tangible assets generates £3.95 in sales.

The working capital ratio

To calculate the working capital ratio we need to identify the stocks, trade debtors and trade creditors. The stocks of £253.2 million are disclosed on the face of the balance sheet. To find the trade debtors and creditors we need to look at the notes to the accounts.

The note on the debtors for the group discloses:

Debtors

	1993 £m	1992 £m
Falling due for payment within one year:		
Trade debtors	160.1	166.6
Amounts owed by group companies	–	–
Prepayments and accrued income	8.1	9.6
Other debtors	14.1	17.1
	182.3	193.3
Falling due for payment after more than one year:		
Trade debtors	0.4	0.4
Amounts owed by group companies	–	–
Other debtors	4.3	7.0
	4.7	7.4
	187.0	200.7

We can see that trade debtors fall into two categories, those falling due within a year and those due in more than a year. Whilst the 0.4 million due in more than a year will have been included in turnover they would normally be excluded from the working capital and debtor days calculation as they are subject to different contractual arrangements. Therefore the debtors used for the working capital would be £160.1 million.

The trade creditors of £101.4 million can be extracted from a similar note, shown in the last chapter.

The working capital used in the ratio will be the total of the stocks and trade debtors less the trade creditors – £311.9 million (253.2 + 160.1 – 101.4). This gives a working capital ratio of:

$$\frac{\text{Working capital}}{\text{Turnover}} \quad = \quad \frac{311.9}{1,064.6} \quad = 0.29$$

IMI needs to find 29 pence in cash to fund every pound's worth of sales that it makes. Consequently any upturn in its sales would increase the working capital requirement proportionately, unless it could reduce stock days, debtor days and increase creditor days.

We now need to look at these to see if there is any scope for improvement.

Control of stocks

There are two ways that we can assess the company's control of stocks, stock turn and stock days. We will calculate both from IMI's accounts.

When looking at stock we have to decide the basis for our analysis. Stock relates to the direct costs used in the period, which are not necessarily disclosed separately on the profit and loss accounts. We have to decide whether to use cost of sales or turnover. Cost of sales more closely reflects the direct costs, but the definition varies from one company to another. Turnover includes profits as well as costs. The choice is largely a personal one, we are unlikely to get an accurate figure anyway as the company will have 'managed' a year end position. Turnover is probably a more useful basis for comparing companies, if they have similar profit margins. We will show both bases for the calculations.

(a) **Stock turn**. This shows us how many times in a year the company converts its stock into sales. The higher the number the better.

Turnover-based:

$$\frac{\text{Turnover}}{\text{Stock}} \quad = \quad \frac{1,064.6}{253.2} \quad = 4.20 \text{ times}$$

Cost of sales-based:

$$\frac{\text{Cost of sales}}{\text{Stock}} \quad = \quad \frac{772.3}{253.2} \quad = 3.05 \text{ times}$$

(b) **Stock days**. This shows us how many days stock the business is carrying. The lower the number the better.

Turnover-based:

$$\frac{\text{Stock}}{\text{Turnover}} \times 365 = \frac{253.2}{1,064.6} \times 365 = 86.81 \text{ days}$$

Cost-of-sales-based:

$$\frac{\text{Stock}}{\text{Cost of sales}} \times 365 = \frac{253.2}{772.3} \times 365 = 119.67 \text{ days}$$

Control of debtors

To identify the company's collection period we look at the debtor days, using the trade debtors' number from the accounts:

$$\frac{\text{Trade debtors}}{\text{Turnover}} \times 365 = \frac{160.1}{1,064.6} \times 365 = 54.89 \text{ days}$$

Control of creditors

To identify the company's payment period we use the trade creditors and look at them in relation to either the turnover or cost of sales.

Turnover-based:

$$\frac{\text{Trade creditors}}{\text{Turnover}} \times 365 = \frac{101.4}{1,064.6} \times 365 = 34.77 \text{ days}$$

Cost of sales-based:

$$\frac{\text{Trade creditors}}{\text{Cost of sales}} \times 365 = \frac{101.4}{772.3} \times 365 = 47.92 \text{ days}$$

13

CASH MANAGEMENT

INTRODUCTION

Cash management is closely interlinked with solvency. A company that manages its cash resources effectively is unlikely to have solvency problems. They should have no difficulty in paying their bills when they are due. Consequently, the way that a company manages its cash is crucial to its long-term survival. It must fund the business in the best way and optimise its cash resources. If we want to understand the company's financial performance, its opportunities and its threats, we must be able to analyse the way that it is managing cash.

To do this we need to look at:

- the operating and financial review,
- the cash flow statement,
- the working capital ratios,
- the loan profile.

THE OPERATING AND FINANCIAL REVIEW

The Accounting Standards board published a document in July 1993 called the *Operating And Financial Review*. This is a 'statement of voluntary best practice' and is intended to cover public companies and any other large company 'where there is a legitimate public interest in their financial statements'. The operating review identifies the main factors that underlie the business, the way that these have varied in the past, and are expected to vary in the future. It gives a full discussion on the operating results and the businesses' dynamics, including the main risks and uncertainties facing the business. The company has to strike a balance beteen the need for disclosure and confidentiality.

The financial review is of particular interest to us, as it should explain:

- the capital structure of the business:
  - maturity profile of debt,
  - types of capital instruments used,
  - currencies,
  - interest rate structure.

- the treasury policy:
  - the control of treasury activities,
  - the currencies in which borrowings are made and cash and deposits are held,
  - the extent of fixed rate borrowings,
  - the use of financial instruments for hedging,
  - the extent to which foreign currency net investments are hedged by currency borrowings, and other hedging instruments.
- the components of the tax charge, if the overall tax charge is 'significantly different from a standard tax charge',
- cash flows from operating activities:
  - a discussion of the cash flows, and any special factors that influenced those flows,
  - segmental cash flows if these are significantly out of line with segmental profits.
- the current liquidity:
  - the level of borrowings at the year end,
  - the seasonality of the borrowings,
  - the peak level of the borrowings,
  - the maturity profile of both the borrowings and the committed borrowing facilities,
  - funding requirements for authorised capital expenditure,
  - restrictions on the company's ability to transfer funds within the group, and any attendant restraints on the group,
  - negotiations with bankers on covenants that restrict the credit facilities,
  - the measures taken, or proposed, to remedy any breach, or probable breach, of banking covenants.
- whether the company is, in the opinion of the directors, a going concern.
- company resources, and strengths, not reflected in the balance sheet.

THE CASH FLOW STATEMENT

Once we have an overview of the cash management of the company we can start to analyse the cash flow during the year in more detail. The cash flow statement shows the cash inflows and outflows during the year. It is discussed in detail in Chapter 4. The cash flows are categorised in a way that makes the movement of cash in a business during the year easy to understand.

We will use the example given below to illustrate the analysis of the cash flow statement.

Cash flow statement

	£
Operating activities	
Cash received from customers	95,000
Cash paid to suppliers	(35,000)
Cash paid to, and on behalf of, employees	(24,000)
Other cash paid	(29,000)
Net cash inflow from operating activities	7,000

Returns on investment and servicing of finance:

Interest received	1,000
Interest paid	(8,000)
Dividends paid	(1,000)

Net cash outflow from returns on investment and servicing of finance (8,000)

Taxation:

Tax paid	(1,500)
Net cash outflow from taxation	*(1,500)*

Investing activities:

Purchase of fixed assets	(15,000)
Disposal of fixed assets	3,000
Net cash outflow from investing activities	*(12,000)*
Net cash outflow before financing	*(14,500)*

Financing:

Issue of ordinary share capital	5,000
Loan	5,000
Net cash inflow from financing	*10,000*
Decrease in cash and cash equivalents	*4,500*

Notes to the cash flow statement

1 Reconciliation of operating profit to net cash inflow from operating activities

Operating profit	10,000
Depreciation	1,000
Increase in stock	(2,000)
Increase in debtors	(5,000)
Increase in creditors	3,000
Net cash inflow from operating activities	7,000

2 Decrease in cash and cash equivalents

Increase in bank overdrafts	4,000
Decrease in cash	500
	4,500

If we are analysing the cash flow we need to look at a number of things.

- How vulnerable is the company's operational cash flow to a fall in cash receipts?
- What is the cash flow interest cover?
- What proportion of the investment in fixed assets is being generated from internal sources?
- Is the company matching long-term sources of funds to long-term applications?

(a) **The operational cash flow**. In this example we have the cash flow from operating activities presented using the direct method. This enables us to see both the receipts and payments in the company and a reconciliation to operating profit. We would not get the same amount of information, and be able to do the same degree of analysis, from a cash flow statement where the operating cash flow is presented using the indirect method. Here we have two pieces of information about the cash flow from operating activities: the net cash inflow from the statement itself and the reconciliation of the operating profit to the net cash inflow, found in the notes.

Firstly we will look at the note reconciling the operational cash flow to the operating profit. The current year's trading will generate £11,000 (the profit plus the depreciation charge). The company has only managed to generate £7,000 because of the net £4,000 that has had to be tied up in the working capital. The increase in stock (£2,000) has been more than covered by the increase in creditors (£3,000), suggesting that the company may be taking longer to pay its suppliers or has reduced stock levels. The big movement in the working capital has come from debtors, which increased by £5,000. We would need to do the debtor days' calculation to see if this meant that customers were taking longer to pay the company.

Now, moving on to look at the cash flow from operating activities. This shows us the movement in cash, during the year, on a receipts and payments basis. The company's cash receipts were £95,000. The company appears to be vulnerable to a fall in receipts. It would take only a fall in receipts of 7.4 per cent (7,000/95,000) for the company to lose the operational cash flow. Whether this is likely to happen would depend on the trend in debtor days.

(b) **Interest cover**. In this example the company is just covering its interest paid with the operational cash flow and the interest received. We can see that the company is close to having difficulties with the bank, but from one year's cash flows are unable to establish a trend.

(c) **Cash flow before investing activities**. The company has a cash outflow of £2,500 before investing activities, therefore there is no contribution towards the purchase of fixed assets from funds generated internally during the year. The net £12,000 spent on fixed assets has had to be funded from existing cash balances and external sources.

(d) **Matching funds to applications**. It is important that a company matches the funds with the applications. Buying fixed assets on overdrafts is risky. The bank can demand repayment at any time, whereas the payback from fixed assets is long-term. If the company is trying to fund seasonal trading then an overdraft would be a suitable source of funds. The general rule is that investment in long-term assets should be funded with long-term sources of funds. The company spent £12,000 net on the purchase of fixed assets, and raised £5,000 from a share issue and £5,000 from loans. The balance of £2,000 was partly funded by using £500 existing cash, the remainder coming from bank overdrafts. A £1,500 'mismatch' on its own doesn't appear serious, but may be indicative of poor cash management.

THE WORKING CAPITAL RATIOS

To calculate these we need information from the profit and loss account and the balance sheet. Calculating these is useful as we have identified that this company has had to have an additional £4,000 invested in the working capital, and that this has contributed to its cash flow problems. We don't know why. Have they become less efficient, or is it arising from an increase in sales? If sales double, we would expect the working capital requirements to double. If the working capital triples, the company is less efficient. The working capital ratios help us identify why the actual cash generated from operations was less than it could have been. Was the company coping admirably with an expansion programme, or had they let the control of working capital slip?

The calculation of working capital ratios is illustrated in Chapter 12.

THE LOAN PROFILE

Looking at the types of borrowing that the company has can tell us a lot about the way the company manages its cash. We are interested in a number of things.

- The types of loans.
- The loan repayment schedule.
- Financial innovation.

Public companies will have disclosed some information in the financial review; the rest can be found by careful reading of the notes.

(a) **The types of loans**. Loans may be secured, or unsecured. Whilst it is common for small private companies to have secured borrowings, it is unusual for large public companies to have their loans secured. When you look at some multinational companies' accounts you may find a small proportion of their borrowings is secured. This tends to relate to their overseas subsidiaries, as in some countries there is a legal requirement for all loans to be secured. Consequently, if you are looking at a large company's accounts and find that previously all loans were unsecured, but are now secured, you have an indication of their bank's level of confidence (or rather lack of) in the company.

It is worth remembering that not all loans have to be repaid. There are an increasing number of convertible loans, usually in the form of bonds. Here the lender has the option, on maturity, either to have the repayment of the loan, or to convert into shares at a price that was fixed when the bond was issued. If the option price is below the current market price of the share, it is unlikely that bondholders will exercise the cash option. Therefore if the company has convertible bonds we need to look at the market price versus the option price to determine the likelihood of repayment in cash.

(b) **The loan repayment schedule**. We have talked in Chapter 11 about the importance of looking at the loan repayment schedule.

By looking at the cash flow statement we can get an idea of whether the loans can be repaid by cash generated within the business. How much cash is being generated before financing? Will the accumulation of this cash flow, taking into account any trends, enable the company to repay the loans? If not they will have only two alternatives that will preserve the existing business:

- a share issue;
- repay existing loans with new loans.

When we have looked at solvency and the investor's view we will have some idea if either are possible.

(c) **Financial innovation**. We talked a little about financial innovation in our chapter on the balance sheet, when we discussed short-term borrowing instruments and bond innovations. A brief look at large company accounts shows there are innovative approaches to managing exchange rates and interest rates. Treasurers in large companies regularly use forward markets, swaps and options to hedge against risk. Whilst these are used to try to avoid risk, they can become risks in themselves.

Large, and public, companies are those likely to be most actively involved in financial innovation. They may have given some information in the financial review that may disclose some of their activities in the following areas.

(i) *The forward markets*. Using the forward markets helps the company to limit its exchange rate exposure. If a company needed to pay for a machine in Deutschmarks in three months' time, it could wait for three months and then take the rate of exchange on the day (the spot rate). Alternatively it could buy the currency 'forward'.

The forward rates are determined by interest rate differentials. Having contracted to buy the currency forward, the treasurer has locked himself into an exchange rate. Whatever happens to exchange rates, he knows the rate that he will get. Sometimes he will do better than the spot rate, sometimes worse. By using the forward market he has 'locked in' an exchange rate, and knows what the machine will cost in sterling. The forward market gives him certainty.

(ii) *Options*. An option is just what it says, if the company buys an option it has the opportunity to buy something at an agreed price. Options can be bought and sold on shares, bonds, currencies, interest rates and futures contracts (a futures contract is a contract to buy or sell something at some agreed date in the future). Let's continue our example of the purchase of the machine. Buying an option to buy the Deutschmarks, rather than a forward contract, gives the company treasurer flexibility. If the option rate is preferable to the spot rate he will take it, if not he can take the spot rate. Unlike the forward contract, he is not committed to buy the marks at the option price.

Options are fine as long as you buy them. They will cost you money, but you will take that into account in deciding whether to exercise the option. The difficulties start when you sell options. In 1991 Allied Lyons lost £147 million, 18.3 per cent of their trading profit, by writing options.

(iii) *Swaps*. Both currency and interest rates can be 'swapped'. Again, this means what it says. For example, a UK company would find it easier to raise money in the UK, where it is known. The company may need dollars to fund an acquisition in the States. It may find it easier, and cheaper, to raise the money in the UK and then swap with an American company that has the opposite problem. Both companies get the currency they want, at the cheapest cost. The arranging bank, as middleman, will have made a profit and everyone will be happy!

Interest rate swaps exploit the credit quality standards between the fixed rate bond market and the floating rate, short-term credit market. These markets have different interest rates for different quality borrowers. To illustrate this, a company rated BBB might be able to borrow short-term at LIBOR + ¾ per cent. A company rated AAA might borrow at LIBOR + ¼ per cent. In the bond market, the interest rate differential widens considerably, the size of the difference is determined by market conditions prevailing at the time but it can be between 1 per cent and 2 per cent. If we assume that the AAA-rated company could issue a ten-year bond at 10 per cent, whereas the BBB rated company would have to pay 11¼ per cent. With a bank as an intermediary they enter into a swap arrangement. The BBB rated company raises short-term variable rate money and the AAA fixed rate money. They swap their interest:

Issues bond   Borrows at
at 10%   LIBOR + ¾%

    10%   Libor + ¾%

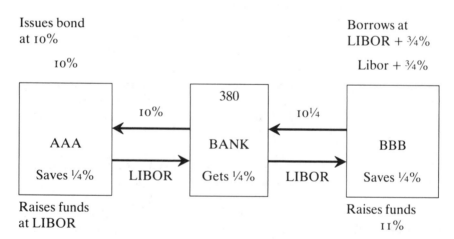

Raises funds   Raises funds
at LIBOR   11%

The AAA-rated company issues a bond at 10 per cent, and the BBB-rated company borrows at LIBOR + ¾ per cent. The AAA-rated company gives the intermediary bank LIBOR, the bank then passes this to the BBB-rated company. The BBB-rated company then pays LIBOR + ¾ per cent on its loan. It gives the bank 10¼ per cent, the bank keeps ¼ per cent, and passes the 10 per cent to the AAA-rated company. The AAA-rated company can then pay its bondholders.

The AAA-rated company has switched out of fixed rates into variable rates and effectively borrowed at LIBOR (a quarter of a per cent cheaper than it can normally get). The BBB-rated company has switched from variable rates to fixed rates, and got a cheaper fixed rate than it can get from the market. The bank has made a profit.

Although everybody seems to win there are two risks in an interest rate swap:

- counterparty failure,
- adverse interest rate movements.

Whilst it is possible to 'unwind', or cancel, a swap this is usually expensive. A number of companies discovered this when Britain left ERM and interest rates fell. They had locked themselves into high fixed rates of interest, and had to pay to get themselves out of the swap.

Interest rate swaps are useful tools for company treasurers as they:

- allow companies to obtain fixed-rate money, when it is impossible to directly access the bond markets,
- reduce the cost of borrowing,
- allow companies to respond to changing economic conditions – moving from fixed to floating rates without changing the underlying debt instrument.

CASH MANAGEMENT IN IMI

In looking at the cash management in IMI we will be looking at the data found in:

- the cash flow statement,
- the financial review,
- the notes to the accounts.

Following the practice of the earlier chapters in this section of the book, we will be looking at where to find the data and how to calculate the ratios. A detailed analysis of IMI's cash management will be given in Chapter 15 when we analyse the financial performance of IMI over the last five years.

The cash flow statement

(a) **The operational cash flow**. When we look at the group cash flow statement we can see that we need to look at the notes to see how they have derived the cash flow from operating activities. Note 26 shows that they are using the indirect method to arrive at the operating cash flow:

Reconciliation of operating profit to net cash flow from operating activities

	1993 £m	1992 £m
Operating profit	79.7	75.6
Depreciation	39.6	38.4
Stocks decrease	4.7	13.2
Debtors (increase)/decrease	(1.9)	0.9
Creditors and provisions (decrease)/increase	(2.7)	4.6
	119.4	132.7

If we add the depreciation charge to the operating profit we can calculate the cash that will be generated from the 1993 sales. We can see that the cash that will be generated from sales has shown a modest increase in 1993, from £114 million in 1992 to £119.3 million in 1993. The big reduction in the operating cash flow has come from the working capital. In 1992 the cash tied up in working capital reduced by £18.7 million, compared to £100,000 in 1993. As turnover increased by almost 6 per cent we would have expected a slight growth in the working capital. Although the cash savings appear small the company is undoubtedly becoming more efficient. This is reflected in the working capital ratios:

	1993		*1992*	
	Turnover	*Cost of sales*	*Turnover*	*Cost of sales*
Stock days	*86.81 days*	*119.67 days*	*95.42 days*	*129.96 days*
Debtor days	*54.89 days*		*60.47 days*	
Creditor days	*34.77 days*	*47.92 days*	*34.45 days*	*46.91 days*

The company has become more efficient in managing its working capital even though the increased cash benefit does not appear large. Had the working capital remained at the 1992 figures IMI would have had to find nearly £42 million!

(b) **Returns on investment and servicing of finance**. The operating cash flow is then used to service the interest and dividends. The cash interest cover was calculated in Chapter 11 at 7.24 times. In 1992 it was 6.6 times. We can see that this improvement came from the fall in interest paid from £20.1 million to £16.5 million. A significant part of this fall would come from the fall in interest rates following Britain's exit from ERM. This view is supported by the fact that interest received also fell during 1993.

Dividends remained constant during the period, and the net cash outflow from returns on investment and servicing of finance increased slightly.

(c) **Taxation**. The cash flow before taxation was £77.6 million (£92.7 million in 1992). The tax paid rose by £3.9 million reducing the net cash flow before investing.

(d) **Net cash flow before investing and finance**. IMI shows this on their cash flow statement, and it is a useful line as one of the things we look at is how much of the capital expenditure programme is funded internally. If this is not disclosed on the statement we would have to calculate it.

We can see that IMI is almost self-funding. All of the fixed asset purchases are covered by the current year's cash flow and only a small proportion of the acquisitions have to be funded from other sources. In both years the cash flow covered over 99 per cent of the net cash outflow from investing activities. Even if they hadn't sold off any assets they would have been able to finance 96 per cent of their purchases and acquisitions.

(e) **Financing and cash and cash equivalents**. There have been small increases in the share capital of IMI as employees' share options matured. The majority of the funds from financing have come from loans, which are reflected in increases in cash and cash equivalents. We can see in the reconciliation of the net borrowings, found at the bottom of the cash flow statement that only £48.8 million of the £101.3 million cash and deposits shown on the balance sheet are cash and cash equivalents. The balance was placed on deposit for longer than three months. All that is happening is that the balance of the maturities within the deposits are changing. The cash and deposits shown on the balance sheet has actually fallen by £58.1 million.

The financial review

A number of interesting things emerge from reading the financial review.

- Brook Street Computers. This was sold for £2.5 million less than IMI paid for it. The company have owned Brook Street Computers since 1990, and it would be interesting to see if they had made a profit on their investment.
- The ratios quoted in the accounts are calculated in a slightly different way to the way that we have calculated them in earlier chapters. Gearing has been calculated excluding goodwill and current asset investments. Interest cover has been calculated using the net debt figure, rather than the interest payable.
- The company has conservative treasury policies, using forward contracts, rather than options, to manage exposure to exchange rates. Overseas investments are matched by matching currency borrowings.

IMI plc
Financial Review

Profit and Loss Account
Turnover increased by 6 per cent from £1006m to £1065m, and profit before exceptional items amounted to £71.7m, which was 5 per cent higher than last year. The trading results from our core industrial activities showed a marked improvement but this was partially offset by losses in the peripheral computer businesses. The results are analysed in detail on page 37.

Brook Street Computers was sold in February 1994, and the loss on disposal of £5.9m, which includes £2.5m goodwill previously deducted from reserves, has been charged as an exceptional item in the 1993 accounts. There is also an exceptional credit of £4.4m from our 30 per cent interest in International Radiator Services Limited which has been accounted for under the equity method from the beginning of 1993.

The interest charge of £10.2m was covered 8 times (1992: 9 times) by profit before interest.

The taxation charge increased from 35 per cent to 36 per cent, partly influenced by the increase in the US federal rate from the beginning of 1993. Although the Group derives significant earnings from overseas it does not have a surplus ACT problem.

Cash Flow
The Group continues to generate strong cash flow from operating activities, which in 1993 amounted to £119m including another pleasing reduction of £5m in stocks. A high level of capital expenditure has been maintained, which amounted to £48m for the year.

During the year we acquired four small businesses, Knorr Bremse, Germany (Fluid Power), CIG Beverage Systems, Australia (Drinks Dispense), Accles & Shelvoke, UK, and Casino Tokens Inc., USA (Special Engineering). The total cost of these acquisitions was £7m which was financed from internally generated cash flow.

Net borrowings at the end of 1993 were slightly lower than last year and gearing was 25 per cent. We continue therefore to be in a strong position to pursue further suitable acquisition opportunities.

Funding and Treasury Management
Net borrowings of £97m at the end of 1993 comprised total borrowings of £198m (including £90m repayable after more than one year) offset by cash and bank deposits of £101m. A detailed analysis of borrowings is given in the notes on the accounts numbered 17 and 19. £10m 7¼ per cent loan stock 1988/93 was repaid at the end of the year and has been replaced by bank loans. The Group maintains banking facilities at a level which is more than adequate to meet foreseeable requirements.

The provision of financial resources and the control of foreign exchange exposures is managed centrally by a small head office team in accordance with overall policies established by the Board. Trading exposures in foreign currencies are largely covered by the use of forward contracts. Where appropriate, the Group hedges net assets denominated in overseas currencies by borrowing in matching currencies.

Financial Controls
Monitoring of financial performance is established centrally. Financial executives report regularly to both their own operational head and to the central financial control function. Subsidiary companies are required to follow strict guidelines and formal procedures relating to financial controls, and their compliance is monitored through regular reviews.

14

THE INVESTOR'S PERSPECTIVE

INTRODUCTION

Despite the determined attempts of some politicians we still do not invest in shares because we have a fundamental belief in wider share ownership – we invest in shares because we want to get richer! No one would invest in a company if they did not believe that they were going to make a return, and preferably one that is better than they could get from a bank, or a building society. There are two ways we make money from shares: a capital gain on the value of the shares, and dividends. These are reflected in many of the ratios that are prepared to express the company's performance from the investors point of view.

Investors are interested in:

- the return on their investment. This can be expressed in two different ways:
  - the overall return, the return on equity,
  - the annual return, dividends.
  - the stock market's view of the future return on their investment:
  - the PE ratio.

Before we look at these ratios, we need to understand two other ratios that are published in company accounts – earnings per share and dividends per share. It is important that we do understand these, as they are used in the calculation of some of the other investment ratios.

In this chapter we will look at the company from the investor's perspective and consider the investment ratios.

EARNINGS PER SHARE

Earnings per share is important to all investors. To the institutional investor earnings per share growth is a key determinant of the investment decision. Companies know this and try to show a nice steady growth in earnings to attract the institutional shareholder. It is this concern that prompts companies to make bad years really bad! (This allows the management to 'turn the business around' in the following year!)

In simple terms earnings per share is the profit attributable to ordinary shareholders, divided by the number of shares in issue. So if our profit was £2,000 and there were 20,000 shares in issue, the earnings per share would be 10p. If you only had one share in this company, 10p of the profit would be yours! You are unlikely to receive this all as dividends, so the immediate cash benefit will be much smaller. However the retained earnings will have an impact on the growth in the capital value of the share.

All listed companies are required to publish earnings per share in the accounts. This is calculated on the basis of:

$$\frac{\text{Profit attributable to ordinary shareholders}}{\text{Number of ordinary shares in issue}}$$

The profit should be the profit after tax, minority interests and preference dividends, and extraordinary items. The number of shares in issue will be the number of shares in issue at the year end; unless there has been an issue for cash during the year, when the weighted average number of shares will be used. (A rights issue is slightly more complicated as we have to account for the discount element in the price.)

The accounting standard (SSAP 3) identifies three ways of calculating earnings per share:

- **Net basis**: this is the simple way outlined above and is the required way of calculating earnings per share in the standard. It is also the method that is used by organisations like the *Financial Times*.
- **Nil distribution basis**: this ignores the tax impact of paying dividends. In Chapter 2 we talked about Advance Corporation Tax. This is the tax that companies pay on behalf of the shareholders, which can be subsequently used to reduce their UK corporation tax bill. Companies that make a significant part of their profits overseas may not generate enough UK tax liabilities to be able to offset their ACT. This means that the payment of dividends can end up costing them more than a company, paying similar dividends, that pays the bulk of its tax in the UK. Companies that have a problem of irrecoverable ACT will often publish their earnings per share on a nil distribution basis, adding the ACT to the profit after tax. This shows what the earnings would have been, had they not paid dividends.

  The accounting standard recommends that earnings per share be shown on the nil distribution basis 'if there is a material difference between earnings per share calculated on the net basis and on the nil distribution basis'.
- **Fully diluted basis**: this shows you what the earning per share would be if all the outstanding share options were exercised. The accounting standard requires that a fully diluted earnings per share figure must be shown if, when the share options are included, there is more than a 5 per cent

dilution in the earnings per share compared to that calculated on the net basis.

In addition to these, analysts use a maximum, or full, distribution, basis. This looks at what the earnings per share would have been if all the available profit was paid as dividends.

When looking at companies' accounts you will now find a multiplicity of earnings per share calculations. FRS 3 encouraged companies to show a number of earnings figures; earnings per share based on continuing operations are often shown in addition to those disclosed on the total business.

DIVIDENDS PER SHARE

Dividends per share is simply the total dividend divided by the number of shares in issue. If the company in our earlier example was paying £1,000 dividends, and had 20,000 shares in issue, the shareholders would be receiving 5p dividend per share.

The dividends can be either net (excluding the ACT) or gross (including the ACT). Gross dividend is used in most of the published calculations of the dividend ratios. Assuming ACT at 20 per cent the gross dividend per share would be 6.25p (5p/0.8).

We now know how much the shareholder will receive in dividend, but is the company being generous, or mean, in its payment of dividends? To find out, we need to look at the dividend cover.

DIVIDEND COVER

This is similar to interest cover, and measures how many times the dividend could be paid out of the available profits. It can be shown in two different ways:

On a total profit basis:

$$\frac{\text{Profit attributable to ordinary shareholders}}{\text{Dividends}} = \frac{2,000}{1,000} = 2 \text{ times}$$

On an individual share basis:

$$\frac{\text{Earnings per share}}{\text{Dividend per share}} = \frac{10p}{5p} = 2 \text{ times}$$

We can see that the company is paying out half of the available profit as dividends. The more the company gives to its shareholders the less it has to put back into the business for next year's development and growth. Determining the size of the dividend is a fine balancing act for most companies. They want to pay enough to maintain a stable share price, but they need to retain funds for reinvestment. Dividend cover at two times is probably verging on the imprudent, almost half of the available profit is being paid as dividends. But like salary increases for staff, the dividend decision is largely determined by expectations, and what everyone else is paying.

For our purposes either of the definitions outlined above would be an adequate definition of dividend cover, but it is worth remembering that *where* the profit is made will have an impact on the dividend cover that we calculate. This arises because of the problems associated with irrecoverable ACT.

DIVIDEND YIELD

The dividend yield tells us what percentage we can expect to get back in dividend if we buy the share at today's price. The market price used in calculating the dividend yield is not quite the same as the cash you would receive if you sold the share. It is the average of the buy price and the sell price – 'the middle price'. The dividend yield is:

$$\frac{\text{Dividend per share}}{\text{Today's market price for the share}}$$

In our example, if the middle price for the share is £2.00 and the company is paying 5p net dividend per share, the net dividend yield would be 2.5 per cent. The gross dividend yield would be 3.125 per cent (6.25/200). The share offers a poor dividend return, but may offer some scope for capital gain. This will all depend on future profit growth, relative to the sector, and to see the market's view of potential we need to look at the PE ratio.

THE PE RATIO (THE MULTIPLE)

These are two different names for the same thing. *The Financial Times* publishes the PE ratio for listed companies, but often talks about the multiple in its articles.

They take the current earnings and look at them in relation to the current price:

$$\frac{\text{Today's market price for the share}}{\text{Earnings per share}}$$

Again the market price used for this ratio is the middle price. The earnings per share figure used in the PE ratio may be different from that shown in the published accounts. Following the implementation of FRS 3 it is not uncommon to see a number of different earnings per share figures in the accounts. They could, for example, be calculated including and excluding exceptional items, or excluding discontinued operations. Whilst this represents a more realistic view of the company's overall performance, it is a problem for businesses like the *Financial Times*, whose readers would find it confusing to be confronted by a number of different PE ratios. Consequently both the *FT* and Extel use the definition of earnings put forward by the Institute of Investment Management and Research (the analysts' professional body). The *Financial Times* uses earnings per share calculated on the net basis, excluding any unrelieved ACT. It then takes the profit attributable to ordinary shareholders and deducts profits, or adds back losses, on sales of assets or subsidiaries. It also adds back any abnormal write-downs in asset values, following a permanent reduction in their values, unless the company intends to sell the assets. The earnings per share figures are updated from the interim figures. They will also use the preliminary figures as soon as they are published, and then update them when the full annual results are available, so the PE ratios will change through the year as different earnings per share figures are calculated.

Therefore it does not represent a measure of sustainable earnings (it includes profit from discontinued operations), but does provide us with a starting point and a comparable basis for measuring the company's performance.

If the middle price for the share was £2.00 and the earnings per share was 10p, the company would have a PE ratio of 20.

We now know how to calculate the PE ratio, but what does it tell us? It says that if we buy the shares at today's price, and profits remain constant, it will take us twenty years to get our money back and still hold the share.

Although we criticise the stock market for its short termism, there are very few of us who would be prepared to wait twenty years to get our money back! Most investors are looking for a payback in five to seven years, depending on the risk profile of the investment. So if someone is prepared to pay twenty times current earnings, but expects to get their money back in five to seven years, they expect the profits to grow significantly over the period. A high PE ratio is usually an indication of an expectation of profit growth (although it could just be that the share is expensive). A low PE usually means that the market has an expectation that profits will fall.

If the market believes that earnings will show considerable growth, and the company gives a profits warning the share price will fall steeply. A share with a high PE is often volatile: small items of good news (supporting the market's view) will cause the price to jump, any bad news (contradicting the market's view) and the price will fall.

PE ratios move in the opposite direction to the dividend yield. If the price of the share rises, the PE ratio rises and the dividend yield falls. If the share price in our example rose to £2.20, the PE ratio would rise to 22 (2.20/0.10) and the gross dividend yield would fall to 2.84 per cent (0.0625/2.20). If the price fell to £1.80 the PE ratio would fall to 18 (1.80/0.10) and the gross dividend yield would rise to 3.47 per cent (0.0625/1.80).

A company's PE ratio should always be considered in the context of the expectations for the sector. The *Financial Times* publishes sector averages in the Actuaries Share Indices. They publish ratios for the sector. It is then possible to look at the company's performance relative to the sector:

$$\frac{\text{PE ratio of the company}}{\text{PE ratio of the sector}}$$

Looking at the company's relative performance within the sector gives an indication of the market's view of its relative performance. We think that a company with a PE of 20 is believed to have a lot of potential for profit growth. But if the sector average is showing a PE of 25, our company is believed to offer less potential than most others in its sector.

Another way of comparing the price to the earnings is the earnings yield, which is also calculated in the Actuaries Share Indices.

THE EARNINGS YIELD

The earnings yield is the reciprocal of the PE ratio, and is calculated in the same way as the dividend yield:

$$\frac{\text{Earnings per share}}{\text{Today's market price for the share}}$$

In our example, with a price of £2.00 and earnings per share of 10p, the earnings yield would be 5 per cent. If we buy the share at the middle price today, and profits stay the same, we can expect to earn 5 per cent on our money.

THE RETURN ON EQUITY

The return on equity is an overall measure of the return on the shareholder's investment. Instead of looking at the investment in the context of the market value, it looks at it in the context of the book value. It takes the profit attributable to ordinary shareholders and divides it by the share capital and reserves:

$$\frac{\text{Profit attributable to ordinary shareholders}}{\text{Capital and reserves}}$$

If the capital and reserves, in our example, were £50,000 and the profit attributable to ordinary shareholders was £2,000, the return on equity would be 4 per cent. It doesn't sound like a good return on our investment, but we would really need to know more information before we were able to take a view. We would need to know:

- what the returns on equity had been in the past,
- what the competitor's returns on equity were,
- the component elements of the capital and reserves. A share issue towards the end of the financial year would have a detrimental effect on the return on equity, so would a revaluation of assets; writing goodwill off through reserves would improve the return.

The return on equity suffers from the same problems as the return on capital:

- Reserves can be increased and decreased by the revaluation of assets.
- Reserves will be reduced if the company's accounting policy is to write off goodwill through reserves, and they have recently acquired a company.

NET ASSET VALUE PER SHARE

This tells you how much of the net assets is owned by each share in the company. It is often described as an indication of the break-up value of the company. However, this largely depends on valuation of the assets being realistic.

It does, however, give us some indication whether the value of the share is underpinned by assets, or whether it is dependant solely upon the company's ability to generate profits.

The net asset value per share is:

$$\frac{\text{Capital and reserves}}{\text{Number of shares in issue}}$$

In our example this would be £2.50 (£50,000/20,000).

MARKET TO BOOK RATIO

This compares the market value of the share with the book value of the share. If we believed the book value, it would give us an indication of the inherent security of the share. If the net asset value is higher than the market value, the shareholder may get his money back should the company go into liquidation. However, there are so many imponderables, and so many differences between companies in the same sector, that this ratio probably has little real value.

$$\frac{\text{Today's market price for the share}}{\text{Net asset value per share}}$$

If we wanted to calculate it for our example it would be 0.8 (2.00/2.50). The market values the company 20 per cent below its net asset value.

IMI's INVESTMENT RATIOS

The investment ratios for IMI are calculated below. Those that require a market price have been shown using the share price at the time of writing.

Earnings per share

IMI publishes two earnings per share figures for 1993 in the accounts: earnings per share before and after exceptional items.

Earnings per share before exceptional items   14.5p
Earnings per share after exceptional items   13.8p

The earnings per share in 1992 was 13.6p, there were no exceptional items. Therefore the growth in earnings per share was 6.6 per cent before exceptional items, and 1.5 per cent after exceptional items.

The two earnings per share figures were calculated on the net basis, by taking the profit for the financial year and dividing it by the 324.4 million average number of shares in issue.

Dividends per share

Dividends had remained constant over the 2 years at 10 pence per share.

Dividend cover

The dividend cover for 1993 is:

Before exceptional items:

$$\frac{\text{Profit for the financial year}}{\text{Dividends}} \quad = \quad \frac{47.0}{32.5} \quad = 1.45 \text{ times}$$

After exceptional items:

$$\frac{\text{Profit for the financial year}}{\text{Dividends}} \quad = \quad \frac{44.9}{32.5} \quad = 1.38 \text{ times}$$

IMI is being very generous maintaining its dividend at these levels as over

72 per cent of its profit is being paid as dividends. Dividends can only be paid at this level if the company is cash generative.

Dividend yield

This can be taken directly from the share information published by the *Financial Times*.

The gross dividend for 1993 is 12.5 pence (10/0.8) and the price of the share, at the time of writing, was £3.57. This was an ex-dividend price, anyone buying the share would not receive the dividend. The price was at the middle of its range for the year as the high was £3.79 and the low was £3.26.

The dividend yield, using the gross dividend, was:

$$\frac{\text{Dividend per share}}{\text{Today's market price for the share}} = \frac{12.5}{357.0} = 3.5\%$$

This is the same as the dividend yield published in the *Financial Times*.

The PE ratio

The price earnings ratio takes today's price and divides it by the earnings per share. The problems is what earnings figure should we use? If we wanted to look at a trend within the company, we would need to use a profit on continuing operations, and before exceptional items. If we wanted to look at the PE relative to the sector we would need to use the same definition of earnings per share that the *Financial Times* uses. (It would then be even easier as we wouldn't have to calculate the PE ratio – we could take it from the paper.)

IMI discloses two earnings per share figures for 1993 in its accounts – 14.5 pence before exceptional items and 13.8 pence after exceptional items. If we were looking at a performance trend we would use the earnings per share before exceptional items in our PE ratio:

$$\frac{\text{Today's market price for the share}}{\text{Earnings per share}} = \frac{357.0}{14.5} = 24.62$$

This is different from the PE ratio shown in the *Financial Times* of 29.9, which is based on an earnings per share of 11.94 pence. (This was based on the preliminary results, the PE was subsequently amended based on a revised earnings per share of 11.78 pence).

This difference arises from the different way that the *Financial Times* calculates the PE ratio. These were discussed earlier in the chapter. The big difference is that it adjusts the profit for unrelieved Advance Corporation Tax. Most of IMI's tax is paid overseas, and therefore cannot be used to offset the ACT paid on dividends. The reported earnings are reduced by the unrelieved ACT, and it is this reduced figure that is used to calculate the PE ratio.

If we do want to compare the PE to the sector we will need to use the published PE of 29.9, and compare it with the PE ratio for the sector shown in the actuarial indices. The PE for the sector shows the markets view of the profit growth prospects of engineering companies. As the economy is moving into recovery we would expect engineering companies to have considerable growth potential, and this is reflected in the sector PE of 32.61.

$$\frac{\text{PE ratio of the company}}{\text{PE ratio of the sector}} = \frac{29.90}{32.61} = 0.92$$

IMI is seen by the market to have a lower profit growth potential than other companies in this sector.

The earnings yield

This is just the reciprocal of the PE ratio and shows us the percentage return on our investment, assuming that the profits remain at current levels. As it is based on the earnings per share figure, we will get different answers using different earnings per share figures:

Published earnings per share before exceptional items:

$$\frac{\text{Earnings per share}}{\text{Today's market price for the share}} = \frac{14.5}{357.0} = 4.06\%$$

Adjusted earnings per share figure used by the *Financial Times*:

$$\frac{\text{Earnings per share}}{\text{Today's market price for the share}} = \frac{11.94}{357.00} = 3.34\%$$

The return on equity

The return on equity shows the return on the shareholders' funds. Any ratio based on them gives us the same problem – what figure should we use? The most comparable definition is the reported shareholders' funds less revaluation, plus goodwill. For IMI in 1993 this was £604.5 million (385.9 – 7.9 + 226.5). With profit for the financial year, before exceptional items, of £47.0 million this would give the following return on equity:

$$\frac{\text{Profit attributable to ordinary shareholders}}{\text{Capital and reserves}} = \frac{47.0}{604.5} = 7.78\%$$

This represented a modest improvement on the 7.36 per cent return in 1992.

This compares with a return on equity based on the reported profit for the financial year and shareholders' funds:

$$\frac{\text{Profit attributable to ordinary shareholders}}{\text{Capital and reserves}} = \frac{44.9}{385.9} = 11.64\%$$

The adjusted return on equity will inevitably be lower as the writeback of goodwill has a major impact on the denominator in the ratio.

Net asset value per share

This shows us the book value of a share in IMI. This is likely to be an underestimate of the real net asset per share as most of IMI's properties are shown at depreciated historical cost. In the directors' report they disclose 'The Directors are of the opinion that on an existing use basis the aggregate market value of the Group's other interests in land and buildings is substantially in excess of their net book value.'

However an asset value per share can be calculated from the book value. This can be taken from the capital and reserves shown on the balance sheet, consequently we will need to show two calculations:

Adjusted shareholders' funds:

$$\frac{\text{Capital and reserves}}{\text{Number of shares in issue}} = \frac{604.5}{325.0} = \text{£}1.86$$

If we were only looking at IMI's performance over time we would probably leave the revaluation reserve in the capital and reserve (this would give a net asset value per share of £1.88). When comparing IMI with companies with different revaluation policies we would need to exclude the revaluation reserve to arrive at a consistent basis for comparison.

The shares in issue is the year end number of shares, not the weighted average that was used for calculating the company's published earnings per share figure.

Reported shareholders' funds:

$$\frac{\text{Capital and reserves}}{\text{Number of shares in issue}} = \frac{385.9}{325.0} = \text{£}1.19$$

Market to book ratio

This compares the market price of the share with the asset value of the share. Its only real relevance is to show what proportion of the share price may be underpinned by the assets.

Adjusted shareholders' funds:

$$\frac{\text{Today's market price for the share}}{\text{Net asset value per share}} = \frac{357}{186} = 1.92$$

Reported shareholders' funds:

$$\frac{\text{Today's market price for the share}}{\text{Net asset value per share}} = \frac{357}{119} = 3.00$$

This suggests that the share price owes more to the expectations of profit improvement than the asset value, although we know that the asset value is understated as their assets are largely shown at cost.

15

IMI

INTRODUCTION

In this chapter we will be analysing and interpreting IMI's financial performance over the last five years. To do this we will be using the summaries of their financial statements that are shown in the following pages. These summaries do not follow the exact presentation of their accounts, as they have been represented in a format that allows companies with different accounting practices to be compared with one another. For example IMI shows income from current asset investments separately, other companies include it with interest received and disclose it in the notes to the accounts.

THE ACCOUNTS

The profit and loss accounts, balance sheets and cash flow statements for the last five years are shown in the following pages. The cash flow statements for 1989 and 1990 have been derived from the published source and application of funds statements.

PROFIT AND LOSS ACCOUNTS

	1989 £m	1990 £m	1991 £m	1992 £m	1993 £m
Turnover	1,079.1	1,029.4	968	1,005.6	1,064.6
Cost of sales	(783.9)	(740.8)	(715.1)	(738.4)	(772.3)
GROSS PROFIT	295.2	288.6	252.9	267.2	292.3
Administration expenses	(65.1)	(64.1)	(63.6)	(79.7)	(85.9)
Distribution costs	(109.1)	(112.9)	(114.4)	(115.6)	(130.6)
Other operating income	3.7	3	3.2	3.7	3.9
OPERATING PROFIT	124.7	114.6	78.1	75.6	79.7
Profit on sale of assets					
Profit on sale of subsidiaries	0.7	(14.7)			(5.9)
Other exceptional items					4.4
Share of profits of associates	4.2				2.1
PROFIT BEFORE INTEREST	129.6	99.9	78.1	75.6	80.3
Interest and dividends received	16.4	18.3	12.5	12.5	6.4
Interest paid – other loans	(2.8)	(2.7)	(3)	(1.8)	(1.5)
Interest paid – bank loans and overdrafts	(17.2)	(15.1)	(14.4)	(18.3)	(15)
REPORTED PROFIT BEFORE TAX	126	100.4	73.2	68	70.2
Tax	(44.3)	(36.9)	(24.8)	(23.8)	(25.2)
REPORTED PROFIT AFTER TAX	81.7	63.5	48.4	44.2	45
Minority interests	(0.5)	(0.1)	(0.1)	(0.1)	1(0.1)
Preference dividend	(0.1)	(0.1)			
Ordinary dividend	(30.5)	(32.2)	(32.4)	(32.4)	(32.5)
RETAINED PROFIT	50.6	31.1	15.9	11.7	12.4
EARNINGS PER SHARE (pence)					
After exceptional items	25.3	19.7	15	13.6	13.8
Before exceptional items	25.3	19.7	15	13.6	14.5
DIVIDENDS PER SHARE (pence)	9.5	10	10	10	10
PROFIT ADJUSTED FOR EXCEPTIONAL ITEMS: ADJUSTED PROFIT BEFORE TAX	126	100.4	73.2	68	71.7
ADJUSTED PROFIT AFTER TAX	81.7	63.5	48.4	44.2	47.1

BALANCE SHEETS

	1989 £m	1990 £m	1991 £m	1992 £m	1993 £m
FIXED ASSETS:					
Tangible assets	188.8	200	230.6	267.4	277.6
Investments	2.5	7.5	2.1	1.8	12.3
CURRENT ASSETS:					
Stocks	258.6	266.1	256.3	262.9	253.2
Total debtors due in a year	202.4	187.7	181.8	193.3	182.3
Debtors due in more than a year	5.8	7.5	11.6	7.4	4.7
Investments and short-term deposits	9.2	9	9	9.3	1.2
Cash at bank and in hand	159.2	142.7	134.9	159.4	101.3
Total	635.2	613	593.6	632.3	542.7
CREDITORS: DUE IN A YEAR					
Bank loans and overdrafts	(64.4)	(77.8)	(144.2)	(157.5)	(107.7)
Current portion of long-term debt	(6.6)	(12.8)	(4)	(11.3)	(1.4)
Trade creditors	(99.3)	(93.9)	(89.4)	(94.9)	(101.4)
Other creditors	(136.6)	(116.3)	(120.5)	(130.4)	(106.5)
Total	(306.9)	(300.8)	(358.10)	(394.1)	(317)
CREDITORS DUE IN MORE THAN A YEAR					
Loans	(108)	(92.6)	(68.6)	(91)	(89.5)
Other	(17.5)	(14.1)	(10.5)	(11.7)	(10.4)
PROVISIONS FOR LIABILITIES AND CHARGES					
Deferred tax	(1)	(0.2)	(0.6)	(1)	(4.6)
Other	(21)	(28.4)	(24.1)	(25.3)	(25.2)
MINORITY INTERESTS	(0.9)				
	371.2	384.4	364.4	378.4	385.9
CURRENT AND RESERVES					
Share capital	81.9	81.4	80.8	81	81.2
Profit and loss account	264.8	282.6	298	323.6	327.7
Revaluation	5.2	3.6	3.6	3.6	7.9
Share premium	63.8	64.8	66.2	67.4	68.8
Other	9.9	14.1	15	15	15
Goodwill	(54.4)	(62.1)	(99.2)	(112.2)	(114.7)
	371.2	384.4	364.4	378.4	385.9
OTHER INFORMATION					
Other goodwill charged directly to reserves	111.8	111.8	111.8	111.8	111.8
Issued shares (millions)	321.3	322.1	323.4	324.2	325
Trade debtors included in debtors due in a year	175.8	162.2	157.7	166.6	160.1
Capital employed	519.6	519.7	468.2	507.4	515.6

CASH FLOW STATEMENTS

	1989 £m	1990 £m	1991 £m	1992 £m	1993 £m
Net cash flow from operating activities	120.2	132.7	133.4	132.7	119.4
RETURNS ON INVESTMENT AND SERVICING OF FINANCE					
Interest received	13.6	17.6	11.6	11.7	6.3
Interest paid	(20)	(17.8)	(17.4)	(20.1)	(16.5)
Dividends received	0.1	0.7	0.9	0.8	0.8
Dividends received from associated undertakings					
Dividends paid	(28.3)	(31.9)	(32.3)	(32.4)	(32.4)
Other income	2.7				
Net cash flow from returns on investment and servicing of finance	(31.9)	(31.4)	(37.2)	(40.0)	(41.8)
TAXATION					
Tax paid	(36.0)	(55.0)	(33.5)	(21.5)	(25.4)
NET CASH FLOW BEFORE INVESTING ACTIVITIES	52.3	46.3	62.7	71.2	52.2
INVESTING ACTIVITIES					
Purchase of fixed assets	(43.8)	(47.9)	(50.2)	(53.9)	(47.7)
Purchase of businesses	(23.9)	(19.4)	(51.7)	(20.4)	(6.7)
Investment in and loans to associated undertakings		(5.5)			
Disposal of fixed assets	3.9	2.6	1.9	2.5	2
Disposal of businesses	31.3	2.7			
Disposal of fixed asset investments	6.6				
Net cash flow from investing activities	(25.9)	(67.5)	(100.0)	(71.8)	(52.4)
NET CASH FLOW BEFORE FINANCING	26.4	(21.2)	(37.3)	(0.6)	(0.2)
FINANCING					
Issue of ordinary share capital	(1.2)	(1.2)	(1.7)	(1.4)	(1.6)
Issue of other share capital					
Bond issue, net of expenses					
Other loans				(41.8)	(17.6)
Capital element of finance lease rentals					
Repayment of loans			36.2		
Redemption of shares		0.7	0.9		
Net cash flow from financing	(1.2)	(0.5)	35.4	(43.2)	(19.2)
CASH AND CASH EQUIVALENTS	27.6	(20.7)	(72.7)	42.6	19
	26.4	(21.2)	(37.3)	(0.6)	(0.2)

RECONCILIATION OF OPERATING PROFIT TO CASH FLOW FROM OPERATING ACTIVITIES

	1989 £m	1990 £m	1991 £m	1992 £m	1993 £m
Operating profit	124.7	114.6	78.1	75.6	79.7
Depreciation	26.6	28.3	33.8	38.4	39.6
Other items	9.6	13.4			
Loss/(profit) on sale of fixed assets	0.7	(14.7)			
Provisions utilised	(7.5)	(7.7)			
Cash to be generated from this year's sales	154.1	133.9	111.9	114	119.3
Decrease/(increase) in stocks	(23.4)	(1.4)	23.2	13.2	4.7
Decrease/(increase) in debtors	(21.2)	18.2	23.3	0.9	(1.9)
Increase/(decrease) in creditors	10.7	(18.0)	(25.0)	4.6	(2.7)
Net cash flow from operating activities	120.2	132.7	133.4	132.7	119.4

ANALYSIS OF IMI's FINANCIAL PERFORMANCE 1989–1993

We will now look at IMI's financial performance over the last five years. Detailed reading of the accounts shows consistent accounting policies and no evidence of creative accounting. The accounting treatment of post-retirement benefits has been revised in the light of new recommendations from a section of the Accounting Standards Board called the Urgent Issues Task Force.

They do use acquisition provisions to increase goodwill arising on acquisitions. These provisions are included in other provisions as part of provisions for liabilities and charges on the balance sheet. The impact of these does not appear to be significant. In 1993 the opening rationalisation provision was £8.1 million. Other provisions were increased by £0.6 million from new subsidiaries. If we were pessimistic and assumed this was all rationalisation provisions it would give a provision of £8.7 million. Exchange adjustments inflated other provisions by 5.7 per cent. If we build this into the rationalisation provision we would have a provision of £9.2 million. The closing provision was £5.6 million, therefore the maximum amount of rationalisation costs not charged to the profit and loss account was £3.6 million (9.2–5.6). Whilst this looks significant in the light of the profit growth 1992–1993 (operating profit grew by £4.1 million) the company had the same accounting policy in previous years. If we apply the same assumptions to 1992 the maximum expenditure on rationalisation that was charged to the provision was £2.9 million. Consequently it is possible that the operating profit growth may have fallen by £0.7 million had rationalisation costs been charged to the profit and loss account.

However there are a number of assumptions in this calculation and the auditors did not feel that the movement on the rationalisation provision was a necessary disclosure for the true and fair view. Consequently it has been ignored in the following analysis.

Solvency

We will look at solvency on the three timescales we discussed in Chapter 11 of this book:

- longer-term solvency,
- short-term solvency,
- immediate solvency.

Both the acid test and the current ratio have been calculated excluding the debtors falling due in more than a year from the current assets, as these debtors cannot be realised in the short term.

(a) **Longer-term solvency**.

(i) *Gearing*. Gearing is one of the important measures of longer-term solvency. There are a number of gearing ratios; we need to look at the balance sheet to decide which is the most appropriate. The balance sheet shows us that IMI has been changing the mix of its debt over the five years, moving from long-term to short-term borrowings. Therefore any measure of gearing must look at total debt. We shall look at all debt and net debt as a percentage of the shareholders' funds. The ratios have been calculated using the reported shareholders' funds in the balance sheet, and adding back the total goodwill that has been written off. This allows us to look at trends, as it ignores the effect that accounting for premium on acquisitions has on the reported shareholders' funds/equity.

	1989	1990	1991	1992	1993
Net debt:equity	1.97%	5.64%	12.67%	15.12%	15.69%
All debt:equity	33.31%	32.81%	37.68%	43.13%	32.43%

IMI is not highly geared. Gearing peaked at 43.13 per cent, on an all debt basis, in 1992 when total borrowings were at £259.8 million. On a net debt basis 1993 was the highest gearing, as the cash and deposits fell by £66.2 million. Their interest cover is satisfactory, although the profit-based interest cover is probably on the low side of acceptable, with bankers looking for minimum interest covers between four and six times, depending on the risk profile of the company.

	1989	1990	1991	1992	1993
Interest cover: profit-based	6.48	5.61	4.49	3.76	4.87

This becomes less important when we look at the cash interest cover. IMI does not have any problem servicing its debt, being able to pay the interest seven times out of the operational cash flow.

	1989	1990	1991	1992	1993
Interest cover: cash based	6.01	7.46	7.67	6.60	7.24

(ii) *Loan repayment schedule*. This was illustrated in Chapter 11. Of the £89.5 million borrowings £23.9 million falls due within two years, £42.7 million between two and five years, and the balance of £22.9 million falls due after five years.

Although IMI has an outflow before financing since 1990 it should not have any difficulties repaying, or refinancing, debt at this level.

(b) **Short-term solvency**. Short-term solvency is reflected in the current ratio, which measures the company's ability to repay its short-term liabilities with short-term assets.

	1989	1990	1991	1992	1993
Current ratio	2.05	2.01	1.63	1.59	1.70

As we would expect, from looking at the balance sheet, the current ratio has fallen until 1992 and then has started to increase. The current ratio reveals that IMI has no short-term solvency problems.

(c) **Immediate solvency**. Immediate solvency is measured by the acid test:

	1989	1990	1991	1992	1993
Acid test	1.21	1.13	0.91	0.92	0.90

The acid test has fallen over the period, but still shows a very solvent business who could pay 90 pence in every pound if asked to pay all of their short-term liabilities immediately. The acid test has fallen for two reasons:

- with the exception of 1992, debtors and cash balances have fallen over the period,
- creditors falling due within a year were steadily rising until 1993, when bank loans and overdrafts and other creditors fell.

IMI is unlikely to be asked to pay all the debt immediately as the banks are unlikely to demand repayment of overdrafts and creditor days are satisfactory:

	1989	1990	1991	1992	1993
Sales based: Creditor days	33.59	33.29	33.71	34.45	34.77
Cost of sales based: Creditor days	46.24	46.27	45.63	46.91	47.92

It is interesting to compare the difference between the creditor days calculated on a sales basis with that on a cost of sales basis. Over the five-year period both show that creditor days have increased by just over a day. But the trend from year to year is different. On a sales basis creditor days fell slightly between 1989 and 1990, whereas on a cost of sales basis they rose slightly. This is likely to happen in businesses where the margins have changed in the period. It reinforces the point that we will never arrive at an accurate number from the ratios (despite the two decimal places!), all we can tell is whether the company is likely to have a problem with creditors.

As we are not comparing IMI with another company the cost of sales basis is probably more appropriate as it will be more nearly right!

(d) **Summary**. IMI should not have any solvency or liquidity problems in the foreseeable future.

Cash management

When we look at IMI's cash flow statement we can see that:

- if you look at the reconciliation of operating profit to the cash flow from operating activities you will see a line that I have called 'cash to be generated from this year's sales'. This shows the cash that will be generated from the sales made during the year. More or less cash could be generated, depending on the company's control of working capital. The cash flow from the sales in the year fell by nearly 30 per cent in the period 1989–1991; from 1992 it has increased slightly. The operational cash flow has been supported by reduced working capital requirements.
- capital expenditure (the purchase of fixed assets) showed a modest increase in the period until 1993, where it fell to £47.7 million. This is only 20 per cent above the depreciation charge in 1993. The company has spent £122.1 million on acquisitions during the period.
- the company's investment activities are largely self-financed. The cash flow before investing covers most of the investing activities (purchase of fixed assets, businesses and investments in associates):

	1989	1990	1991	1992	1993
Cash flow before investing as a % of investing activities	77.25%	63.60%	61.53%	95.83%	95.96%

In the first three years the cash before investing activities did not cover the purchase of assets and acquisitions. In 1989 the shortfall was covered by £31.3 million cash that was received from the sale of businesses. In 1990, the problems stemmed from the increase in tax paid and in 1991 IMI made relatively large acquisitions, spending £51.7 million to buy six companies. The cash requirements were largely met by existing resources.

- The cash flow statement shows a business living within its means. Only in 1990 and 1991 did they have significant cash outflows before financing.
- There have been no significant share issues during the period. Shares have only been issued through the exercise of options on share save schemes.
- Borrowings increased in 1992 and 1993; this was reflected by similar increases in net cash and cash equivalents.
- With the exception of 1990 and 1991 the long-term sources of funds have matched the long-term applications. A company should match the investments that are made in the long term with sources of funds that will be available on a long-term basis.

The long-term sources of funds available to the business are:
- cash flow before investing activities,
- disposal of fixed assets, businesses and fixed asset investments,
- share issues,
- loans.

The long-term applications are:
- purchase of fixed assets, businesses and fixed asset investments,
- loan repayments,
- share redemptions.

The long-term sources of funds as a percentage of the long-term applications were as follows:

	1989	1990	1991	1992	1993
Long-term sources of funds as % of long-term applications	115.66%	69.20%	47.70%	157.34%	134.93%

To summarise, IMI's management of cash over the period has been conservative. They have tried to be as self-funding as possible. This may have constrained the development of their business, as they limit the size of their expansion. However, in the light of the uncertainty in many of their markets during this period, the company has probably steered the safest course. It will be interesting to see how the company develops in 1994, when a number of their markets should start to show an upturn.

Profitability

(a) **Return on capital**. We will start to analyse their profitability by looking at their return on capital employed. This has been calculated in two ways: firstly, using the published figures, and secondly using the profit before exceptional items and an adjusted capital employed figure. The revaluation reserve has been deducted and goodwill added back to arrive at a capital employed figure that is comparable across the five-year period.

Both calculations show a marked decline:

	1989	1990	1991	1992	1993
Based on published figures	28.10%	22.74%	19.35%	17.36%	16.82%
Adjusted for profit, goodwill and excluding revaluation	21.45%	17.13%	13.41%	12.10%	12.01%

We can see that the return on capital has fallen significantly during the period, and must now identify whether this has arisen from falls in profitability, poorer asset utilisation or both. To do this we must look at the profit margin and the asset turn.

	1989	1990	1991	1992	1993
Profit margin (based on adjusted profit)	13.53%	11.48%	9.36%	8.76%	8.28%
Asset turn (adjusted for goodwill and revaluation)	1.59	1.49	1.43	1.38	1.45

The answer is both. The profit margin, based on profit before interest and tax, has fallen from 13.53 per cent to 8.28 per cent and IMI is only managing to generate £1.45 in sales for every pound of capital invested compared to £1.59 in 1989. This is a combination of the increase in tangible assets (they have increased by 47 per cent in the five years) and the fall in turnover during the period. (Turnover fell by over 10 per cent in the period 1989–1991, in 1992 it rose by 3.9 per cent, and in 1993 by 5.9 per cent to end the period just over 1 per cent below the 1989 figure.)

(b) **Operating Profit**. Operating profit is the prime element of the profit in the return on capital.

	1989	1990	1991	1992	1993
Operating profit margin	11.56%	11.13%	8.07%	7.52%	7.49%

We can see that the operating margin has shown a similar fall. To try to understand why, we need to look at some of the segmental information.

(c) **Divisional performance**. IMI has four main divisions, with drinks dispense being the only division consistently to grow in turnover and profits during the period. The return on operating assets is not analysed as IMI changed its divisional structure in 1992 and the operating assets for the new structure are only available from 1992 onwards.

(i) *Building products*. The turnover of the building products division has fallen by nearly 25 per cent in the period, reflecting the downturn in the construction industry. However, the company has improved its profit margins in the last two years, almost returning them to 1989 levels. Any growth in turnover should have a significant impact on the reported operating profits.

	Turnover	Operating profit	Operating margin
	£m	£m	
1989	404	36.7	9.08%
1990	380	31.6	8.32%
1991	319	21.5	6.74%
1992	296	22.4	7.57%
1993	306	27.6	9.02%

(ii) *Drinks dispense*. The turnover in drinks dispense has grown by nearly 39 per cent in five years. Profit margins have fluctuated from one year to the next, but in 1993 are the largest in the group.

	Turnover	Operating profit	Operating margin
	£m	£m	
1989	185	21.8	11.78%
1990	188	22.8	12.13%
1991	207	22.9	11.06%
1992	230	28.6	12.43%
1993	257	30.0	11.67%

(iii) *Fluid power*. The fluid power division saw turnover falling for the first three years in the period and rising for the last two. Profits and margins have more than halved in the period.

	Turnover	Operating profit	Operating margin
	£m	£m	
1989	214	35.9	16.78%
1990	210	32.5	15.48%
1991	196	22.2	11.33%
1992	207	16.9	8.16%
1993	220	16.7	7.59%

(iv) *Special engineering*. Special engineering is a diverse division with a wide range of products including production of titanium, special valves, coins and ammunition. Turnover fell until 1993, when it increased by 6.6 per cent. Profits and margins also rose in 1993, having previously fallen since 1990.

	Turnover	Operating profit	Operating margin
		£m	£m
1989	281	30.2	10.75%
1990	265	33.4	12.60%
1991	249	14.0	5.62%
1992	228	12.0	5.26%
1993	243	15.9	6.54%

The changing fortunes of the divisions have impacted on the profitability of the company. In 1989 Fluid Power and Special Engineering with their large profit margins accounted for just over 53 per cent of IMI's profits. By 1993 their profit margins had almost halved and they accounted for around 41 per cent of the company's profits. However all of the divisions have considerable growth prospects, drinks dispense with the worldwide spread of fast food chains and the other divisions with an upturn in the world economy. Drinks dispense was the only division to have a fall in its operating margin in 1993; profit margins rose in all other divisions.

(d) **Geographical performance**. IMI is an international business, generating most of its turnover and profits overseas. This is illustrated below in the analysis of turnover and operating profit for 1993:

	Percentage of total turnover	Percentage of total operating profit	Operating profit margin
UK	46.86%	39.05%	6.25%
Rest of Europe	21.41%	24.47%	8.55%
The Americas	26.76%	30.49%	8.53%
Asia/Pacific	4.98%	5.90%	8.87%

This means that their profits are less exposed to the performance of one economy. When one economy moves into recession another should be moving out. However, their profits over the last five years have been eroded as unfortunately all their main markets were in recession together.

Having a clearer idea of why the company's profit margins have fallen, we should now look at their asset utilisation.

Asset utilisation

(a) **Tangible asset turn**. The tangible asset turn fell steadily until 1992, and showed a modest increase in 1993:

	1989	1990	1991	1992	1993
Tangible fixed asset turn (adjusted for revaluation)	5.88	5.24	4.26	3.81	3.95

In 1989 each pound of capital invested in tangible assets managed to generate £5.88 in sales; by 1993 it had fallen to £3.95. This measure indicates that the company should have excess capacity and would therefore be able to cope with increased demand.

(b) **Control of working capital**. The company has become more efficient in managing its working capital in 1993 and this is reflected in the working capital ratio:

	1989	1990	1991	1992	1993
Working capital ratio	0.31	0.32	0.34	0.33	0.29

In 1989 every pound of sales required 31 pence cash tied up in the working capital; this rose to 34 pence in 1991 and has fallen in the last 2 years to 29 pence. Obviously if their turnover increases with their markets coming out of recession, IMI will have to find more cash to fund its expansion programme unless it can reduce its working capital requirements further.

To ascertain if this is possible we need to look at the individual working capital ratios.

As we are not comparing IMI's performance with another company in the sector, cost of sales is the most appropriate basis for calculating stock and creditor days.

(i) *Stock days*. Stock days rose in 1990; since then they have fallen:

	1989	1990	1991	1992	1993
Stock days (cost of sales based)	120.41	131.11	130.82	129.96	119.67

(ii) *Debtor days*. Debtor days were rising steadily until 1992; in 1993 the company improved the collection period to just under fifty-five days:

	1989	1990	1991	1992	1993
Debtor days	59.46	57.51	59.46	60.47	54.89

(iii) *Creditor days*. The payment period was more or less constant between 1989 and 1990, fell in 1991, and has risen in both 1992 and 1993.

	1989	1990	1991	1992	1993
Creditor days	46.24	46.27	45.63	46.91	47.92

(iv) *Summary*. The improvement in the working capital ratio in 1993 came from improvements in all three areas of working capital control.

The investor's perspective

You will find that you will be unable to calculate a lot of the ratios that were discussed in Chapter 14, as they need the then current share price. Unless you have kept track on how the share price has moved over a period you will be unable to establish trends in:

- the dividend yield,
- the PE ratio,
- the earnings yield,
- the market to book ratio.

All these ratios require a current share price. However you will be able to establish trends in:

- earnings per share,
- dividends per share,
- dividend cover,
- return on equity,
- net asset value per share.

(a) **Earnings per share**.

	1989	1990	1991	1992	1993
After exceptional items	25.3p	19.7p	15.0p	13.6p	13.8p

Reported earnings per share fell by 54 per cent from 1989 to 1992; in 1993 it increased by 1.5 per cent. The increase was more significant when exceptional items are excluded from the calculation:

Before exceptional items	25.3p	19.7p	15.0p	13.6p	14.5p

Earnings per share had increased by 6.6 per cent, before exceptional items, in 1993.

(b) **Dividends per share**. Dividends per share showed modest growth in 1990, but have subsequently been maintained at a constant 10 pence:

1989	1990	1991	1992	1993
9.5p	10.0p	10.0p	10.0p	10.0p

(c) **Dividend cover**. IMI has maintained dividends out of falling earnings, therefore the dividend cover has fallen until 1993:

1989	1990	1991	1992	1993
2.66	1.97	1.49	1.36	1.38

(If exceptional items are deducted from the calculation the dividend cover rose to 1.45 times in 1993.) IMI is only able to maintain dividend payouts at this level because it is relatively cash generative.

(d) **Return on equity**. Return on equity is shown below and is based on both the published figures and adjusted for exceptional items, goodwill and the revaluation of assets.

	1989	1990	1991	1992	1993
Published profits and shareholders' funds	21.85%	16.47%	13.25%	11.65%	11.64%
Profit before exceptional items as a percentage of adjusted shareholders' funds	15.24%	11.41%	8.45%	7.36%	7.78%

As we would expect, the return on equity has fallen over the period, as profits have fallen and the shareholders' funds have increased, although the adjusted return on equity showed a slight improvement in 1993.

(e) **Net asset value per share**. Net asset values are shown below calculated using both published shareholders' funds and adjusted shareholders' funds:

	1989	1990	1991	1992	1993
Reported shareholders' funds	£1.16	£1.18	£1.13	£1.17	£1.19
Adjusted shareholders' funds	£1.66	£1.71	£1.77	£1.85	£1.86

The net asset value per share fell based on the reported shareholders' funds in 1991 as the share capital increased at the same time as the shareholders' funds reduced, following a write off of goodwill.

The adjusted net asset value per share is probably a more realistic reflection of the underlying trend in asset values.

(f) **Summary**. Shareholders have had falling returns over the last five years and will be hoping for the recovery to be reflected in improved levels of profitability and dividend returns.

Summary of IMI's financial performance

IMI is a conservatively managed engineering company. Its profits have fallen in the five-year period under review but would be expected to rise in future years as its markets recover. Despite the fall in profits it has maintained its expenditure on research and development, vital for its continued success, with it only falling in 1991:

1989	1990	1991	1992	1993
£8.7m	£10.3m	£9.0m	£10.3m	£11.7m

It would appear to be in a relatively healthy condition, given the apparent improvement in the ratios discussed above. If, as seems likely, the profit decline was largely due to the decline of some of its key markets, as the markets recover IMI should be in a good position to, literally, profit from the recovery. This expectation of profit growth is already built into the share price and any failure to deliver the anticipated profits could lead to shareholder disaffection.

Part III

HOW CAN I USE MY ANALYSIS?

16

INTRODUCTION

In the first part of this book we looked at the information that we could find in a set of accounts, in the second part we learnt how to analyse and interpret the data. This part of the book is concerned with how to apply our analytical and interpretative skills. We will now look at the four main areas where managers are most likely to use financial analysis.

- Analysing suppliers' accounts.
- Analysing customers' accounts.
- Analysing competitors' accounts.
- Identifying the acquisition potential of a company.

Most managers have a good commercial understanding; it is in the area of finance that they usually feel most exposed. Once they can add financial analysis to their existing knowledge about their suppliers, customers and competitors, they will have a comprehensive understanding of their company's position in the marketplace. We have looked at all aspects of financial analysis. When we use this analysis in conjunction with our existing information base we start to get a real understanding of our company's strengths and weaknesses, and of the threats and opportunities facing us.

This section of the book shows you how to apply your knowledge. It looks at each application and identifies:

- the main concerns,
- the relevant ratios.

A lot of the analysis in each section will be similar, especially when looking at profitability, but the emphasis will be different. Each of the sections is intended to be able to be referred to separately, so much of the discussion will be common to all.

17

SUPPLIERS' ACCOUNTS

INTRODUCTION

The viability of suppliers is essential for the long-term survival of any company. No one wants to squeeze a supplier so hard on price and payment terms that they go into liquidation. The analysis of suppliers' accounts is an integral part of the negotiating process. We need to understand their business, and the threats and opportunities facing them, if we are to protect our own business.

When looking at suppliers' accounts we will have a number of concerns.

- Will they be able to deliver the order if we give it to them?
- Have we got a good deal?
- What's the strength of our negotiating position?

Financial analysis helps to address all of our concerns about our suppliers. There are two aspects to our first concern. The first part relates to our suppliers' manufacturing ability – will they be able to deliver the right quality product, on time. Unfortunately, no amount of financial analysis can answer this question. It can, however, help in the second part of our concern that relates to their financial viability. We need to reassure ourselves that our suppliers will continue in business and will not be forced into liquidation.

To answer the second concern we must look at the three main elements of the deal.

- **The price**: we need to reassure ourselves that our suppliers are not ripping us off! If the market is very competitive we are likely to have had a number of different quotations from alternative suppliers, but it becomes more difficult when there are fewer alternatives.
- **Stock levels**: we may have agreed that suppliers will carry our stock, or have some form of consignment stock arrangement that will reduce our working capital requirements, but increase theirs. Can they afford to do this?
- **Credit terms**: are we getting the same credit terms as their other customers? If we are paying faster, shouldn't we get a better price?

The third concern raises the question of how important you are to them. You will have a different negotiating position if you are 1 per cent of their business than if you are 20 per cent. You may find that they need your business more than you need them!

This chapter of the book addresses these concerns and shows you the relevant ratios to use when analysing suppliers' accounts.

RELEVANT RATIOS

Most of the ratios discussed in previous chapters have some relevance in the analysis of suppliers' accounts; the ones selected in this chapter are particularly useful in satisfying our main concerns.

We must, however, remember that ratios will never be a totally accurate reflection of our suppliers' business. We must always bear in mind the inherent problems of using information from published accounts. Whilst published accounts must conform to the Companies Act and accounting standards, they are also a marketing brochure and represent the best 'true and fair' picture that the company can show the outside world. This is why looking at trends is so important. Every year the company tries to show the best picture: is the best getting better, or worse?

Solvency

We need to ensure that our suppliers will be able to deliver the goods that they have promised. We do not want our suppliers to go into liquidation, consequently we need to ascertain their ability to pay their bills when they fall due. The solvency of a potential supplier is critical to the sourcing decision.

We need to identify their likely relationships with their suppliers: are they likely to be put 'on stop'? If their suppliers won't deliver goods to them because they are slow payers, they are unlikely to be able to deliver the goods to us on time. Our other concern is their probable relationships with their bankers: are the banks likely to pull out of the business? Our prime concern is with any possible short-term problems, but if we envisage them being a supplier in the medium term we must consider some of the other, longer-term, solvency ratios.

Consequently we would need to use the following ratios in our analysis:

- creditor days,
- acid test,
- current ratio,
- gearing,
- interest cover.

We would also need to look at the loan repayment schedule.

(a) **Creditor days**. Creditor days can be calculated using either purchases, cost of sales or sales as the basis for the calculation. When we are analysing suppliers' accounts we are not trying to make any comparison of one company's payment period against another. We are trying to assess the possible risk of dealing with a specific supplier. Consequently purchases (for companies using a Format 2 presentation of the profit and loss account) or a cost of sales based calculation (Format 1) is probably more appropriate. These will more nearly reflect the payment terms. Therefore the most appropriate ratio to use is:

$$\frac{\text{Trade creditors}}{\text{Cost of sales/Purchases}} \times 365$$

(b) **The acid test**. This measures the company's liquidity, and its ability to pay all their short-term liabilities instantly. Whether this is likely depends on our analysis in other areas. If the creditor days calculation showed that the company is taking so long to pay its suppliers that they are likely to be pressing for immediate payment, this would be an appropriate ratio. Another situation where it would be an important ratio is where a company has such a poor relationship with its bank that they are likely to withdraw overdraft and short-term borrowing facilities.

The acid test is defined as:

$$\frac{\text{Liquid assets}}{\text{Creditors falling due in a year}}$$

The liquid assets are those that the business could convert into cash at very short notice. For most businesses this would be debtors, short-term investments and cash, but this obviously varies from business to business. A retailer would find it easier to convert stock than debtors. Some manufacturing companies would also find that stock can be easily converted into cash. A good example is Johnson Matthey, who process precious metals. They would be able to sell their gold stocks in the same way as a grocer could sell their food stocks.

We would not necessarily expect a company to be able to repay all of its short-term liabilities from liquid assets. We are interested in whether the company is becoming more, or less, liquid and why. We need to know whether this is likely to become a problem.

(c) **The current ratio**. The current ratio looks at the company's ability to repay short-term liabilities out of short-term assets. It is:

$$\frac{\text{Current assets}}{\text{Creditors falling due in a year}}$$

The size of the 'ideal' current ratio varies from one industry to another. It largely depends on the length of the company's production cycle. The longer it takes the company to turn the raw materials back into cash the larger the current ratio needed. Companies, like grocers, where the buying decision is made daily and they get cash from their customers before they have to pay their suppliers, will not have enough current assets to pay their short-term creditors. But grocers are unlikely to be major suppliers to a company. If one of our suppliers doesn't have sufficient short-term assets to cover their short-term liabilities, the liabilities will have to be repaid by selling fixed assets. If our suppliers have net current liabilities we need to identify the likelihood of them having to be repaid. (The creditors could be largely short-term borrowing instruments that could be 'rolled over' as long as the company still appears credit-worthy.)

It is also worth remembering that we would expect the current ratio to be falling over time, as companies become more efficient in controlling their working capital.

(d) **Gearing**. We discussed a number of different gearing ratios in Chapter 11. The most generally applicable gearing ratio is the one calculated on the net debt basis:

$$\frac{\text{All debt} - \text{cash and short-term deposits}}{\text{Capital and reserves}}$$

This ratio is useful because it considers long- and short-term debt. It is probably the most relevant ratio for smaller suppliers who are unlikely to be able to raise much in the form of long-term borrowing, and will be forced to have most of their borrowing in the form of bank overdrafts and short-term loans. These short-term borrowings would not be picked up in the more conventional definitions.

(e) **Interest cover**. Interest cover is one of the most important solvency ratios as it looks at the company's ability to service their debt. It can be calculated from the profit and loss account, or from the cash flow statement:

Profit-based:

$$\frac{\text{Profit before interest}}{\text{Interest payable}}$$

Cash-based:

$$\frac{\text{Operational cash flow}}{\text{Interest paid}}$$

The higher the cover the less likely it is that the company will have any difficulties with its bank. If the interest cover is above six times the company should not have too many difficulties raising extra finance. Whereas a company with a two times interest cover would find it almost impossible to raise extra funds, as half its profits are going to service its existing debt. A fall in profits, or a rise in interest rates, could easily mean that the interest charge was greater than the available cash.

(e) **Cash generation and the loan repayment schedule**. The company could have future solvency problems if the rate of cash generation was insufficient to repay the debt. It is worth looking at the cash flow before financing and comparing this with the loan repayment schedule. If the company is only generating an average of £40 million a year and has to repay £300 million in the next two years, it could have a problem! There are a number of ways that the problem could be resolved:

- it could have a rights issue,
- it could take out more loans to repay the existing debt,
- it could sell some assets.

Our analysis in other areas would help to identify if any of these options are likely to be available to the company.

Ability to finance the order

If we are giving a supplier a large order we need to check that the company will be able to generate sufficient finance to be able to deliver the goods. If we are placing an order for £1 million the supplier will have to fund the working capital requirements associated with our order. We need to identify how much cash they are likely to have to find and whether they will be able to raise it.

There are two ways of approximating the cash that will be required to fund the order: the first is to look at the existing working capital ratio, and the second is to try to calculate the specific working capital requirements associated with the order.

(a) **The working capital ratio**. This is simply calculated:

$$\frac{\text{Stock} + \text{trade debtors} - \text{trade creditors}}{\text{Turnover}}$$

This tells us, on their existing business, how many pence they will need to have tied up in the working capital to fund a pound's worth of sales. So, for example, if they need 30p per pound of sales, the £1 million pound order probably means that they will either need to:

- find £300,000 to fund the order, or
- reduce their working capital requirements. If they reduced their stocks

and debtors and increased their creditors it is possible to use the same amount of working capital to fund an increased level of sales.

Our analysis should help us identify if either option is possible.

(b) **The working capital requirements of the order**. This involves a number of assumptions being built into our calculations:

- the materials cost percentage,
- the length of the production cycle (the lead time is a good approximation for this),
- the labour cost percentage,
- the overhead cost percentage,
- the probable profit margin on the order.

If you are fortunate enough to have an 'open book' relationship with your suppliers (where they have to give you a breakdown of their costs and cost structure) you could work with more realistic numbers and have to make fewer assumptions. Otherwise you will need to look at the cost structure revealed in their profit and loss account, and flex it for any probable differences in your order. You may decide that you have to make so many assumptions that the current working capital ratio would give you a good enough guide to the cash requirements of the order.

To illustrate how the working capital requirements for the order could be calculated, we will consider the following example:

Order size	£1 million
Credit terms	60 days
Materials costs	50% total cost
Labour cost	30% total cost
Overheads	20% total cost
Profit margin	5%
Lead time	2 months
Ratios calculated from the company's accounts:	
Raw materials stock days	30 days
Finished goods stock days	15 days
Creditor days	50 days

The profit and loss account for the order would be:

Turnover	1,000,000
Material costs	475,000
Staff costs	285,000
Overheads	190,000
Profit	50,000

To complete the order the supplier would have to fund the working capital requirements. They would have to hold stock, wait the agreed credit period, and this would be offset by the credit they could take from their suppliers.

The supplier has to fund the three components of stock: raw materials work in progress, and finished goods.

Cash required to fund raw materials:

$$\frac{30}{365} \quad \times \quad 475,000 \quad = 39,041$$

Only the materials costs are included at this stage. Although some over-heads are incurred in carrying stock, the bulk of the overheads will start to be incurred on manufacture.

Cash required to fund work in progress:

$$\frac{60}{365} \quad \times \quad 950,000 \quad = 156,164$$

Once the product is started to be manufactured all of the costs will begin to be incurred, so we have based the calculation on the total cost.

Cash required to fund finished goods:

$$\frac{15}{365} \quad \times \quad 950,000 \quad = 39,041$$

The total cash that will be tied up in stock is £234,246.

The cash required to meet our credit terms will be:

$$\frac{60}{365} \quad \times \quad 950,000 \quad = £156,164$$

The costs are used for the calculation, not the sales, as the company will not have to fund the profit, only the costs.

This will be offset by the credit that the supplier is able to get from his suppliers:

$$\frac{50}{365} \quad \times \quad 950,000 \quad = £130,137$$

In this calculation we are assuming that the company gets the same period of credit from all of his suppliers. We could do a more detailed analysis looking at the probable credit terms for each category of costs. However, we are unlikely to have costs presented in the format shown in this example.

This gives a cash requirement, before financing costs, of:

$$£234,246 + £156,164 - £130,137 = £260,273$$

We would need to reflect on whether the business is likely to be able to raise another £260,000 to satisfy our order. Or reduce their stocks and debtors and increase their creditors, making the same amount of working capital generate more sales. The last thing we would want to do is to give a supplier an order that would cripple their business!

The profitability of the supplier

Companies have a dilemma when dealing with suppliers; they want them to be profitable (in the long run you need to be profitable to survive), but they don't want them to be too profitable (that might mean that they are ripping you off)! In looking at suppliers' accounts we need to look at trends in both the return on capital and the operating profit.

(a) **Return on capital employed**. In Chapter 12 we discussed the determinants of return on capital. We saw how it could be improved in one of two ways, improving profitability, or improving the utilisation of assets. Customers can have a large impact on the return on capital of suppliers. The negotiated price will affect the profitability. Customer requirements for stockholding and extended credit terms will affect asset utilisation. When we look at suppliers' accounts we are interested in identifying:

- what is their return on capital?
- is it acceptable?
- is it improving?
- why? improved profitability? improved asset utilisation?
- is our order likely to have an impact on their return on capital?

We need to look at the ratios in the return on capital.

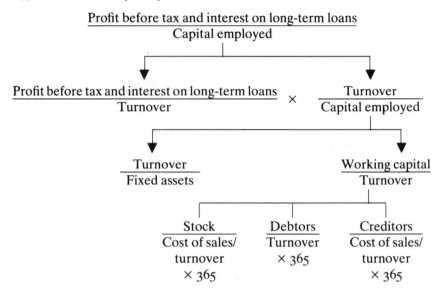

If the profit margins have changed we would need to check whether this is from operating profit or profits and losses on assets or subsidiaries. Have exceptional items had an impact on profitability?

The most appropriate fixed asset turn is calculated by using the tangible assets, less any revaluation. (This eliminates any differences in potential suppliers revaluation policies, and takes the numbers back to a common base.) If this is falling, the tangible assets are being used less effectively and the company probably has excess capacity. If it is increasing the company is being more efficient, but may be approaching maximum capacity.

The working capital ratios are important in supplier analysis, particularly debtor and creditor days. We have discussed the use of creditor days in looking at solvency. Debtor days are a useful tool for negotiation. Are you paying faster than their average customer? If you are paying in forty-five days and their debtor days are seventy-five days, other customers are taking longer to pay and this should be reflected in the price. You should be buying the goods at a discounted price.

(b) **Operating profit**. Remember that we want our suppliers to be profitable, but not too profitable! If operating profit is changing it is useful to reflect on what might be causing the change.

It could be a change in price feeding through to the turnover; a rise in prices would reflect in increased turnover, a fall in prices in reduced turnover. But increases and decreases in turnover do not always reflect changes in price. Changing volumes will also impact on turnover. Unfortunately we are unable to determine which of these has caused the change in turnover.

It could be a change in the product mix. We might be able to find some information about this in the segmental information disclosed in the notes to the accounts, where companies disclose their turnover, operating profit and operating assets by class of business and geographical segment. This would show us if the source of the company's profits has changed to any significant degree.

Profitability could improve through cost reduction. Alternative, cheaper materials may be used, staff costs and overheads may have been reduced. We will be able to see if there have been any changes in the disclosed costs, including staff numbers and total staff costs. If the company has managed to improve its overall profitability through cost reduction, wouldn't you as a customer want a share of the improvement? Maybe there is scope for a price reduction?

The importance of the order

If you want to identify the strength of your negotiating position you need to know how important your business is to your supplier. What percentage is your business of their total turnover? This is when it is useful to get hold of the individual company's accounts. Your order may be totally irrelevant to the group, but could be 20 per cent of the individual company's business. If you are a large customer, you have a strong negotiating position, but often can't afford to drive too hard a bargain. If you negotiate price reductions and extended credit terms you may force the company into liquidation, or the parent company may decide to close or sell the business. If you have a key supplier, where you are also a key customer, in financial difficulties you have a strategic dilemma. Should you continue to negotiate hard, or should you structure the negotiation to help the supplier? It is often cheaper to pay a better price, or faster than to look for alternative suppliers. Being a large customer is a two-edged sword: with the power comes responsibilities!

SUMMARY

Financial analysis is an integral part of the sourcing decision. Before we place large orders, we need to ascertain the financial viability of suppliers and the impact that our order will have on their viability. Sometimes companies go into liquidation because they are expanding too fast. They can get the orders, but can't get the cash to fund the orders!

Financial analysis is not just important in vetting suppliers, it can also play a useful role in the negotiating process. It helps us to identify our best negotiating position.

18

CUSTOMERS' ACCOUNTS

INTRODUCTION

If we want to develop a close relationship with our customers it is essential that we understand their business. We need to appreciate their strengths and weaknesses in order to understand our opportunities and threats. Clients' accounts are a useful addition to our normal market intelligence as they will quantify the success, or otherwise, of their marketing plans, and some of the threats and opportunities facing their, and consequently our, business. In the accounts we can see:

- where they are making their sales:
  - by type of business,
  - geographically.
- which parts of their business have real sales growth opportunities,
- where they are making their profits:
  - type of business,
  - geographically.
- where their profits have grown,
- their cost structure,
- where they get the best return on their operating assets,
- the other companies in the group (they could represent sales opportunities),
- the areas of the business they intend to develop in the future.

The accounts will contain the financial information and the factors influencing the business' performance will be disclosed in the operating review. The operating review is part of the operating and financial review statement proposed by the Accounting Standards Board in 1993. It is not a mandatory requirement (it is intended to be a 'statement of best practice') but is found in most large companies' accounts. It represents a balance between disclosure and discretion. Best practice requires a number of detailed disclosures, some of which may be seen as confidential or commercially sensitive.

The operating review should disclose the factors, and the trends, that underlie the company's performance, together with those factors that are expected to impact on the company's future performance. It should divulge any industrial or environmental changes that will affect the company's results. These include the development of new products, acquisitions, disposals and changes in:

- market conditions,
- market share,
- exchange rates and rates of inflation,
- turnover and margins.

It should also disclose the company's investment for the future. This may be in the form of capital expenditure, or revenue expenditure that is expected to generate some future benefit. This could be in the form of maintenance, training, marketing and advertising campaigns, or research and development. It is easy to see how full disclosure of all these items could be compromising for the company. However, despite its general nature the operating review does contain some interesting information about our customers' businesses. It will certainly give us an understanding of how they see their performance and their focus for the future. It may provide us with a starting-point for a more detailed discussion with our clients. If we are selling capital equipment we will be able to see their current level of capital expenditure and some indication of their likely future spend.

When we are looking at our clients' businesses we have a number of concerns.

- Will they be able to pay us?
- Will they be in business next year?
- Is there potential for increasing our sales?
- What is the best way to structure the sales negotiation?

Financial analysis will help to address some of these concerns, and will give us information that may be useful in focusing our sales negotiations.

RELEVANT RATIOS

One of our immediate concerns is whether the company will be able to pay us for our sales. If our client is part of a group we may find it useful to look at both the group accounts, and those of the individual company. The individual company accounts will reflect the company's position within the group. You can have an individual company that is not commercially viable on its own, but the parent, or the group, have guaranteed the borrowings. Alternatively, the individual company could be viable, but the group goes into liquidation because of problems in other parts of the group. The group accounts may be useful in other ways: they will disclose the group's principal subsidiaries and associated undertakings. These could represent sales opportunities. If you are a supplier to one part of the group, you should be acceptable to the rest. Whilst some companies operate a system of centralised purchasing, with approved suppliers, a lot of groups allow individual companies to select their own suppliers.

SOLVENCY

The company's solvency and creditor days are important ratios, as they address two of our concerns. They indicate whether we are likely to have a credit control problem and whether the company is likely to stay in business.

(a) Creditor days

As we are not trying to do any comparative analysis creditor days based on cost of sales or purchases will be the most appropriate measure to use:

$$\frac{\text{Trade creditors}}{\text{Cost of sales/purchases}} \quad \times \quad 365$$

(b) The acid test

Customers will try to extend payment terms if they have a problem with liquidity, so the acid test is a useful ratio:

$$\frac{\text{Liquid assets}}{\text{Creditors falling due in a year}}$$

This measure represents the worst view of solvency; we are assuming that all of the short-term liabilities fall due for immediate repayment. This will only happen if the bank is losing patience and the creditors have already been waiting an inordinately long time for payment. Things generally have to be bad for a trade creditor to resort to liquidating the company. They are a long way down the creditor queue and are unlikely to see much money back if the company is liquidated. They would probably be better off if they waited, rather than liquidated.

Liquidation tends to be initiated by banks and preferential creditors (people like DHSS and Customs and Excise) who stand a greater chance of getting their money back.

Consequently we would not necessarily expect a company to be able to pay all of its short-term liabilities out of its liquid assets, but is the company becoming more or less liquid? Is this a result of a disproportionate change in liquid assets, or in short-term liabilities? Is it more, or less, liquid than our other customers?

(c) The current ratio

For most businesses the difference between the current assets and the liquid assets is stock. This should be reflected in a stronger current ratio:

$$\frac{\text{Current assets}}{\text{Creditors falling due in a year}}$$

We would expect the company to have a positive cover (the current ratio should show more than a pound in current assets for every pound of short-term liabilities). The main exception to this is retailers, where it is not unusual to have net current liabilities. If your client does not have a positive cover, this means that they would have to sell off their fixed assets to repay their short-term liabilities. They are relying on the continued support of suppliers and the bank.

(d) Interest cover

To see whether they may be having problems with the bank we can look at the interest cover. This can be calculated in two ways, based on cash or profit:

Profit-based:

$$\frac{\text{Profit before interest}}{\text{Interest payable}}$$

Cash-based:

$$\frac{\text{Operational cash flow}}{\text{Interest paid}}$$

The cash-based measure is probably the most appropriate, as interest is physically paid out of cash, not profit. If the company receives interest as part of its normal operations, the interest received should be added to the operational cash flow, to arrive at the cash before interest paid figure. The bigger the cover the less likely that the company will be having difficulties with the bank. If the company can't cover its interest with the operational cash flow it will have to resort to selling assets, or having a share issue to pay the bank interest and is likely to have real problems in repaying the loans

Only short-term borrowings are reflected in the acid test and the current ratio. Not all loans are short-term; we need to look at gearing and the loan repayment schedule to see if the company may have future difficulties with its bankers.

(e) Gearing

Gearing looks at the relationship between debt and equity and tells us whether the company has borrowed more funds than it has raised from the shareholders, or has left in the business. The most popular definition of gearing is probably the most useful, as it allows us to calculate this regardless of whether the debt is short- or long-term:

$$\frac{\text{All debt} - \text{cash and short-term deposits}}{\text{Capital and reserves}}$$

Being highly geared is not necessarily bad, in fact it may be good for the shareholders in times of expansion. They stand to make more money than those shareholders who have invested in a company with low gearing, as the increased profits will be shared between fewer shareholders. However, being highly geared with a low interest cover is likely to be bad news. It will not take much of a fall in profits (or a rise in interest rates) before the company starts to have problems with its bankers.

(f) Loan repayment schedule

Having considered whether the company has borrowed a lot of money our next step is to see if the company will be able to repay the loans. To do this we need to look at the loan repayment schedule and compare it with the cash being generated by the company. Looking at the trends on cash flow before financing tells us if the company is likely to be able to repay the loans out of cash flow. If not they have three options:

- repay the old loans with new loans,
- have a share issue to repay the loans,
- sell assets to repay the loans.

Our analysis should be able to identify the most likely option.

PROFITABILITY

We have considered their solvency, we now need to look at their profitability. We want to know whether our customers have growth potential. Are their sales increasing or decreasing? The profit and loss account will reveal the trends on turnover and profits. However, it is unlikely that we will be involved in their total business. Our products may be used in only one part of their business. If we are only selling to a specific part of their business we may find the segmental analysis, given in the notes to the accounts, a more meaningful basis for analysis. (This was discussed in Chapter 7.) We are interested in what is happening in the part of our customers' business that we sell to, and how this compares to the results that they are getting from other parts of their business. They are likely to focus their investment and energies on the part of their business that is generating the best return and the best prospects. Consequently we have to be interested in the relative performance our client's business. Any part of their company that is under-performing is likely to be sold off, or closed down, any area that is perform-ing well will be developed and strengthened. (The only exception to this is where you have companies generating relatively low profits in mature markets. these may be retained by the company if they are cash generative, they can become 'cash cows'.)

The segmental analysis will give us useful information about the relative performance of different parts of our client's business, and performance in different geographical markets. It will analyse turnover, profit (usually profit before interest), and operating assets by class of business and geo-graphically. It enables us to work out the profit margins and return on operating assets for different parts of their business. It does not, however, analyse cash flows which may not reflect the profit.

Having identified where the company is making its profits we need to consider how it is trying to improve its profitability. To do this we need to consider the hierarchy of ratios, shown in Chapter 17:

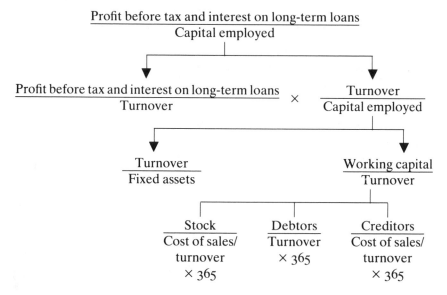

Firstly, we need to identify the return on capital itself. Is the business generating a better, or worse return than it used to? What has changed? Is it the profitability or the asset utilisation?

If it is the profit we need to consider whether any improvement in the return is sustainable. To do this we need to consider where the profit has come from.

It could have arisen from:

- operating profit,
- interest received,

- profits or losses on sale of fixed assets, or subsidiaries,
- other exceptional items.

Operating profits should be sustainable, interest received may or may not be. This depends on the type of business and whether interest received is a normal component of profit (for example, retailing). If it isn't then any improvement in return on capital arising from interest received may be of short-term benefit. Profits on sale of assets, subsidiaries and other exceptional items are best treated as 'one offs'.

If the company is looking at profitability driving improvements in return on capital and we are selling them revenue items they will be looking for price reductions in the negotiations. (This would be particularly relevant if our product represented a major cost. If they can negotiate a 5 per cent reduction on something that is 40 per cent of their total cost, they will be generating a significant improvement in their profits!)

If the company is using better asset utilisation as a way of improving return on capital it will also have an impact on the negotiations. Are they trying to use their fixed assets more effectively? Perhaps we have a machine, or tooling, that can extend life? If they are trying to control their working capital it will affect our negotiations. If we find that the company's creditor days are longer than our payment terms, are they paying us faster than their other suppliers? The company's buyer will be trying to extend the payment terms in the negotiation, to bring our terms into line with those of his other suppliers. If they are trying to reduce stocks, they will be looking for an improvement in delivery times and may be asking us to carry some of their stock. Perhaps we should look at the possibility of a consignment stock arrangement?

SUMMARY

Financial analysis is a useful tool for the salesman. It gives us a wealth of additional information and can often be a guide to future negotiations. By using financial analysis in conjunction with our market intelligence we should be able to turn our customer's threats into our opportunities!

19

COMPETITORS' ACCOUNTS

INTRODUCTION

Curiosity is a human trait. We are always intrigued by the financial performance of our competitors: are they performing better or worse than we are?
We see their marketing activities, and have some idea about their commercial strategies, but how does this translate into their financial performance? We need to know whether their marketing activities are more, or less,
successful than ours. We know that this will be reflected in their profitability
and the way that investors feel about the business.

We have three main concerns about our competitors.

- **Relative profitability**: who is the most profitable company in the sector?
  Why?
- **solvency**: will they be able to continue trading? Do they have so much
  cash that they can support an aggressive discounting policy to gain
  market share?
- **Relative investment potential**: does the stock market rate them as a
  better investment than our company? Why?

Financial analysis helps us address these concerns. It identifies whether
their marketing activities are successful, whether they are likely to survive
and their perceived investment potential.

RELEVANT RATIOS

We are likely to have different competitors in different markets, and may
not compete with them in the full range of their business activities. Consequently we are more likely to be interested in individual company accounts,
rather than groups, and probably more interested in their profitability within
specific business segments than the total.

Solvency

We are obviously interested in whether our competitors are likely to continue trading in the future and so examination of their solvency will be an

integral part of our financial analysis. We want to know whether they are likely to be having difficulties with their suppliers. If the company is always 'on stop' they are unlikely to be able to meet delivery deadlines. Creditor days is a good measure of supplier relationships. When we use creditor days in competitor analysis we are using it comparatively. We are trying to compare their creditor days with those of other people in the industry. Therefore we need to have a measure that is comparable across companies. This means that measures based on purchases (does everyone in the industry use a Format 2 presentation for the profit and loss account?) or cost of sales (does everyone in the industry define cost of sales in the same way?) are unlikely to be used. Turnover would probably give a better basis for comparison: it largely depends on how the other companies in the industry are preparing their accounts. The only problem with using turnover is when you have companies with widely different profit margins. As long as there are no real differences in profitability within the industry, at least we would be consistently wrong! Consequently we are likely to use the following formula for calculating creditor days:

$$\frac{\text{Trade creditors}}{\text{Turnover}} \times 365$$

If the company appears to be taking a long time to pay its suppliers we are interested in looking at the acid test:

$$\frac{\text{Liquid assets}}{\text{Creditors falling due in a year}}$$

The liquid assets will be determined by the nature of the business, but for a manufacturing company they are likely to be debtors receivable within a year, short-term deposits and cash. This is the most pessimistic view of solvency, as we are assuming that all of the creditors ask for immediate repayment. As long as the company doesn't appear to be having problems with its bankers or suppliers the current ratio is probably a more accurate reflection of the company's solvency:

$$\frac{\text{Current assets}}{\text{Creditors falling due in a year}}$$

This measures the company's ability to pay its short-term liabilities out of short-term assets. If the company has net current liabilities (its creditors due within a year are larger than its current assets) it is likely to have solvency problems, unless it is a retailer. It will have to sell fixed assets to be able to repay its short-term liabilities.

Gearing looks at the relationship between debt and equity. The most popular definition of gearing is probably the most useful, as it allows us to compare companies with a range of borrowing maturities:

$$\frac{\text{All debt} - \text{cash and short-term deposits}}{\text{Capital and reserves}}$$

A highly geared company is one where the shareholders will fare badly in a recession and well in a recovery. Interest will have to be paid regardless of profits, whereas dividends are determined by the company, and whether it can afford to pay. When sales and profits increase, a highly geared company will be able to reward its shareholders, as the increased profit will be spread amongst relatively fewer shares. Whether high gearing is a problem is influenced by two things: the economic outlook, and the interest cover.

Interest cover looks at the company's ability to service its existing debt. It can be calculated from the profit and loss account, or from the cash flow statement:

Profit-based:

$$\frac{\text{Profit before interest}}{\text{Interest payable}}$$

Cash-based:

$$\frac{\text{Operational cash flow}}{\text{Interest paid}}$$

A company with a low interest cover (anything below three times) is exposed to falls in profits and rising interest rates. The late 1980s recession saw the two occur together and this forced several large companies into liquidation. Interest cover also influences a company's ability to raise additional funds from the bank. Banks are reluctant to lend to companies with low interest cover, as the company could have problems servicing its existing debt, let alone any additional debt. On the other hand, a company with a high interest cover (over seven times) would find no difficulty supporting additional loans.

If a company has loans, a sad fact of life is that they must be repaid. We are interested in our competitors' ability to repay its existing debt. What is their loan repayment schedule? How does this compare to the cash flow before financing? Looking at the trends, will they be able to repay the loans from cash flow? If not, looking at their interest cover is it likely that they will be able to get new debt to repay their existing debt? If not, are they likely to be able to raise additional share capital to repay the loans? If not, do they have any under-utilised assets that they can sell? Or are they likely to have to re-negotiate the terms with their bankers, and maybe have a debt equity conversion programme?

Looking at our competitors' solvency is useful as it helps us identify whether the company has the following:

- current, or potential problems with suppliers and banks.
- sufficient financial strength to support a price-led market penetration programme. We know that any reduction in price requires a disproportionate increase in volume to maintain profits at current levels. Any company engaging in marketing activities that drive the price down has to have a strong balance sheet to survive and realise the benefits of the increased market share.
- the ability to absorb an increase in the working capital. They may be under pressure to carry their customer's stock and extend debtor days. If they have solvency problems then they are unlikely to be able to respond to any of these requests from their customers.

Profitability

We know the level of prices charged by our competitors, and have a fair idea of their service levels. What we want to know is how does this translate into profitability. Are they more, or less, profitable than us? We are interested in the two measures of profitability: operating profit and the return on capital. Are their operating margins similar to ours? If not, do we have any information in the profit and loss account that would tell us about cost differences? We can look at the disclosures on salaries and staff. (But beware, some companies disclose total employees, others disclose full-time equivalents. In industries where part-time working is common, the comparisons can be very misleading.) We would expect operating margins within the same industry to be fairly similar. If a competitor in the same market has a very different operating margin they have either:

- identified a new market,
- developed a new manufacturing process/different method of distribution,
- practiced creative accounting.

The last option is of interest, but the first two could be of major concern. Careful reading of the notes to the accounts would help verify, or eliminate, the creative accounting option.

The return on capital employed is the other measure of profitability that we are interested in. This is important as it will influence the outsiders' view of the business. When looking at the return on capital it is useful to use the hierarchy discussed in Chapter 12:

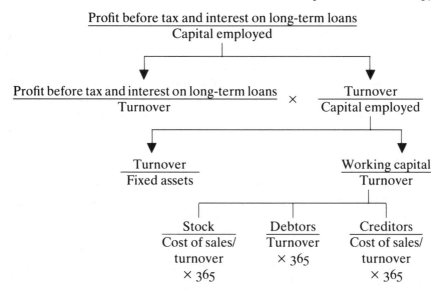

Firstly, we need to identify the return on capital itself. Is the business generating a better, or worse return than other companies in the industry? Is their return sustainable? To determine this we need to look at where the profit has come from. It could have been generated from:

- operating profit,
- interest received,
- profits or losses on sale of fixed assets, or subsidiaries,
- other exceptional items.

Operating profits should be sustainable, interest received may or may not be. This depends on the type of business and whether interest received is a normal component of profit (for example, retailing). If it isn't then any improvement in return on capital arising from interest received may not be sustained. Profits on sale of assets, subsidiaries and other exceptional items are best treated as 'one offs'.

Having looked at the profitability element of return on capital we move on to look at the asset utilisation. Are they managing to generate more, or less, sales per pound of capital tied up in the business? Are any differences arising from their utilisation of fixed assets, or their control of working capital? The working capital ratios are always interesting, as stock days and debtor days affect their relationships with their customers. It is useful to analyse stock into its component parts, working out stock days for raw material stock, work in progress and finished goods stock. If our competitors are carrying more raw material stock they may be better able to cope with rush orders and shorter delivery times. A difference in the work in progress may reflect a difference in manufacturing times, which will work through into delivery lead times. A difference in finished goods stock may reflect their willingness, or otherwise, to carry stocks for their customers.

The debtor days calculation is important as it gives us an indication of their credit terms with customers, as creditor days does with suppliers.

The analysis of the return on capital hierarchy gives us some useful insights into competitive advantages and disadvantages. It is possible to use our analysis to identify the probable success of our marketing plans.

The investor's perspective

If the competitor is a public company, or part of a public company, we need to identify how the business is performing from the investor's point of view. (This is less relevant for private companies whose owners tend to be the directors of the company.) Our starting point is the earnings per share and dividends per share shown in the accounts. Institutional investors are looking for earnings per share growth in advance of inflation. They also want to see real dividend growth (this is very important as the actuarial valuation of pension funds is based on income, i.e. dividends, not market value). A share is more likely to attract the institutional investor if it can show steady growth in earnings and dividends. They are also likely to be attracted to a company if the dividend payout is reasonably certain. This is reflected in the dividend cover ratio:

$$\frac{\text{Profit attributable to ordinary shareholders}}{\text{Dividends paid to ordinary shareholders}}$$

This follows the same principle as interest cover. The higher the cover the greater the chance of the dividend still being paid, and even increased, if profits fall.

The return to the shareholders is also reflected in the return on equity:

$$\frac{\text{Profit attributable to ordinary shareholders}}{\text{Capital and reserves}}$$

This shows the return on the shareholders' funds, but suffers from the problems of accounting for goodwill and revaluation. It tends to be more widely used overseas, where goodwill is shown as an intangible asset and revaluations are not allowed. This makes the equity figures more comparable.

We can see the stock market's expectation of profit growth reflected in the share information found in the *Financial Times*. In Chapter 14 we discussed the stock market's view of a company's future performance. A PE ratio between five and seven is indicative of an expectation of no real growth in earnings. These shares are likely to have relatively high dividend yields, reflecting an approximation to interest rates (the alternative opportunity for deposits with zero capital growth). A high PE indicates that the markets believe that profits will grow. If we are looking at competitors' accounts we are interested in whether the stock market believes that their profits will grow faster, or slower, than other companies in the same industry. Consequently we need to look at the PE relative to the sector, and compare our competitors' PE ratios with our own.

A high PE ratio relative to the sector is indicative of the market's view that profit growth will be higher in this company than the others. Remember that this relatively high PE will make the share more volatile. The stockmarket expects profits to grow faster than other companies in the sector, therefore if there is any bad news from the company the market will over-react, sending the share price tumbling. Good news will support the market's view and the price will rise.

A company's growth prospects may not be fairly reflected in the PE ratio. The share price can be influenced by all sort of extraneous factors. Who is running the company can be important. Some people have 'city cred', others don't. That will influence the way the share price moves. The board's presentation of their future plans may have been unconvincing (or too convincing)! You must remember that the stock market is the same as any other market: it is full of people. The personal relationships are as important within the market as they are in any other industry. A company's shares can underperform in the market, in the short-term, because some leading analysts don't like, or trust, the board. Some companies are very good at establishing relationships, others ignore the 'teenage scribblers' (how some companies see the analysts!). This will be reflected in the share price. We should always remember that a PE ratio is someone's view about the way that profit will move. The market is not always right!

SUMMARY

Financial analysis can give us some useful insights into our competitor's business. We can identify the success of their marketing, potential problems facing the business, and see how they might respond to their customers.

Most managers already understand the strengths and weaknesses of their own products, and their position in the market place. They know their competitors' marketing strategies, strengths and weaknesses. Financial analysis helps us to have a more rounded view of our competitors' performance and may help us identify ways of improving our own.

20

IDENTIFYING THE ACQUISITION POTENTIAL OF A COMPANY

INTRODUCTION

Companies become acquisitive to enhance profitability and this can be achieved in a number of different ways:

- improving market share,
- gaining economies of scale,
- gaining a better, or more complete, product range,
- acquiring cash.

Companies in the same industry may decide to merge to get economies of scale, and greater market share. We could decide to buy a company because it has developed improved technology or products. The acquisition could be the cheapest way of improving our own products and transferring their technology. Acquisition may be the only way to acquire them as they may be protected by patents.

Other companies become acquisitive because they want to diversify. This motive often drives the one-product companies who are exposed to changes in their markets. They may want to move from declining industries into expanding ones, or they may feel that a diverse company offers better protection against the vagaries of the economic cycle.

This all sounds simple and very obvious, but many companies seem less profitable after an acquisition than they were before. So what makes some companies have more success with acquisitions than others? The successful predators seem to follow similar criteria.

- Firstly they buy businesses they understand. They avoid the glamorous acquisitions. Either they stay within their own sector, or integrate vertically – buying into suppliers or customers. Any diversification outside of their existing business is in mature established markets producing everyday products. They do not buy companies with sophisticated technologies operating in emerging markets. The risks are too great.
- Secondly the business must have the potential to be cash generative. Most

successful predators like to see significant amounts of cash being generated by the acquisition within the first year. The cash could be generated in a variety of ways.

- The business could in itself be cash generating. The predator could use the company as a 'cash cow', stripping the cash from the subsidiary through dividend payments.
- The company might have subsidiaries that could be sold off to generate cash. There have been a number of occasions where this has proved so successful that the remaining business is more profitable without its subsidiaries than it was with them. Five minus two can equal seven! This is called 'unbundling'.
- The company may have under-utilised assets that could be sold off. If a company has prime commercial property that has not been revalued they may be vulnerable to 'asset stripping'. This tends to be more common in times of rising property prices and shortages of good commercial property.
- The company could be badly managed. If they have more cash tied up in the working capital than other companies in the industry the installation of proper stock and credit control procedures could rapidly generate cash.

- Thirdly the company is 'asset backed': its asset value is greater than its market value. This means that the company is less exposed to losing money on the acquisition.
- Fourthly the company should be performing relatively poorly. This gives the predator scope for turning the company around. If they can improve profits, they will always be able to sell the business later for a profit. A poorly performing asset-backed business is always attractive to the conglomerates. It gives them options for the future.
- And finally they are pessimists, not optimists. They always look at what can go wrong, not what may go right. Our personal experience tells us that this has to be the right approach. What can go right rarely does, but what can go wrong usually does, plus a load of other things you never thought of!

In summary the successful predators are risk averse. They tend to buy companies that are undervalued by the market because of poor performance, not because they are exposed to technical risks. Their acquisitions are always cash generative, or at worst potentially cash generative when the underlying performance of the business has improved. Their asset backing gives them greater security; under-utilised assets can always be sold to generate cash.

As managers, we are unlikely to be involved in identifying acquisitions for diversification programmes. We are more likely to be involved in the acquisitions of competitors, particularly smaller competitors who have found a niche in the market place. They may or may not be looking to sell their business. Financial analysis can be used, in conjunction with marketing information, to identify the acquisition potential of a company. If we take a leaf out of the successful predator's book, we are looking for companies that have:

- relatively poor financial performance,
- cash generation potential,
- a greater asset value than market value.

In this chapter we will look at how you can use financial analysis to identify the acquisition potential of a company and ensure that it will meet the above criteria. We will look at the ratios that you would use and the bases that can be used to determine the price paid for an acquisition.

RELEVANT RATIOS

If we are looking for a business where we have scope to improve the profitability we must start with the profitability ratios. We need to look at the return on capital employed as this will give us some indication of both the profitability and the potential of the target company to generate cash.

The return on capital

We need to look at each of the elements of the return on capital hierarchy illustrated in Chapter 12. This will show us both where the profit is coming from and whether there may be any scope for generating cash from the businesses' assets.

(a) **Profitability**. The profit figure used for the return on capital has three elements:

- operating profit,
- profit on sale of fixed assets or subsidiaries,
- interest received.

The profit on sale of assets or subsidiaries is a reflection of the asset values shown in the accounts. If the company is consistently making profits on sales of assets this tells us that the assets are undervalued on the accounts; if they are making losses the assets are overvalued.

Profits and losses on sale of assets are best used as a guide to the asset valuations, they do not form a basis for sustainable profit growth!

If the company is receiving interest it must have money on deposit. If we know the average interest rates during the period we can get some idea of their average cash balances. We would then need to reflect on the nature of these cash balances. They may be permanent, in which case they can be transferred to the acquiring company, or seasonal, reflecting the nature of the business.

Only operating profit will offer sustainable profits in the long term. It is useful to see where the company is making its profits. If they are a large private company, or a public company, they will give segmental information in the notes to the accounts. This will analyse turnover, operating profit and operating assets by class of business and geographical segment. We want to know where they are making their profits: it may be that they are strong in markets where we are weak or vice versa. The segmental analysis will give us some idea about whether the company would be a good fit with our own.

We would expect the operating profit to improve after the acquisition. The company will be absorbed into our infrastructure and staff costs should reduce. We may be able to close some of their offices and factories and relocate the business to our sites. This would reduce our overhead costs. As a larger business we may be able to get better terms with our suppliers, and reduce our costs.

However they may have some customers who prefer to do business with them because they don't want to do business with us! We should expect to lose a proportion of the sales following the acquisition. If you know the market place, and the customer base, you should be able to 'guesstimate' a likely post-acquisition turnover.

We should then be able to look at the current level of profit and extrapolate a post-acquisition profit, taking into account the likely cost savings that should arise following the acquisition. We would then need to do some sensitivity analysis, remembering that successful predators are risk averse, always looking for things that can go wrong. What would be the effect of us losing another 10 per cent of the sales, of only achieving 50 per cent of the planned cost reduction? We need to generate a number of profit projections, to help us identify the maximum price that we would be prepared to pay.

(b) **Asset utilisation**. The asset turn is probably less important than the two constituent ratios: the tangible asset turn and the working capital ratios. The tangible asset turn is a useful measure that helps us identify if the company's assets are being used effectively. If they used to generate £5.00 sales for every pound invested in tangible assets and are now only managing to generate £3.00, they probably have excess capacity. We could either use this capacity ourselves, or we could sell off the assets and generate cash.

The condition of the assets would determine whether we were able to sell them and realise a significant amount of cash. Unfortunately we only have limited information about the likely state of the assets from the accounts. The cash flow statement would disclose the level of capital expenditure in recent years. As a general rule you would expect a company to be investing at a rate greater than the depreciation charge. Depreciation is based on historical costs and historical technologies. Whilst it is dependant on the industry, we would expect a company's expenditure to have to exceed the depreciation charge just to stand still. We may be able to get some indication of the age of the assets by looking at the note to the fixed assets in the accounts. This will show the cost, the depreciation to date and the book value. If the book value is 20 per cent of the cost, the assets are 80 per cent through their lives. The note on depreciation in the accounting policies will disclose the asset lives. There are however two problems to bear in mind when looking at this.

- The analysis can never be accurate, the calculation can be distorted by recent capital expenditure.
- The bands given for the asset lives may be so broad (for example, three to twenty years) that we cannot calculate the age of the assets.

The working capital ratios are important as they can be indicative of three things:

- the efficiency of the management. An efficient management would be trying to reduce the working capital. As the potential acquisition is likely to be involved in a similar industry you can see how their working capital ratios compare to yours.
- the cash generation potential of the company. If we can reduce the investment in working capital we will generate cash.
- the profit potential of the company. We know that if we can reduce the investment in working capital it will not only generate cash, it will also improve the return on the company's operating assets (these are the assets that are involved in the generation of profit).

It is worth analysing stocks into the three elements and calculating stock days for raw materials, work in progress, and finished goods stock. Calculating the work in progress days gives you some idea of the length of the production cycle and you will be interested in whether they take longer to produce the goods than your company. A higher finished goods stock may arise from a decision to carry stocks for their customers.

Debtor and creditor days will be important as they may reflect, in part, their relationships with their customers and suppliers.

The cash flow statement

The cash flow statement is important as it will show us the company's potential to generate cash. However, if we are looking at a small private company we would have to prepare a cash flow statement, as they are not required to prepare one under FRS 1.

(a) **Operational cash flow**. We would start by looking at the operational cash flow. This can be divided into two parts, the cash flows arising from sales during the year and the cash flows from working capital. We have seen in earlier chapters that if we take the operating profit, add back depreciation, losses on sale of assets and then deduct profits on sale of assets and any utilisation of provisions, we can identify the cash flow from sales. This may not be the same as the cash flow from operating activities, as the working capital requirements could have increased or decreased. We would ideally be looking for a company with a strong cash flow from sales, but an increasing investment in working capital. This could arise from either poor management or expansion, either way it would be a short-term problem and the company could subsequently become cash generative. It would then become even more cash generative when the anticipated cost reductions have materialised.

(b) **Returns on investment and servicing of finance**. We have talked about the importance of the company's profits in the acquisition decision. We don't just buy profits, we also buy assets and liabilities. A combination of the two will be reflected in the price that we are prepared to pay. If we buy a company we take over their debts, and we are interested in the company's ability to service its debts out of the current cash flow. The cash-based interest cover is important. If the company is having difficulties with its bank it may be more likely to accept a low offer.

We are not just interested in the company's ability to pay interest, we also need to look at its ability to pay us dividends. We buy a company to gain access to their cash. The subsidiary will have to pay the parent a cash dividend. They may not be able to do this in the short term, but they will have to be able to do so in the long term.

(c) **Taxation**. If our plans for improving the profitability of the company work, it will have to pay more tax on the increased profits. More tax means less cash available for investing activities.

(d) **Investing activities**. We would want the acquisition to be self-funding and would hope that the cash flow before investing activities would cover the capital expenditure. To quantify this we would really need to have some idea of the state of their current fixed assets before we could take a view on the likely level of future investment. We can get some idea of the age of the assets from the notes to the accounts, which will have also disclosed the additions. We are only likely to see the assets when negotiations have started.

(e) **Cash flow before financing**. Ideally we would want to see a positive cash flow, or potentially positive cash flow, before financing. This should be sufficient to repay any borrowings when they fall due.

We have seen how the cash flow statement can help us identify the company's ability to generate cash. We will now consider how we might value a company.

COMPANY VALUATION

Whilst it is unlikely that managers will be involved in determining the price on an acquisition (this will be determined by the board of directors) they are often asked to help the company spot potential acquisitions. If we are trying to identify the acquisition potential of a company, we are looking for companies that can improve the profitability of our own organisation. Essentially we are looking for bargains! If we want to know whether a company would be a good buy, or not, we have to have some idea of how to value a company. There are three different bases for valuing companies:

- an asset basis,
- a profit basis,
- a dividends basis.

The first two are appropriate for valuing acquisitions, the dividends basis is only relevant when you have a small stake in a company. (It is useful when you are looking at the potential return on your investment and comparing it with the price of the share.)

(a) **Asset-based valuation**. This looks at the net worth of the company and is a useful starting point in company valuation. The net worth is simply the bottom line of the balance sheet. This tells us the value of the company using the company's valuation policies. Once we have read these policies we will have a clearer idea of the relevance of this valuation. The policies may undervalue or overvalue the company. You will remember that IMI showed most of its properties at depreciated historical cost. Therefore the book value of £385.9 million understated the value of the company. We would undoubtedly need to adjust this figure to arrive at a closer approximation to the market value. The fixed assets will be an important element of the valuation. To get some idea of a market valuation of the assets we would have to ask the following questions.

- Land and buildings.
  - Are they owned or leased?
  - How long does the lease have to run?
  - Have they been revalued?
  - When?
  - By whom?
  - What was the basis for the revaluation?
- Plant and machinery.
  - Has the company been replacing its machinery?
  - How old is the equipment?
- Other fixed assets.
  - What are they?
  - How have they been valued?

- Stock.
  - What is it?
  - Are the stock days larger than the industrial average? (This could be a sign of inefficiency, or it may mean that they have obsolete stock that has not been written off. This happens in smaller companies who are often reluctant to make provisions because of the effect on profitability and net worth.)
- Debtors.
  - What is included?
    - trade debtors,
    - other debtors,
    - prepayments,
    - debtors due in more than a year.
  - Are the debtor days larger than the industrial average? (This could be a reflection of management inefficiency or it may be that they have not been writing off their bad debts.)
- Creditors.
  - What is included?
  - How much is debt?
  - Is it secured?
  - On what?
  - What is the repayment schedule?

We would have to look at all of these and make an assessment of the likely net worth of the company. This will be our view of what the company may be worth; someone else may well have a different view. The only asset we know the value of is cash, but even that is open to debate. The amount of cash in the business is bound to be different from the year end position.

(b) **Profit-based valuations**. When we buy a company we are buying assets and future profits. Therefore any valuation of the company has to reflect the two. There are two different ways of approaching a valuation based on profits:

- return on capital,
- price earnings ratio.

(i) *Return on capital*. All companies are trying to improve their return on capital employed, so the last thing that they would want is to make an acquisition that would reduce it. Consequently return on capital is likely to be one of the key acquisition criteria. It can also be used to value a company. When we have considered the return on capital, in other parts of this book, we have used the pre-tax profit. If a company is considering buying another company they would normally look at the post-tax profits. All companies tax plan, and will be concerned about the tax impact of the acquisition. We discussed, earlier in this book, how companies make acquisitions to alleviate their Advance Corporation Tax problems.

Consequently, most companies would use an after-tax return on capital employed. To calculate the price that they would be prepared to pay for the acquisition they would apply the target return on capital percentage to the profits of the company they are considering acquiring.

To illustrate this we will consider the following example.

A company has a post-tax return on capital criterion of 10 per cent. The company they are considering acquiring is currently averaging £500,000 after-tax profits, however the predator believes that this can be increased to £600,000 following the acquisition. The return on capital can be used to value the company:

Based on current profits:

$$\frac{£500,000}{10\%} = £5,000,000$$

This would form the basis for the original offer.

Based on anticipated future profits:

$$\frac{£600,000}{10\%} = £6,000,000$$

This would be the maximum price that the company is prepared to pay.

(ii) *The price earnings ratio.* This is the alternative profits-based valuation method. This uses the PE ratios of quoted companies and applies them to the potential acquisition. It is often a useful guide to the price that the owners might expect to receive from the sale of the company.

Using the PE ratio involves another element of judgement, as we will have to identify similar companies, with similar growth prospects. We need to consider the growth prospects as these are reflected in the PE ratio.

Continuing with our example, if a similar company had a PE ratio of 14 the owners might expect to receive at least 14 times current earnings, £7,000,000. However, this exceeds the maximum amount suggested by the return on capital criterion. The owners of the company may expect to receive more for the business than we are prepared to pay.

We would look at all three valuation methods to try to find a company where the price that we would have to pay is:

- within our return on capital criterion,
- less than the asset value of the company.

SUMMARY

Companies attempt to buy other companies for a variety of reasons, often more to do with long-term strategic gains than short-term profit enhancement.

However, irrespective of the reason for the acquisition, a structured analysis of a company's past and current financial performance will provide valuable information for both the selection and negotiating process.

Whilst many of the ratios are the same as used in other contexts, they enable us to look at the acquisition potential of a company. A company's net worth and its ability to generate cash and profits will be reflected in the price that we are prepared to pay.

21

THE AVAILABILITY
OF ACCOUNTS

WHERE CAN I GET ACCOUNTS FROM?

In the UK accounts are readily available for all companies. Suppliers and customers will normally provide you with their accounts. However we may need to analyse more than one set of accounts. If they are part of a much larger group they will usually provide you with the group accounts. It may be necessary to analyse the accounts of the individual company, as well as the group accounts. The accounts of the group may not reflect the same risks as those of the individual company. The subsidiary company that we are dealing with may be viable, but the group may be in financial difficulties. Alternatively the group may be viable and the subsidiary isn't and will shortly be sold, or closed. By looking at the two we would get a greater understanding of the risks facing the company and the commercial opportunities.

Accounts are available from three sources.

The company itself: most public companies will send potential investors a copy of their accounts.

Financial Times Annual Report Service: this offers a free service to readers of the *Financial Times*. There are currently over 700 company accounts available from this service. They are sent within the next working day, unless new accounts are to be published shortly, when they are sent on publication. Companies whose accounts are available from this service are marked in the *Financial Times* with a club symbol. To order accounts, you should ring 081 770 0770 or fax 081 770 3822 and quote a code number given daily in the *Financial Times* within the information about the London Share Service. This is found with the share information in the Companies and Markets section of the paper.

Companies House: all companies must file accounts at Companies House, although there are proposals for exempting certain small companies from this requirement. Accounts are available as a photocopy (costing £7.00 per set, if posted) or as a microfiche (costing £5.50, if posted). The microfiche records usually contain the last three years' accounts and annual returns from the company. The annual return includes:

- the registered office address,
- details of the company secretary and directors,
- a summary of the share capital,
- a list of members/changes in members since the last annual return.

The microfiche is much better value (it would cost £21.00 to get three years' accounts) but you need to have access to a microfiche reader to be able to use it. If you need accounts quickly they can be faxed at a cost of £20.00 per document. Companies House guarantee transmission within the hour.

Accounts can be ordered over the phone, as long as you are paying by credit card or direct debit. The phone numbers and addresses to contact are:

Companies registered in England and Wales:
Postal Search Section,
Companies House,
Crown Way,
Cardiff.
CF4 3UZ
0222 380 801

Companies registered in Scotland:
Postal Search Section,
Companies House,
100–102 George Street,
Edinburgh
EH2 3DJ
031 225 5774

Companies registered in Northern Ireland:
Registry of Companies and Friendly Societies,
IDB House,
64 Chichester Street,
Belfast,
BT1 4JX
0232 234 488

FORMAT OF ACCOUNTS FILED AT COMPANIES HOUSE

The accounts filed at Companies House may not be as detailed as the ones we discussed in Section 2. Small- and medium-sized private companies can opt to file modified accounts, whereas large private companies and public companies will file their full accounts. These modified accounts filed by smaller companies are a summarised version of the ones prepared for shareholders. This has been designed to ensure that smaller companies do not have to disclose to the general public information that will be harmful to the business. These modified accounts restrict the scope for financial analysis, as it is impossible to analyse profitability using modified accounts. We can only analyse the solvency of small companies using the modified accounts.

We discussed in Chapter 1 the changing accounting requirements for smaller companies, with two sets of accounting practice beginning to emerge. Large companies are required to comply with increasingly detailed accounting rules and disclosure requirements. Whereas smaller private companies comply with a shorter, restricted set of rules that reduce the amount of disclosure in the accounts. This is reflected in the accounts filed at Companies House for small- and medium-sized private companies (a definition of these is given in Chapter 1). In its full accounts a small private company may elect to use a shorter format for the balance sheet. This combines many items treated separately under the Companies Act provisions. They are allowed to file an even shorter version of this balance sheet.

Accounts for small private companies

A small company is required to file:

- a modified balance sheet. This is illustrated below and only shows the totals for each balance sheet category. It is a less detailed balance sheet than the one included in the accounts prepared for the shareholders, which may be available from the company if they are a supplier or a customer.
- notes to the accounts to disclose:
  - accounting policies,
  - debtors falling due in more than a year,
  - creditors falling due within a year,
  - creditors falling due in more than a year,
  - authorised and allotted share capital,
  - details of any shares allotted during the year,
  - analysis of the cost and depreciation of fixed assets (only for the major categories disclosed in the abbreviated balance sheet),
  - details of indebtedness,
  - the basis of converting foreign exchange into sterling,
  - the previous year's figures.

Modified balance sheet filed by small companies at Companies House

Fixed assets
    Intangible assets
    Tangible assets
    Investments

Current assets
    Stocks
    Debtors
    Investments
    Cash at bank and in hand
    Prepayments and accrued income

Creditors: amounts falling due within a year

Net current assets

Total assets less current liabilities

Creditors: amounts falling due after more than a year

Provisions for liabilities and charges

Accruals and deferred income

Capital and reserves
    Called up share capital
    Share premium account
    Revaluation reserve
    Other reserves
    Profit and loss account

You will notice that whilst we have some disclosure of the company's assets we have very little information about their specific liabilities.

Accounts for medium-sized private companies

There are fewer exemptions for medium-sized companies, who must file:

- a directors' report
- a balance sheet
- a modified profit and loss account. This starts at gross profit and doesn't disclose turnover or cost of sales.

INDEX